Temba Tupu!

AUTOBIOGRAPHY: WATER / ANCESTORS MIDD / FAMILY GHOSTS
THE ELLA GALLUP SUMNER AND MARY CATLI COLLECTION FUND

TEMBA TUPU!
(Walking Naked)

The Africana Woman's
Poetic Self-Portrait

Edited by

Nagueyalti Warren

Africa World Press, Inc.

P.O. Box 1892
Trenton, NJ 08607

P.O. Box 48
Asmara, ERITREA

Africa World Press, Inc.

P.O. Box 1892
Trenton, NJ 08607

P.O. Box 48
Asmara, ERITREA

Book design: Saverance Publishing Services
                  (www.saverancepublishing.com)
Cover design: Ashraful Haque

Library of Congress Cataloging-in-Publication Data

Temba tupu! (walking naked) : the Africana woman's poetic self-portrait /
edited by Nagueyalti Warren.
      p. cm.
ISBN 1-59221-239-5 -- ISBN 1-59221-240-9 (pbk.)
1. Poetry--Women authors. 2. Poetry--Black authors. I. Warren,
Nagueyalti.

PN6109.9.T45 2008
808.81'99287096--dc22

                        2008011879

to my husband, Rueben, who cradles my dreams,

carefully shielding them from mordant criticism

until they are strong enough to fly.

CONTENTS

Womanhood (Identity)

Contents

Womanhood (Physical Appearance)

Contents

Motherhood

Aging

Relationships (Spiritual)

Relationships (Family, Friends and Others)

Contents

Relationships (Love and Sexual)

Contents

Relationships (Political)

Tributes (for women famous and ordinary)

Acknowledgement

I wish to express my gratitude to all who have contributed to the completion of this book and to espacially thank Ms. Brenda Nix who exerted great effort to locate various poets and to organize and keep records; and to my student workers, Audrey Powell, Shaquanda Jacobs, Kiara Reed, Corey Wallaby, and Clarissa Walker, many thanks for your time and energy. Acknowledgement and thanks are due to my editor Angela Ajayi who was undaunted by the size of the manuscript and gave it her enthusiasm and full support.

And I remember
walking
as a little girl to school
on the savannahs of Westmoreland
walking from our hillbound village
walking along steep hillsides
walking carefully so as not to trip and plunge
walking into the valley

—Afua Cooper from "And I Remember"

Nudity is...a strong and fearless image that says we do not
believe that our bodies are inferior or ugly, or open to assault of any kind.

—Jocelyn Maria Taylor from "Testimony of a Naked Woman"

INTRODUCTION

*Oppressed people resist by identifying themselves as subjects, by defin-
ing their reality, shaping their new identity, naming their history, telling
their story.*

— *bell hooks*

I

After viewing the popular summer movie, *What Women Want*, in which
Mel Gibson's character has the capability of hearing the thoughts of any
woman he encounters, my son confided to me that he wished he, too, could
know what women think. "It's not magic," I told him. "It's easy. If you want to
know what women think, just read what they write." He stared at me blankly.
He stared because he is nineteen, and his adolescent body could not imagine
intellectualizing desire. Second, because he occupies a world in which men do
not routinely read the works of Black women, the idea was to him a strange sug-
gestion. As a consequence of the efforts of university departments of women's
studies, the increased number of women faculty and some enlightened men, a
few women's works are now required reading in the university setting. There-
fore, as a college sophomore, my son is not completely clueless; nonetheless,
he never thought to read women outside the classroom as a way of measuring
what they think and how they feel. After encountering a few poems by women,
he was surprised to find that their poetry usually does not focus on, nor, for the
most part, is it about men, but instead reveals who they are and how they see
themselves.

In spite of efforts in the academy to diversify curricular choices, Black
women's poetry has not received its due critical attention.[1] In a world that all
too often still equates blackness with maleness, aside from a few exceptions,
Black women poets generally lag behind Black men and their sister novelist
both in exposure and accolades. The nature of Black women's poetic expression
contributes to the problem. They so often express their poetic imagination in
mother wit, signifying, testifying, calling folks out, or in call and response modes
and poetic motifs involved in every day life, that their poetry too often passes
unrecognized or challenged because it fails to conform to white standards.

What is poetry, my students often ask. In 1971, Nikki Giovanni gave the
following definition: "Poetry is the culture of a people. We are poets even when
we don't write poems; just look at our life, our rhythms, our tenderness, our sig-

nifying, our sermons and our songs"(27). Invariably this definition fails to satisfy my students, familiar as they are with Aristotle's Poetics. They ask, but what of language, harmony or symbols? June Jordan's definition extends Giovanni's, and I insist that they become acquainted with both. Jordan writes: "Poetry tells feeling. A poem tells relationship. Poetry turns the individual drama of being human into words[;] it is an art open to all vocabulary made personal. Poetry changes life into a written drama where words set the stage and where words then act as characters on that stage" (xiv). Generally speaking, women poets use language for clarity, not to obscure but to reveal. In her comments about women poets, Mary Mackey observes that "right off the bat they tend to commit the unpardonable sin of speaking clearly. Poems by women often make statements that can be understood by everyone . . . Why a poem [that is blunt] is positively unprofessional. If everyone went around writing poetry like that, they'd have to give up teaching it in the universities" (179 Juhasz). Africana[2] poets appear to make a concerted effort to resist poetry as elite discourse by privileging the vernacular.

When Black women poets define themselves as part of a so-called universal[3] poetic tradition it means embracing the language techniques of western patriarchal societies—heroic couplets, poetic diction, obscure symbolism, cryptic illusions—and adopting only lofty themes. Phillis Wheatley and other early poets did, in fact, adopt what Cora Kaplan describes as "high language"—language that is public, political and literary (188 Montefiore). Many poets however, refuse the confinement of their inherited languages. In her early poetry, Giovanni announced that she would speak through English and imbue her usage with black meaning. African poets writing in the languages of colonialism face a similar difficulty. The answer for these poets has been to create their own tradition and claim the "shared themes, topoi, and tropes" that comprise Africana heritage (39 Gates, *Loose Canons*) and expresses in the West as a creolized language and in Africa as Pidgin English.

This anthology is a collection for which my students and I have wished. My Black women's poetry course necessitates the purchase of many books in order to study the complex and collective genius of Africana women. "Temba Tupu!" represents in a single volume the writing of poets from the United States, Canada, the Caribbean, Central and South America, Africa, and Europe and the subcontinent of India. To be sure, excellent anthologies have been published within the past decades. *The Routledge Reader in Caribbean Literature* (1996) edited by Alison Donnell and Sarah Welsh; Stella and Frank Chipasula's groundbreaking collection, *The Heinemann Book of African Women's Poetry* (1995); *Motherlands: Black Women's Writing From Africa, the Caribbean and South Asia* (1992) edited by Nasta Sushelia; *Enfim . . . Nos/Finally . . . Us* (1995) a bilingual collection of poetry edited by Miriam Alves and Carolyn Richardson; *Sisterfire* (1994) edited by Charolette Watson Sherman; Illona Linthwaite's *Ain't I a Woman: Classic Poetry by Women From Around the World* (1987) and *Whistling Bird: Women Writers of the Caribbean* (1998) edited by Elaine Campbell and Pierrette Frickey, are excellent and welcome additions to the study of black women's poetry. None, however, focuses exclusively on Africana women poets and how they see themselves, and none brings together the collective gynocentric vision of the African Diaspora. The central aim of this collection, then, is to present the voices and peculiar angle of vision of the Africana woman poet and in doing so, explicate the politics of identity. Like members of the Combahee River[4] Collective, the poets included in this collection demonstrate the radical politics that come directly from their identity. Unfortunately, many poets that I first sought to include had to be eliminated because of my inability to obtain permission to reprint. Conducting the research for this project has made it apparent that Black women writing anywhere inspire Black women writing everywhere. We buy our books and read each other. In fact, women may be their own best audiences. African American women have taken the lead with popular book clubs in homes and online. One example is the Go On GIRL! Book Club with more than 420 members and 35 chapters throughout the country (Brown). This club is one of the largest—but by no means the only—Black women's on-line reading group. These readers are gaining economic power with New York publishers, influencing them to invest in books that might otherwise have gone unpublished. In other countries, publishing appears to be even more difficult than it is for Blacks in the United States. The difficulty is compounded in countries where women have low literacy rates.

In Africa, women historically have been the keepers of tradition and culture. The poetic tradition is no different, although scholarship—that until recently marginalized or ignored Africa's women poets—makes it seem otherwise. Fortunately, the introduction to *The Heinemann Book of African Women's Poetry* urges "women to reclaim their historic role as singers of the songs that constituted a major part of [the African] poetic experience" (xvii). The publication of Africana women's poetry is increasing, and the poets recognize their relationship to each other and to the Pan-African spirit that has enabled their survival. They write to, for and about each other. From Great Britain, Africana women have declared that

> Even centuries of slavery, oppression and sexual abuse, of attacks on our culture and on our right to be, have not succeeded in breaking black women's spirit of resistance. Instead of distancing us from the African heritage which has sustained us, the thousands of miles we have travelled and the oceans we have crossed have simply strengthened our collective senses of self-worth (239 *The Heart of the Race*).

All women would benefit from a collective sense of self-worth because in the United States—the Western world, the East, the Third World—and in fact—the whole world, there appears to be hatred toward women. A cursory glance at the daily news reveals the high numbers of women and girls stalked, beaten, raped, and murdered or splayed and painted across advertiser's layouts on any given day and exposes societal disdain for women. Male violence against women and girls demonstrates the extent to which white-supremist, capitalist, patriarchy[5] will go to maintain power. Nikolay Solty's murder of his pregnant wife and family and his admission that he did it "for her tongue," [6] clarifies not only the misogynistic nature of society that contributed to his machisimo, but points to the courage it takes for women to speak up and out and not just black women but all women. To speak openly is still the male prerogative. Articulate women threaten to usurp male power and authority. Mr. Solty inscribed his deranged act of power by writing a note on the back of his murdered wife's photograph, "For her tongue"—silencing her and claiming for himself the language that Holderlin [7] declared the "most dangerous of possessions, . . . given to man . . . so that he may affirm what he is" (IV 246 Heidegger). Women are often feared and hated for what they are not: men. This animosity compounds for Black women because they are not white and a profound antipathy of Blacks still exists. Heinous crimes against Black women rarely receive national media attention, seldom are sensationalized, and almost never result in massive police manhunts. Thus Audre Lorde writes: "This woman is Black/ so her blood is shed into silence/ this woman is Black/ so her blood falls to earth/ like the droppings of birds/ to be washed away with silence and rain."

Angry voices erupt from this collection. Some poets respond to the pervading male contempt for women that seems to traverse the boundaries of race and class. Anger, an essential political emotion, for women, is an "outlaw emotion." [8] For Black women the angry, black and evil stereotype functions to oppress her outrage even more. Nevertheless, Africana poets embrace their anger. Infuriated by the rape of Joan Little [9] and other Black women, African American poet, Jayne Cortez in the final stanza of "Rape" explodes: "We celebrated day of the dead rapist punk/ and just what the fuck else were we supposed to do"[.] Ai's poetic monologues accept anger and outrage as the normal consequence of violence, and Toi Derricotte's "On the Turning Up of Unidentified Black Female Corpses" reveals the fear of living in a society that does not value women's lives. Her final stanza asks, "How can I protect myself? Even if I lock my doors, / walk only in the light, someone wants me dead."

A frightening conundrum of societal hatred is the insidious way it internalizes in the targeted group—the way it forces women into collusion with the oppressor. Anger and fear produce depression, insanity, disease and death. Ntozake Shange's "Crack Annie" interprets the devastating results of anger and fear turned inward. Africana women struggle with self-hatred and low esteem in their own psyches, the result of the external onslaught on their being, particularly in the form of popular culture. Black music is one culprit. Beverly Bryan, Stella Dadzie and Suzanne Scafe critique the song lyrics played in popular British nightclubs and conclude that the songs make Black people appear "defined and obsessed by our own sexuality"(219). The British Heptones' song lyrics, "I need a fat girl tonight," pale in comparison to African American rap lyrics in "Female Funk" or "2 Bitches," or "Ain't no Bitches," or "All my Bitches are Gone," or "Blow Job Betty," or "Tramp," or "Invasion of the Flat Booty Bitches." These songs and others like them, replete with references to Black women and girls as "bitches and hos" sell to millions and contribute to male contempt by defining women and girls as sexual prey. The interplay of external images with internal self-doubt creates reflections not unlike the illusion Colleen McElroy writes about in her poem of the same title. She creates the "wide mouth black girls/ they sneer at mousy mongoloid blondes . . ." In "Spotlight Politics" Ruth Forman captures the image of the girl affected by the words of popular culture and mirroring back what that culture reinforces. Forman wisely concludes, "she embarrass you huh"[?]

While Rap and Reggae represent current examples of negative stereotyping of women in their song lyrics, Black music has a long sexist history. In the 1940s, Blues singer Lightin' Hopkins' lamented, "Black gal, O black gal, what make your doggone nappy/ head so hard[?]" The singer attacks the lack of submissive behavior in Black women, but more vitriolic is his use of "black" before it was declared beautiful, and "nappy" before it was a hairstyle. Una Marson, Jamaican poet now deceased, responded with her own lyrics. Using the blues timbre she affirms in "Kinky Hair Blues": "I like me black face and me kinky hair" but concludes that she must change in order to "win" a man. Lyrics by Wade Newton, "Go on black gal, don't try to make me shame/go on black gal don't try to make me shame/ Cause your hair is so short I swear to God I can smell/ your brains" (89 Cook) may help explain why hair weaving is a thriving commodity in Black communities—a preference for long hair seems to be embedded in our popular collective consciousness.

The character Caledonia is another familiar allusion in the Black musical tradition. Louis Jordan's 1940 Tympany Five band rendition asked, "Caledonia! Caledonia! What makes your big head so hard?" McElroy's poem "Caledonia" turns the stereotypical image on its head, creating positive images—"Mama and aunt jennie both hardheaded/ and lean on words/"—that teach her ". . . love, like hate/ is always acted out." Stephen Henderson's now classic essay, "Survival Motion," says "Caledonia is a black woman; that's why her head is hard. Black women are evil. Every Negro knows this" (89 Cook). Henderson explains that the lyrics are indicative of self-hatred and the low self-esteem of Black men projected onto their alter egos. Hip-Hop as culture, Rap as music, and Raggae all inherited anti-feminine sentiments from a sexist male tradition that women sometimes supported by singing demeaning blues lyrics that claimed they would rather "my baby haul-off and hit me, than to jump up and quite me." The practice continues today with women rappers calling other women "bitches and hos." Hackneyed images in popular music are not limited to the United States and Great Britain. Famous Nigerian musician, Fela Anikulapo-Kuti's popular song, "Lady," continues the trend. Professor Nkiru Nzegwu's essay, "African Women and the Fire Dance," charges that Fela's catchy tempo and convincing social message are damaging. The lyrics, "African woman go dance/ e go dance the fire dance/ e know im lord and master/ e go cook for am/ e go do anything he say . . ." Nzegwu claims

> deploys imageries that are so compelling and intuitively true about what many believe to be the masculinist patriarchal continent of Africa. The song plays on multiple levels: It glorifies a certain [submissive] image of African woman; it denigrates the image of a woman in charge; it instructs us on how a real African woman occupies space and carries herself; it prescribes what the proper relationship is between spouses; and it ridicules any traits that are perceived to be foreign and alien (1).

Nzegwu questions how Fela can extol the virtues of African womanhood as docile and subordinate to men when his own African mother whom he loved and respected was an extraordinary and politically powerful figure. Funmilayo Ransome-Kuti traveled the world keeping political commitments while the Reverend Israel Oludotun Kuti, her husband, kept their home. She questions why Fela does not examine his father's life for lessons that teach other men how to be supportive of their wives. He could have drawn from his father's life the "principles of sharing family responsibilities" (2). He chose not to tell men that women value caring and loving traits in men and find them manly. Instead, he presents an image of the African woman that his own family experience proves untrue. The ethos of sexism and masculine desire for power, not to mention money, supported by society often is a stronger sway than personal relationships. Fela, like the Rappers, Reggae, and Blues musicians, will say whatever sells, regardless of what he believes. White supremacist, capitalist, patriarchy willingly supports and pays handsome rewards for music that denigrates women.

Against this background, the poets in this collection write to subvert and deconstruct the wicked popular representations of themselves. Africana women poets not only seek to articulate an excluded identity but to replace a deranged one as well. The sexist affronts to Africana womanhood are clear.

Patricia Hill Collins summarizes the racist insults that are both extensive and familiar when she writes:

> The controlling images of Black women that originated during the slave era attest to the ideological dimension of Black women's oppression. Ideology represents the process by which certain assumed qualities are attached to Black women and how those qualities are used to justify oppression. From the mammies, Jezebels and breeder women of slavery to the smiling Aunt Jemimas on pancake mix boxes, ubiquitous Black prostitutes, and ever-present welfare mothers of contemporary popular culture, the nexus of negative stereotypical images applied to African-American women has been fundamental to Black women's oppression (5).

These poets do not ignore the racist, capitalist, patriarchal backdrops of the United States, Canada, Great Britain, Columbia, Bolivia, and South Africa. Brazilian poet, Marta André writes clearly about "white supremacist, capitalist, patriarchy" when she says:

> ... with the swindler's wad of money and the footsteps/ of the past/ became a sugar mill./ In the disorderliness of time/ no one became a people/ because of the negligence of the imperial stroke of the pen.

The political climate and context in which the poems are created determine the extent to which the poets focus on issues of race. The Black Consciousness Movement in South Africa, the revolutionary movements in 1975 in Angola and Mozambique, and the 1960s fall of colonialism in West Africa, the labor strikes in Great Britain, the Black Power/Black is Beautiful movement in the United States have all affected the poets' attitude toward race and racism and the attendant politics. Some of the poets especially in Africa are revolutionary freedom fighters in the literal sense. A Mozambique guerrilla, Josina Machel's poem is a call to arms. The final stanza states: "This is the time to be ready/ and firm/ The time to give ourselves to the Revolution."[10] During the armed struggle for independence, African women fought along side their men—bearing arms as well as babies. The Civil Rights and Black Power Movements in the United States provoked African American women poets to focus more often on racism than in periods following those social movements. Nikki Giovanni's poem "Reflections on April 4, 1968"[11] illustrates one response to race in the United States. Giovanni asks:

> What can I, a poor Black woman, do to destroy america? This is a question, with appropriate variations, being asked in every Black

heart. There is one answer—I can kill. There is one compromise—I can protect those who kill. There is one cop-out—I can encourage others to kill. There are no other ways . . . ." (279 Henderson).

This outlaw emotion—justifiable rage—resulted in a labeling of the poets as militant, radical, rabid, homicidal and worse, landing them on the FBI's list of dissidents.

Various literary movements have produced images of Africana women that the women poets have revised, rewritten or challenged in their own poems. One movement to come under scrutiny is Negritude. An African and male-centered crusade for cultural equity, Negritude was the brainchild of three men, Léopold Senghor of Senegal, Aimé Césaire of Martinique, and Leon Damas of Guyana. These poets were students in Paris during the 1930s, all were colonial subjects and disillusioned with the treatment they received when they arrived in France. Responding to the French's negative attitudes toward African culture and aesthetics, these poets embraced and celebrated their African heritage and traditions. However, Negritude romanticized and objectified women or ignored them all together. According to Mercer Cook, Senghor, speaking to a group of students at Howard University in 1966, thanked the male writers of the Harlem Renaissance, naming Alain Locke, W.E.B. DuBois, Marcus Garvey, Carter G. Woodson, and the poets, Langston Hughes, Sterling Brown, Claude McKay and others, for inspiring the Negritude poets. The women poets of the Renaissance, while ignored by Senghor and others of the Negritude School addressed some issues never broached by the men, including women's love for each other, their idea of beauty and issues of race. Maureen Honey's *Shadowed Dreams: Women's Poetry of the Harlem Renaissance* examines the contributions of these unsung poets. They were the sophisticated and intellectual equals of their male counterparts to whom Senghor refers. They connected sexism and racism in ways the men appeared oblivious to—drawing a relationship to the destruction of nature. Anne Spencer's "White Things" critiques colonialism when she writes: "blanched with their wand of power; / and turned the red in a ruby rose to a poor white poppy-flower." Spencer's poem addresses a Pan-African audience, although she is un-acknowledged.

Langston Hughes claims that usually the poet has his hand on the emotional pulse of the people (11), but the poet cannot take the pulse of a man and measure the heartbeat of a woman. Thus, for all of its good intentions, the Negritude Movement, its preoccupation with color, the beauty of the black race, and its romanticizing of the African woman ultimately came under the attack of less self-conscious writers and women demanding realistic images. The Negritude School was composed mainly of poets from Francophone African and Caribbean countries. Wole Soyinka probably best sums up the

Anglophone response to Negritude with his now famous quip: "A tiger does not need to proclaim his tigertude!" and the African novelist Mariama Bâ spoke for many women when she wrote that

> The nostalgic songs dedicated to African mothers which expresses the anxieties of men concerning Mother Africa are no longer enough for us. The Black woman in African literature must be given the dimensions that her role in the liberation struggles next to men has proven to be hers, the dimension which coincides with her proven contribution to the economic development of our country (145 El Naga).

Ama Ata Aidoo argues that "male African writers . . . can only portray women the way they perceive them" (146 El Naga). Senghor sang of feminine beauty when he wrote: "Bare woman, black woman/ Clad in your color which is life/ in your form which is beauty" (14 Cook). His lines may, as Mercer Cook suggests, have caused the "African woman to regally adjust her boubou and walk with renewed assurance" (14); however, Senghor undercut those noble sentiments when he chose a Caucasian woman for his bride.

In the United States during the Black power and Black is Beautiful movements, the practice of extolling the beauty of black womanhood and choosing white women for mates facetiously was referred to as "talking black, sleeping white." Too often, when women pointed to the contradictions in the Black is Beautiful rhetoric, they were silenced by accusations from the infamous Moynihan Report,[12] charging them with emasculating Black men. Eldridge Cleaver even named the space between Black men and women "the naked abyss of negated masculinity" (206). Thus, Black women critiquing the movement were accused of betraying Black men and their analysis equated with attacks.

Perhaps the space between Black women and men equally is the abyss of negated femininity. Since Sojourner Truth first posed the question "Ain't I a woman?" in 1851, Black women poets have answered saying that they indeed are phenomenal women. Sojourner Truth's physical appearance, however, her size and her force of character challenged the notion of feminine frailty. The Africana woman recognizes her own strength while understanding that often it is her undoing, as Giovanni's "Woman Poem," poignantly reveals: "It's a sex object if you're pretty/ and no love/ or love and no sex if you're fat/ get back fat black woman be a mother Grandmother strong thing but not woman" (13 Cade). Society claims woman is a weak thing—strength therefore places Black women between a rock and a hard place. Through their acceptance of the past, embrace of the present, and faith in the future, Black women poets claim the rocks and the hard places. Their poetry celebrates life with all its seemingly unfair contradictions.

II

THE POLITICS OF POETRY: SPEAKING OF THEORY

The philosophy of the poet is . . . in the poem . . .
—Margaret Walker

In *The Poisonwood Bible*, Barbara Kingsolver questions how whites live with the history of colonialism, imperialism and the arrogance of oppression. One way to "live with it" (9) is to announce the death of history or to deconstruct, rename, turn it into tropes and write it off. Her question coincides with popular post-colonial, post-modern theories. These theories provide a way, Joyce Ann Joyce contends, to avoid confronting historical deeds and misdeeds. That said, aspects of post-modern theories can be instructive for reading Africana poetics. Jacques Derrida's proposition that challenges the nature of reality is a necessary opening for the *interdicted*[13]—for *freeplay*[14] and for the rupturing of the center to occur. The center of the masculine matrix undone leaves a free space occupied by neither sex, but enables different readings for both. With a vacated center no otherness exists. There is but one Mind where individuals express various states of consciousness in that Mind. All have access to the Mind's ideas with the individual consciousness acting as filter. Afrocentric, Eurocentric, phallocentric, and gynocentric theories express various states of consciousness. None expresses the whole, but some enable an enhanced reading of a particular consciousness. Since ideas exist in a metaphysical realm without race or gender, Alice Walker's lucid description of writers "black writers and white writers . . . writing one immense story—the same story, for the most part—with different parts to this immense story coming from a multitude of different perspectives" (5) is apropos.

Ideas ultimately come from a realm quite beyond the individual personalities who propose them; nevertheless, once the original, primary and unlimited thought enters the word or logos it is subjected to the experiences, practices and interpretation of the personality. Thus, this collection centers on Black women's consciousness: self definitions, their questions regarding the complexities and contradictions of race and gender, their spiritual and inner lives, and their search for Truth. In her seminal essay, "The Darkened Eye Restored," Mary Helen Washington identifies the "single distinguishing feature of the literature of black women—and this accounts for their lack of recognition—it is this: their literature is about black women; it takes the trouble to record the thoughts, words, feelings, and deeds of black women, experiences that make the realities of being black . . . look very different from what men have written"(35). As such, Africana poetry requires a separate analysis and its own theory.

Some critics suggest that black writing generally lacks a theoretical base, but in "Gender and Theory: Dialogues on Feminist Criticism," Barbara Christian cogently argues that, "People of color have always theorized—but in forms quite different from the Western form of abstract logic." Black theory often is a narrative form, a story or proverb. Theory erupts in the play with language. Christian points to "dynamic rather than fixed ideas" that character-ize our theories (114). Christian's discussion of literary criticism is especially useful for analyzing Africana poetry. She outlines three tiers: The highest one contains discourse, theory, and the literary canon; the middle consists of the classroom and reading texts. The lowest tier—the one most applicable to Afri-cana poetics—consists of stories, poems, plays, the language of the folk, and reader responses like, "I sure know what she is talking about," or "I don't want to hear that," "Her words move me," and/or "That poem changed my life"(51). Christian, well aware that the hierarchy is artificial, arbitrary, and provoked by the politics of criticism, subverts the high/low categories by including the descriptions of audience response to the works. As long ago as the first century A.D. Longinus understood the importance of audience response. He defined the Sublime as the quality that produces *ekstasis* within the audience; that is, the work emotionally moves the audience. While Longinus's concern was only with the lofty or highest tier, *ekstasis* exists in the so-called low world. Christian urges revaluation of that world, for it is here that the language of Black folk and the poetry of resistance reside.

More than an act of resistance, writing poetry for many of these women constitutes a survival motion and emotion. Pam Ward's poem, "Don't Get Killed on Your Kitchen Floor," exemplifies the urgency in many of the poems. The poetic stance that emerges from this florilegium, Gynocentric Pan-African Poetics, joins the hands of sisters around the globe as they attempt to clarify and comprehend the complexities of female experiences, a woman-centered way to understand blackness, a way to embrace color and a politics of poetry that begins with the self. Christian articulates the concept when she calls up

> the vision of women moving all over the world . . . In the spaces
> created for us by our foremothers, by our sisters in the streets, the
> houses, the factories, the schools, . . . now able to speak and to listen
> to each other, to hear our own language, to refine and critique it
> across time and space, through the written word (48 "The Highs
> and Lows of Black Feminist Criticism").

Our ancestors speak many languages, but when they walk the walk and talk the talk of our collective experiences, we hear clearly their instructions. Makeda, the Queen of Sheba advises if we fall, do not be destroyed. Centuries later Jodi Braxton responds: "you's a black Queen Sheba. great black great-grandmom/ i love the you/ that works in my flesh." The dialog found in this collection is worldwide and crosses the bridge of space and time.

Gynocentric Pan-African Poetics, as a mode of discourse, opens "a many-voiced palaver of thought/feeling, image/language that moves us . . . toward a world where, like Alice Walker's revolutionary petunias, all of us can bloom" (48 Christian). My introduction of this term, Gynocentric Pan-African Poetics, initially raises more questions than it answers, but I hope that it will provoke conversation and not vituperative debate that serves no purpose. This poetics leads to theorizing about Africana women's poetry and to more productive readings of Africana women's poems. Theory itself is germane only in so far as it illuminates the text. In attempting a definition for a feminist poetics, Jan Montefiore concludes that finally a feminist poetics "means, primarily understanding the significance of woman's poetry"(1). Tools of analysis will aid in understanding Africana women's poetry. The theoretical framework used for men may not be valid for women's poetry; and the dangers of essentialist reductivism and assumptions of a monolithic Black female experience lurk in the shadows of theoretical frameworks. Theories emerging from the Black Arts Movement come immediately to mind. What started out as efforts of critique and analysis of Black Art developed into straightjacket definitions of what it ought to be and do. In 1968, Ron Karenga[15] addressed the Organization of Black American Culture in Chicago and called for a Black aesthetic that he defined as "a criteria for judging the validity and/or the beauty of a work of art" (5). The proscription for a poem to be valid according to Karenga was that it "expose the enemy, praise the people and support the revolution"(6). This theory projected a monolithic Black experience, one that excluded women, gay men and lesbians, as well as any expressions that were contrary to the rhetoric of the movement. The lessons to be learned from the Black Arts Movement and Black Cultural Nationalism are clear. Privileging one Black experience as universal only produces a skewed view of reality. Women's experience is both individual and collective.

Gynocentric Pan-African Poetics, then, does not suggest that race or blackness is the only criteria for evaluating the poetry of women from different cultures and class backgrounds. Racial identity in multiracial societies indeed is problematic, as several poets here indicate. The Haitian poet, Gilda Nassief, in "Blacksister," asks, "where does black start/where does white start/ among all the infinite shades?" This collection embraces the identities these women have assigned to themselves. Certainly theoretical diversity also appears in this collection. Thus, "the dance of difference"[16] is valued and maintained.

Regardless of the pitfalls lurking in theory, women poets face what Suzanne Juhasz names "a double bind" and what for Black women poets becomes a tripartite vise. Juhasz states that, "If and when a woman chooses to be a poet, the double bind exists within the writing itself . . . her criteria and standards of excellence have been created by men describing the work of men"(3)—thus the need for a different framework for evaluating the works of Africana women poets—gynocentric, pan-African poetics.

> *I had rather speak five with my understanding, that by my voice I might teach others also, than ten thousand words in an unknown tongue . . . Let your women keep silence . . . for it is not permitted unto them to speak.*
>
> *—I Corinthians 14:19, 34*

Stealing the Fire: Reclaiming Our Own Words

Africana poets have answered Medusa's[17] laugh in challenging the hegemony of male language with our own linguistic variety—with our mother's tongue. In her 1929 essay, "A Room of One's Own," Virginia Woolf bemoaned the use of male language[18] by women writers. She wrote only about white women and before the poetry of Una Marson and Louise Bennett, that captured the potent language of ordinary Black womenfolk. Africana poets have a language and a tradition. In *Black American Women's Writing*, Eva Birch notes that their writing "is not only black, but also distinctively female, characterised by celebratory embracing of the writers' African cultural heritage, and a determined retrieval of their mother's stifled creativity"(10). Audre Lorde's essay, "Poetry is not a Luxury," demands that Black women reclaim what they once owned. In traditional African society, in African American, as well as West Indian cultures the woman is storyteller. Lorde suggests that from the stories that we rightly own, we can speak the truth of our lives.

Black speech, its musical quality and underpinnings comprise the linguistic heritage of Black poetry. Black scholars, among them Houston Baker, Imamu Baraka, Barbara Christian, and Stephen Henderson have analyzed this heritage. However, none other than Christian has attempted a definition of a feminist poetic. She outlines the African stylistic motifs or call and response, a musical tradition in Black poetry. Further, she points out that women poets tend not to romanticize and worship European physical characteristics as have their male counterparts as well as some early women novelist. Instead, they embrace African physical features as natural and desirable.

Defining Africana poetry is essential to understanding it. In discussing the poetry of the Black Arts Movement, Henderson uses appropriate terms. His is "a critical framework . . . flexible enough to facilitate discussion of the entire range of Black poetry"(67). The linguistic gestures of dropping a word, turning a phrase, free-rhyming word play, using compressed and cryptic imagery, or choosing certain words characterizes Black women's poems. Henderson classifies these poetic elements as "Virtuoso Naming and Enumerating." "Worrying the Line," another useful term taken from the melismatic singing, characteristic of the Black musical tradition, in its altering the pitch of a note is expressed in the verbal parallel of repetition, frankness, bluntness of language, obscenity or a kind of social dissonance. The "complex galaxy of personal, social, institutional, historical, religious and mythical meanings that affect everything we say or do as Black people sharing a common heritage," (41) Henderson defines as "Soul-Field." Another useful term for reading Africana poetry is "Saturation," Henderson's most problematic term because it attempts to measure the blackness of a poem. Nevertheless, it is useful for identifying gynocentric elements—that poetic tone that shows the depth and quality of the experience of womanhood. Saturation displays itself most clearly in theme. All poems written by Africana women are not saturated, although the ones included here are by virtue of the overarching focus of the collection.

Amandina Lihamba's description of African orature forms also is appropriate in explaining the relationship between poet and audience. Orature form, like African American call and response, penetrates the distance between poet and audience. Relying on the participatory nature of African orature forms, poets use it to engage an audience. The public nature of orature versus the private character of poetry when combined produces ironic and contradictory elements. According to Lihamba, "Orature forms have survived in Africa in spite of and because of colonialism. Because of the antagonism and repression unleashed by colonialism against African people and their culture, to actively engage in cultural practice became an act of political resistance"(xix). Orature form is an African survival born in the Diaspora as call and response. The use of orature is an act of inclusion as opposed to exclusion, and for women poets establishes a relationship between poet and audience that is equal as opposed to hierarchical.

Matriot[19] words form the basis of gynocentric pan-African poetics. These words have massive concentrations of feminine energy, resonate with maternal culture and offer a powerful vocabulary of fire words capable of creating new metaphors. Matriot words include first blood, menses, uterus, birth, period, cramps, labor-pain, cycle, change-of-life, breast, womb, Kotex, vagina, panties, bra, hair, lips, hips, legs, rape. These words resonate feminine energy and belong to women, but when women use them they seem to strike fear in men who have sometimes appropriated them for their own use and attempted to universalize them as abstract terms. When women use these fire words, they are accused of being too personal. Houston Baker's observation that "The most theoretically sophisticated act . . . in our era is an autobiographical one—on metalevels" (143 *Afro-American Literary Studies in the 1990s*) addresses the objection. He explains that the objection to the personal is usually made because "Morality and objectivity demand transcendence of the merely personal . . ."(144). T.S. Eliot of course comments on the issue of eccentricity in poetry, "one error . . . is to seek for new human emotions to express; and in this search for novelty in the wrong place . . . discover[s] the perverse"(10). Women's experience is often thought to be perverse. Ntozake Shange's poem, "You're Just Like a Man," speaks directly to Eliot's idea of perversion when she writes:

> so anyway they were poets/ & this guy well he liked this woman's work cuz it wazn't 'personal'/ i mean a man can get personal in his work when he talks politics or bout his dad/ but women start alla this foolishness bout their bodies & blood & kids & what's really goin on at home/ well & that aint poetry . . .

These Africana poets claim the right to be as personal as they want to be—to be explicit with their fire words—letting the flames consumes what they must.

Women's movements worldwide have made it clear that the personal is political and that the political can indeed become poetical. This collection of poetry by Africana women is an indication of the vibrancy of Black women in Africa and the Diaspora—how they see themselves as women, as daughters and mothers, as sexual beings, lovers, wives, spiritual and political beings, workers, thinkers, and as artists, restricted or fulfilled. The Africana woman's angle of vision reflects her culture, geography, class and economic background, education, age, religious and sexual orientations in addition to gender and race. These poets see with an unflinching gaze the multiple dimensions of identity—power, glory, faults and dangers inherent in Black womanhood regardless of their "pools of origins."[20] They praise, criticize, see beauty in themselves and others, in their own scars and ugliness; and in the distortions thrust upon them by societies that want from them everything or nothing, they claim the right to be free. When these poets ego-trip, they are well aware of their actions—singing praise songs to themselves and embracing a conflicted past too long denied, one that has molded and continues to shape their poetic sensibility.

Artistic validity and thematic relevance guided the selection of these poems. Some of the poets are famous; others have written their poems out of the sheer need to express themselves with little or no expectation of having their works published. Some appear here in print for the first time. Classic voices, early poets, modern and contemporary poets are here for a comparative look at changes in style, tone, and texture from one period to the next. The collection falls easily into three sections: Passages, Relationships and Recognition, the first of which focuses on poems about the growing self, girlhood, womanhood, physical appearance, sexuality, pregnancy, motherhood, grand-motherhood, aging, and death, the next: spirituality, friendships, violence and abuse, lovers, family, and politics, and the last section pays tribute to women famous and ordinary. Within each section, the poets appear in chronological order of the periods during which they wrote, with the older poets appearing first.

The poets assembled here range from mild-mannered to outrageous. Gladys Casely-Hayford, African lesbian poet of the 1930s in the words of her own mother was the latter. Many of the poets here are famous. In fact, two—the late Gwendolyn Brooks and Rita Dove—have both received well-deserved recognition, as, respectively, the first African American recipient of the Pulitzer Prize for poetry in 1950 for *Annie Allen* (1949); and the latter named the first African American Poet Laureate of the United States from 1993 to 1995. Dove won the Pulitzer Prize for *Thomas and Beulah* (1986) in 1987.[21] While not as widely known as Brooks and Dove, Pinkie Gordon Lane was the first African American named Poet Laureate of Louisiana, serving from 1989-1992. Perhaps the most prolific African American poet, June Jordan has twenty-two books to her credit, and the most beloved popular poet, Maya Angelou, as well as Audre Lorde and other lesbian poets are included, as are aspiring new poetic voices.

Poets from outside the United States may be less well known, but some have achieved fame in other genres. For example, well-known Ghanaian playwright, Ama Ata Adioo also has published poetry. Jamaican poet Una Marson who in 1937 proclaimed:

> I regret nothing—I have lived/ have loved/ I have known laughter/ and dance and song, / I have wept, / I have sighed, / I have prayed. I have soared on fleecy clouds/ To the gates/ of heaven, / I have sunk/ Deep down/ In the pit of hell . . .

received some recognition and was published in Jamaica and in Great Britain. Some poets from obviously privileged backgrounds contrast with others from urban ghettoes, or with those who have escaped rural poverty and other oppressive and uninspiring environments. Their talents, skills and techniques vary, yet what emerges from the collection is a "literary sisterhood" [22] that draws ancestral threads from Lucy Terry and Phillis Wheatley to Frances Harper and Gwendolyn Brooks in the United States, from Una Marson and Louise Bennett to Grace Nichols in the Caribbean, and from Queen Hatshepsut to Mabel Segun to Stella Chipasula in Africa. Coming to voice in the works of these poets then is a poetic tradition not born yesterday. Not only was Lucy Terry the first African in America to leave a written record of her poem, "Bars Fight" (1746) and Phillis Wheatley the second with the publication in 1773 of *Poems on Various Subjects, Religious and Moral*, but for women in Africa the written tradition dates from the Eighteenth Egyptian Dynasty and includes a long poetic obelisk inscription composed by Queen Hatshepsut, one of the few women pharaohs. Queen Hatshepsut also was known as Hashepsowe, a moniker she used when she ruled as a man not as queen—thereby subverting the category called (wo)man.

The poems collected here echo Gwendolyn Bennett's "Song . . . of waters shaken from firm brown limbs/ Or heads thrown back in irreverent mirth." These poets sing "the heart of a race/ While sadness whispers/ . . . the cry of a soul." The particular elements in Africana poetry are race and gender, the universal, their soulscript, to borrow the title of June Jordan's 1970 anthology. Soulscript transcends race, gender, time and space to communicate the spiritual and eternal. Their poems expose their naked innermost selves. Walking naked is a metaphor that says Africana women move through the world unprotected, unadorned, and uninhibited as themselves. Their poems focus on defining moments, historical instances, and articulate the ever-differing difference of woman's voice.[22] Collectively these poems offer a gestalt. They challenge generally held beliefs about Black women, that for one, we do not lose our minds because we are too spiritually grounded, for example. However, we all know someone like Sylvia Hamilton's "Crazy Black Luce." The word is that Black women do not commit suicide; still we know women like "Crack Annie." Sometimes suicide is slow, taking a lifetime to commit.

Part One of this collection, "Passages," represents the female journey, from girlhood to maturity, old age and death. What is the meaning of girlhood for non-white, poor, female children? Maya Angelou has said that growing up and realizing all that you are not is the "Rust on the razor that threatens the throat" (6), but Nikki Giovanni says that during her childhood, even though her family was poor, all the while she was quite happy. Memories of childhood run the gamut. This section begins with Harlem Renaissance poet Gwendolyn Bennett's (1902-1981) "To a Dark Girl" and is one of the first poems by a woman to embrace an African aesthetic. The descriptions of girls move from the color brown to black, and the section ends with contemporary poet from Great Britain, Sista Roots' (Ras Tina) poem, "She," describing the life of a girl growing into womanhood in a constricted patriarchal society.

Womanhood

When Elizabeth Cady Stanton announced, "Woman feels the invidious distinctions of sex exactly as the black man does those of color" (13 Oakley), she committed an act of omission that continues to plague white feminists—the inability to see the Black woman. Black women feel both sex and color simultaneously. Wherever whites are in power, Blacks feel their color, and wherever men are, women feel as other.

The womanhood section begins with "Ain't I a Woman," Sojourner Truth's powerful poetic statement and trope on the prevailing definitions of womanhood. Seizing upon the negative characteristics of woman personified in Eve, Truth uses metalepsis—a trope-reversing trope, a figure of a figure—to engage her method of signifying. Employing hyperbolic imagery, frankness, bluntness of language and the repetition of her few choice words, "Ain't I a Woman?" she turns her phrase on the conjunction "If" and gives power and agency to all women when she declares: "If the first woman God ever made/ was strong enough to turn the world/ upside down, all alone/ together woman ought to be able to turn it/ rightside up again." Harlem Renaissance poet, Anita Scott Coleman's "America Negra" opens the door to multiple identities of Africana women especially in the Diaspora stating "I am Indian . . . I am Irish and Scotich and Welsh . . . I am Africa." Womanhood means embracing anger as one encounters limitations. Maureen Ismay rejects what has come to typify Africana women, an image fired by the legends of Truth and Tubman. In "Frailty Is Not My Name," Ismay resists being straitened by these legendary women, declaring "I'm no mythology . . . I'm not a big strong, black woman/ iron hard and carrying/ all the sorrows of the world on my back." In an apostrophe to Sojourner Truth, Ismay rejects also the false concept of frailty. Beverly A. Russell in the tradition of Langston Hughes'"I Too Sing America," claims that she too is "The Fair Sex." This poem challenges in ways much like Truth's "Ain't I a Woman?" by exposing the "knight in shining armor rescue myth" that fails to save her—nonetheless, she is the fair sex. Unlike Sojourner's rhetorical question, the contemporary poets move from interrogative to declarative with many poems stating "I Am Woman." Mari Evans' poem states "I Am a Black Woman" and talks back to Angela Grimke who wrote "The Black Finger" introducing "A straight cypress" image. Over forty years later Evans in a formal revision of the "Black Finger" writes, "I am a black woman/ tall as a cypress."

Part of Africana identity is work; hard physical labor as set forth by Sojourner Truth's description of womanhood. Black women's lives are tied up with work from slave days to nowadays. In the Caribbean, the women called their work "double days." What Truth pointed out as custom in the United States was true also in the islands. Whites made no distinction between black male and female labor, making women equal to men. The women concluded, "But in our eyes, we were more than equal to men, for having completed our work on the estate, it fell to us to tend to the children and perform domestic duties such as preparing food and cultivating any available plot of ground for provisions" (17 Bryan, et.al). Poems that deal with work include Natasha Trethewey's "Domestic Work," and Ayanna Black's "Rag Dolls." The majority of these poems show the women working for whites; however, Micere Mugo's "Wife of the Husband" captures most deftly woman working for man.

The primary focus of Africana poetry is not on man—Mr. Charlie nor Mr. Lover Man—but on the woman in the mirror and the change within. Part of defining womanhood is the poet's description of the physical aspects of identity. One feature stands out more than any other in a Black woman's physical appearance: hair. Rebecca Carroll, editor of *Sugar in the Raw: Voices of Young Black Girls in America*, understands well the issue of coping with and learning to appreciate black hair that starts with young girls and for some women is an unending problem. Carroll writes:

> Young black girls and older black women alike battle with hair in a similar way that young white girls and older white women battle with weight[,] . . . Our hair grows out rather than down, it is kinky as opposed to silky, it is thick as opposed to thin, it is ornery as opposed to obedient, it is sensual as opposed to sexy. And in a white, puritanical, and patriarchal society, all of these things don't quite add up (143).

The ideal beauty in America and around the world is not black. To sing of Black beauty and fully embrace the physical aspects of blackness takes tremendous courage, a healthy self concept, and as Alice Walker might say, it takes getting whiteness off the eyeball. Una Marson's "Kinky Hair Blues" introduces the section on physical appearance. In the poem she openly celebrates her natural self. It is a well-known saying that Man is God's glory, woman is man's glory, and hair is woman's glory . . . the more hair the better, the straighter the better. To cut a woman's hair and go natural were extreme acts of deconstructing the meaning of beauty. Black women were afraid of the natural look because not just whites but more importantly Black men told them that nappy was ugly.

Natasha Trethewey's poem, "Hot Comb," captures the Africana woman's effort to assimilate Black hair into a non-Black aesthetic. Karen Williams's, "There's a History in My Hair" questions the politics of hair. A fascinating example of hair politics is the case of Joan Little, the same young woman in Jayne Cortez's poem, "Rape." In the United States hair is so politically volatile that Little's defense team urged her to change her short Afro hairstyle to one more acceptable. Her refusal might have resulted in a guilty verdict; thus—to save her own life—Little straightened her short hair.[24] Trethewey's poem commemorates the place where Africana women get their hair "fixed"—in "Naola Beauty Academy" and Javacia Nicole Harris counters with "Don't Tell My Hair to Relax."

Physical identity includes also the shape of women's bodies, but this subject is all but missing from the poems of the older poets. Maureen Honey highlights Michael Cooke's description of poetry from the early period as "indirect, coded, wrung free of overt anger" (17). However, some of the older poets use nature to reflect woman's body and her beauty and others, who mention body parts, focus mainly on hands or eyes to portray feminine beauty. Octavia Wynbush's poem, "Beauty," says "beauty lurks for me in black, knotted hands." Harriet Jacobs' "about our hips" marks the departure from the elegiac, controlled tone of earlier poets. Poems in this section include African poets who use the African continent and physical landscape as metaphor for woman's body. Abena Busia's "Mawu of the Waters" is an example.

Body weight for Africana women generally is not the distressing and sometimes pathological obsession as it is for some Caucasian women and girls, whose problems result in eating disorders and even death. Social science research confirms this tendency but also reports that with regard to real obesity Black women have the worst health statistics of any group of women on nearly all of the major health indices. Being overweight relates to or exacerbates many other diseases. The discrepancy lies between medical obesity and culturally defined voluptuousness. While the Africana woman has maintained a positive body image in her own mind, she is nonetheless aware of the negative stereotypes that exist about her. One poet reacts to the negative type: fat-black-ugly-mammy/Jemima, deftly creating a positive image with her volume of poetry entitled, *The Fat Black Woman Poems*. Grace Nichols with verve and good humor announces in "The Fat Black Woman Remembers:" ". . . her Mama/and them days of playing/the Jovial Jemima/ tossing pancakes/to heaven . . . But this fat black woman ain't no Jemima/Sure thing Honey/Yeah." Signifying on fat, Nichols's "Fat Poem" is an excellent example of naming and enumerating. "Fat is/as fat is/as fat is/Fat does/as fat thinks/Fat feels/as fat pleases." This entire section opposes the western interpretation of pulchritude, setting forth its own theory of that which is lovely.

Beauty articulated in the poems of Africana women is essentially interconnected with color. Una Marson announced her color claiming, "My blackness is a beautiful cloak/of selfhood that permeates the soul." Other poets, however, decry the difference color makes. Cheryl Clarke's "If You Black Get Back" included in the Girlhood section portrays the stinging repudiation of black skin by some Black people unable to resist society's definition of blackness. "Vashti ... was an ugly and dirty little black girl/whose nappy hair could not hold a curl/whose name nobody even wanted to say/much less to play/with her/so in awe of browns and tans we were." Maya Angelou's classic poem of pride and self-acceptance, "Phenomenal Woman," concludes the section on Africana physicality.

Motherhood

Africana women have written of and to their mothers, perhaps even more than have men, but what they have to say is different. Maybe they see the woman in the mother whereas men see mostly mythical mothers. African women poets are changing the poetic identity of the African mother. Their images are neither nostalgic nor symbolic. Included in this section are two perspectives on motherhood: the mother's and the daughter's. Frances Harper's "The Slave Mother," opens the section. Poems to or about being grandmothers and other mothers—surrogates through extended family ties or other relationships are here as well. Abena Busia's poem, "Though I Have Sworn," describing pregnancy in a strange land, opens the section on pregnancy and childbirth. Other pregnancy and childbirth poems include Kristina Rungano's "Labour," and Amelia Blossom Pegram's "Birthing."

Poems from the mother's perspective include Carole Stewart's "Don't Call me Mama" that demands people see her as a woman. Rita Dove's two poems, "Motherhood" and "Mother Love," both from the mother's perspective, challenge the assumptions about mother love and mothering. From the daughter's perspective motherhood is memory that captures frozen moments like Saundra Sharp's "Double Exposure," that invites her mother to get off her face. Stella Chipsula's "I Am My Own Mother Now," accepts responsibility for mothering the mother. Wanda Coleman and Audre Lorde close this section with "Dear Mama," and "Black Mother Woman" respectively, each from a daughter's stance.

Some poems clearly reject motherhood. Georgia Douglas Johnson's poem, "Black Woman," says: "Don't knock at my door, little child, /I cannot let you in." Included are poems on abortion. Gwendolyn Brooks's "The Mother" with its poignant opening line, "Abortions will not let you forget ...," and "Voodoo" about abortion by Miriam Alves appear in the Motherhood section; however, laina mataka's, "Just Be Cuz U Believe in Abortion Doesn't Mean U're Not Pro-Life," is categorized by its overtly political content as opposed to the apolitical tone the Brooks and Alves poems create.

Sarah Webster Fabio, and other daughters and granddaughters recall grandmothers in their poems. Margaret Walker's classic, "Lineage," memorializes the grandmother's strength. Maya Angelou reinforces the image of strength with her poem, "Our Grandmothers," but Alda Do Espirito Santo's poem,

"Grandma Mariana," softens and extends the image with her "mad old woman [that] does not have land anymore." The image is not a tower of strength but a woman wizened and worn-out by life.

Aging

Women age differently from men and in different cultures for women aging often is complex. Africana culture reveres age, and often women only gain respect in old age. Poems on aging and death include Mary Eliza (Perine) Tucker Lambert's "The First Grey Hair," which opens the section and Gladys May Casely Hayford's "The Palm Wine Seller," which looks at the aging African woman that the men do not see because of their wine-induced illusions. Marjorie Oludhe Macgoye poem exposes the fear children sometimes have of the elderly.

The poets approach the subject of death from various perspectives. African women, especially those in exile, focus on the significance of funerals. Abena Busia's "Exiles" is an example. The final poem in this section, June Jordan's "Ghaflah," reveals the pain of losing a loved one. For the most part, the poets are as accepting of death as they are of old age.

Relationships

Relationships include spiritual, family, sexual and political. This section opens with Africana poets' relationship to the spiritual universe. The spiritual orientation of these poets spans from the divine feminine of the Thunder Perfect Mind to the Christianity of Penny Jessye's "Good Lord in That Heaven," to Luisha Teish's "Hoodoo Moma." The beginning of the section contains excerpts from The Thunder Perfect Mind, the Nag Hammadi Library, the Obelisk Inscription of Queen Hatshepsut, Makeda, by the Queen of Sheba, and the Shulamite's contribution of the Song of Songs. "Good Lord in That Heaven," a traditional African American spiritual is here credited to Penny Jessye who set it to music. The section ends with the contemporary works that include Alice Walker's "Pagan," and captures the Africana woman's return to traditional African spirituality.

"Ancestors on the Auction Block" by Vera Bell introduces the section on family, friends and significant others, followed by Maggie Pogue Johnson's "Old Maid's Soliloquy" and Gwendolyn Brooks' "Sadie and Maud." This section reveals women's interconnections and kinship. It also covers violence and abuse of women by lovers, family members and others. Examples are Pat Parker's "Womanslaughter," Jayne Cortez's "Rape" and Riua Akinshegun's "Hands" among others.

Love and sexual relationships include women who love men as well as women who love other women. "Lines to an Old Dress," Mary Eliza (Perine)

Tucker's poem about the long ago joys and pains of a relationship now gone opens the topic, followed by Georgia Douglas Johnson's "I Want to Die While You Love Me," and Jessie Fauset's "Touché." Gladys May Casely-Hayford's "Rainy Season Love Song," introduces lesbian love succeeded by Kathleen Tankersley Young's "Hunger" for the woman whose "body is a dark wine." These early poems are followed by contemporary poetic statements: Pat Parker's "My Lady Ain't No Lady," and Sandra Royster's "Love Ain't Hip," Carolyn Rodger's "Now Ain't That Love," and Grace Nichols's "My Black Triangle," help to define love and sexuality.

Political relationships begin with an excerpt from "To The Right Honorable William Earl of Dartmouth" by Phillis Wheatley, followed by "White Things" by Anne Spencer and "Women Together" by Mabel Segun of Nigeria. The political context introduced by these poems acknowledges that the personal is indeed political. Sylvia Hamilton's "Shoes," demonstrates how the simple act of shopping for shoes for the Africana woman can be an encounter with racism. Hamilton is a Canadian poet. S. Pearl Sharp using the same metaphor of shopping explores the privileges that capitalism and class create in the United States. Her "The Never Woman" ". . . will never catch a May Co. white sale/on 200 thread percale." Sharp recognizes that her "tears," read as poems, "are no ablution for the/never hanging in [the never woman's] eyes." The politics of poverty, the body politics of pregnancy and abortion, of colonialism, imperialism, and sexism appear in this section. "Fact," by Esmeralda Riberio clearly exhibits these themes. This sections ends with Audre Lorde's paradigmatic poem, "Need: A Chorale For Black Woman Voices" that questions violence and wonders how women can use the pain of their experiences to create and live better lives.

Tributes

The final section of this anthology is a collection of praise poems to women who are famous and to those whose names no one will recognize. The section opens with a praise song to Ella Fitzgerald. Famous women saluted in this section include Phillis Wheatley, Sojourner Truth, Harriet Tubman, Frances Harper, Stagecoach Mary, Lucy Prince, and more from Pat Parker's "Movement in Black." Gwendolyn Brooks, Nikki Giovanni, Fannie Lou Hamer, Billie Holiday, Ma Rainy, Bessie Smith, Alberta Hunter, Josephine Baker, Ella Baker, Anne Nzinga, Rosa Parks, and Mary Muthoni Nyanjiru are also among the many women praised. In her poem for Josephine Baker, Jayne Cortez praises and chastises. The section ends with Giovanni's classic "Ego Tripping (there may be a reason why)" and Grace Nichols's "Epilogue." Both of these poems begin in Africa and end in the Diaspora. Giovanni's poem reclaims our soul, saying, "I can fly like a bird in the sky" while Nichols recovers our voice with her "new tongue" that "has sprung," where the old one was lost in the oceans we have crossed.

In an anthology such as this, there are, unavoidably, many omissions even though I have made a concerted effort to be inclusive of age, class, political persuasion, sexual orientation and writing styles. Perhaps this offering will inspire others to take up the task of editing more Africana women's poetry.

Nagueyalti Warren
Atlanta, Georgia

Works Cited

Alves, Miriam and Carolyn Richardson, eds. *Enfim . . . Nos/Finally . . . Us.* Colorado Springs: Three Continents Press, 1995.

Angelou, Maya. *I Know Why the Caged Bird Sings.* New York: Random House, 1969.

Baker, Houston and Patricia Redmond, eds. *Afro-American Literary Studies in the 1990s.* Chicago: U of Chicago P, 1989.

Baraka, Imamu. *Blues People: Negro Music in White America.* New York: William Marrow, 1968.

Birch, Eva. *Black American Women Writing.* New York: Harvester, 1994.

Brown, Ann. "Support for Black Books: African American Women Tackle Publishers," *Black Enterprise* (September 2001): 194.

Brown, Lyn Mikel. *Raising Their Voices: The Politics of Girl's Anger.* Cambridge: Harvard UP, 1998.

Bryan, Beverley, Stella Dadzie, and Suzanne Scafe, eds. *The Heart of the Race: Black Women's Lives in Britain.* London: Virago, 1985.

Cade, Toni, ed. *The Black Woman: An Anthology.* New York: Signet, 1970.

Campbell, Elaine and Pierrette Frickey, eds. *The Whistling Bird: Women Writers of the Caribbean.* Bolder and London: Lynne Rienner, 1998.

Carroll, Rebecca. *Sugar in the Raw.* New York: Crown, 1997.

Chipasula, Stella and Frank, eds. *The Heinemann Book of African Women's Poetry.* Oxford: Heinemann, 1995.

Christian, Barbara. *Gender and Theory: Dialogues on Feminist Criticism.* Ed. Linda Kauffman. NY: Blackwell, 1989. 113-32.

_____. "The Highs and Lows of Black Feminist Criticism." *Reading Black, Reading Feminist.* Ed. Henry Louis Gates. New York: Meridian, 1990. 44-52.

Cixous, Helene. "The Laugh of the Medusa." *SIGNS* 1 (4) 1976: 875-894.

Cleaver, Eldridge. *Soul on Ice.* New York: McGraw-Hill, 1968.

Collins, Patricia Hill. "The Politics of Black Feminist Thought." *Black Feminist Thought: Knowledge, Consciousness, and the Politics of Empowerment.* NY: Routeledge, 2000.

Cook, Mercer and Stephen Henderson. *The Militant Black Writer in Africa and the United States.* Madison: U of Wisconsin Press, 1969.

Derrida, Jacques. "Structure, Sign and Play in the Discourse of the Human Sciences," *The Structuralist Controversy: The Language of Criticism and the Sciences of Man.* Eds. Richard Macksey and Eugenio Donato. Baltimore: The Johns Hopkins UP, 1972.

Donnell, Alison and Sarah Welsh, eds. *The Routledge Reader in Caribbean Literature.* London and New York: Routledge, 1996.

Eliot, T.S. "Tradition and the Individual Talent," *Selected Essays.* New York: Harcourt, Brace, 1950.

El Naga, Shereen Abou, "The Theme of Motherhood in Sub-Saharan Women's Poetry," *ALIF* 17 (1997): 143-160.

Gabbin, Joanne, ed. *The Furious Flowering of African American Poetry*. Charolettesville, VA: U VA Press, 1999.

Gates, Henry Louis, Jr., "Talking That Talk," *Critical Inquiry* 13 no.11 (1986): 203-10.

_____. *Loose Canons: Notes on the Culture Wars*. NY: Oxford UP, 1993.

Giovanni, Nikki. *Gemini: An Extended Autobiographical Statement on my First Twenty-Five Years of Being a Black Poet*. New York: Viking, 1971.

Harris, Wilson. "Art and Criticism," *Kyk-over-al* 3 no. 13 (December 1951): 202-05.

Heidegger, Martin. "Holderlin and the Essence of Poetry," *Existence and Being*. Trans. Douglas Scott. London: Vision, 1949.

Henderson, Stephen. *Understanding the New Black Poetry*. New York: William Marrow, 1973.

hooks, bell. *Talking Back: Thinking Feminist, Thinking Black*. Boston: South End Press, 1989.

Honey, Maureen, ed. *Shadowed Dreams: Women's Poetry of the Harlem Renaissance*. New Brunswick: Rutgers, 1989.

Hughes, Langston, ed. *Poems From Black Africa*. Bloomington: Indiana UP, 1963.

Johnson, Barbara. "Metaphor and Metonymy in *Their Eyes Were Watching God*," *Black Literature and Literary Theory*. Ed. Henry Louis Gates, Jr. New York: Methuen, 1989. 205-219.

Jordan, June. *Soulscript: Afro-American Poetry*. New York: Doubleday, 1970.

Joyce, Joyce Ann. *Warriors, Conjurers and Priests: Defining African-Centered Literary Criticism*. Chicago: Third World Press, 1994.

Juhasz, Suzanne. *Naked and Fiery Forms*. New York: Octagon Books, 1976.

Karenga, Ron. "Ron Karenga and Black Cultural Nationalists," *Negro Digest* 17 no. 3 (January 1968): 4-9.

Kingsolver, Barbara. *The Poisonwood Bible*. New York: Harper Collins, 1998.

Lihamba, Amandina. "Introduction." *My Mother's Poems and Other Songs* by Micere Mungo. Nairobi: East African Educational Publishers, 1994.

Linthwaite, Illona, ed. *Ain't I a Woman: Classic Poetry by Women from Around the World*. London: Virago Press, 1987.

Lorde, Audre. "Poetry is not a Luxury," *Sister Outsider: Essays and Speeches*. [1984] New York: Quality Paperbacks, 1987.

Mackey, Mary. "Women's Poetry: Almost Subversive." *Naked and Fiery Forms*. Ed. Suzanne Juhasz. New York: Octagon Books, 1976.

Montefiore, Jan. *Feminism and Poetry: Language, Experience, Identity in Women's Writing*. London: Pandora, 1994.

Mungo, Micere Githae. *My Mother's Poems and Other Songs*. Narobi: East African Educational Publishers, 1994.

Nzegwu, Nkiru. "African Women and the Fire Dance," *West Africa Review*. 2 no.1 (2000) [iuicode:*http://www.icaap.org/iuicode?101.2.1.11*].

Richter, David H., ed. *The Critical Tradition: Classic Texts and Contemporaary Trends*. Boston: St. Martin's, 1998.

Sherman, Charolette Watson, ed. *Sisterfire*. New York: Harper, 1994.

Susheila, Nasta, ed. *Motherlands: Black Women's Writing From Africa, the Caribbean and South Asia*. London: Women's Press, 1992.

Walker, Alice. *In Search of Our Mother's Gardens*. New York: Harcourt Brace, 1983.

Walker, Margaret. *On Being Female, Black, and Free*. Ed. Maryemma Graham. Knoxville: U of TN Press, 1997. 15.

Washington, Mary Helen. "The Darkened Eye Restored: Notes Toward a Literary History of Black Women." *Reading Black Reading Feminist*. Ed. Henry Louis Gates. New York: Methuen, 1989. 30-43.

Notes

1. *The Furious Flowering of African American Poetry* (1999) Joanne Gabbin's excellent collection of essays considers critically the work of only three women poets, lucille clifton, Alice Walker and Gwendolyn Brooks. The rest are devoted to African American men poets. Ann Venture Young's research on *The Image of Black Women in Twentieth-Century South American Poetry* (1992) is a valuable source but deals mostly with the works of men. Tanure Ojaide and Tajan M. Sallah, editors of *The New African Poetry: An Anthology* (1999) present an informative overview of African poetry and include the works of several women. One of the best critical examination of African poetry, Ojaide's *Poetic Imagination in Black Africa* (1996), contains but a few pages devoted to women poets.

2. The term Africana refers to women of Black African descent and is interchangeable with the term Black.

3. It cannot be universal when it excludes them.

4. A river in South Carolina where during the Civil War General Harriet Tubman led a military campaign freeing 750 slaves. The Collective, a group of African American feminist in Boston, took its name from this river. Founded in 1974, they struggle against all forms of oppression.

5. The term bell hooks introduced into currency and uses to complicate and highlight the nuances and complex web of racism and sexism as they occur in an economic context.

6. Mireya Navarro, "Sacramento's Shaken Ukrainian Residents Hold Funeral for 6 slain Relatives," *The New York Times* (August 27, 2001): Doc 78465.

7. Friedrich Holderlin the German poet, quoted in "Holderlin and the Essence of Poetry," by Martin Heidegger.

8. Allison Jagger's term used in Lyn Mikel Brown's, *Raising Their Voices: The Politics of Girl's Anger*. Cambridge: Harvard UP, 1998, 10.

9. Little, an African American imprisoned in North Carolina, forced to perform oral sex on a prison guard, killed him in self-defense. Charged with first-degree murder, she was acquitted in 1975, after an outcry from feminist groups and the support of the NAACP.

10. Her entire poem is not included due to copyright problems.

11. Date of the Reverend Dr. Martin Luther King, Jr.'s assassination.

12. The report, "The Negro Family: The Case for National Action," produced in 1965 by Daniel Patrick Moynihan, defined the Black family as pathological, blaming the Black woman's strength rather than poverty and racism for emasculating Black men.

13. From *interdite*, "forbidden, disconcerted, confounded, speechless." Translated by Richard Macksey and Eugenio Donato.

14. The disruption of presence, *freeplay* is always an interplay of absence and presence.

15. Black cultural nationalist; founder of the Los Angeles based US Organization and creator of Kwanzaa.

16. Term used by Kimberly W. Benson in "Performing Blackness: Re/Placing Afro-American Poetry." *Afro-American Literary Study in the 1990s*. Eds. Houston Baker, Jr., and Patricia Redmond. Chicago: U Chicago Press, 1989. 184.

17. Helene Cixous' essay, "The Laugh of the Medusa," states: "If a woman has always functioned 'within' the discourse of man, a signifier that has always referred back to the opposite signifier which annihilates its specific energy and diminishes or stifles its very sounds, it is time for her to dislocate this 'within,' to explode it, turn it round, and seize it, taking it in her own mouth, biting that tongue with her very own teeth to invent for herself a language to get inside of" 887.

18. Language of the white male English speaking intelligentsia.

19. Micere Githae Mugo's term for heoric mothers. Adapted here to function in the same capacity as Henderson's mascon words concerning blackness. Mascon words have massive concentrations of black experiential energy and cultural resonance. Examples are words like "rock, roll, jelly, and jam."

20. Term borrowed from Wilson Harris, "Art and Criticism," *Kyk-Over-al* 3 no. 13 (December 1951): 202-05.

21. Natasha Trethewey has won a Pulitzer Prize in 2007 for her collection *Native Guard*.

22. In a *New York Times Book Review* of Mary Helen Washington's *Invented Lives*, Henry Louis Gates coined the term to describe Black women's fiction.

23. Barbara Johnson describes the writer's task as one needing to narrate the appeal and the injustice of universalization, "in a voice that assumes and articulates its own, ever differing self-difference" 218.

24. Milton Jordan. "Joan Little: From Petty Thief to Celebrity, A Young Black Woman Discovers That Her Image Is What Others Want it to Be," *Charlotte Observer*. August 14, 1975: 1A, 4A.

PASSAGES

GIRLHOOD

The girl is mother of the woman

To a Dark Girl
Gwendolyn B. Bennett | *United States*

I love you for your brownness
And the rounded darkness of your breast.
I love you for the breaking sadness in your voice
And shadows where your wayward eye-lids rest.

Something of old forgotten queens
Lurks in the lithe abandon of your walk
And something of the shackled slave
Sobs in the rhythm of your talk.

Oh, little brown girl, born for sorrow's mate,
Keep all you have of queenliness,
Forgetting that you once were slave,
And let your full lips laugh at Fate!

At the Carnival

Anne Spencer | *United States*

Gay little Girl-of-the-Diving-Tank,
I desire a name for you,
Nice, as a right glove fits;
For you—who amid the malodorous
Mechanics of this unlovely thing,
Are darling of spirit and form.
I know you—a glance, and what you are
Sits-by-the-fire in my heart.
My Limousine-Lady knows you, or
Why does the slant-envy of her eye mark
Your straight hair and radiant inclusive smile?
Guilt pins a fig-leaf; innocence is its own adorning.
The bull-necked man knows you—this first time
His itching flesh sees form divine and vibrant health
And thinks not of his avocation.
I came incuriously—
Set on no diversion save that my mind
Might safely nurse its brood of misdeeds
In the presence of a blind crowd.

The color of life was gray.
Everywhere the setting seemed right
For my mood.
Here the sausage and garlic booth
Sent unholy incense skyward;
There a quivering female-thing

Gestured assignations, and lied
To call it dancing;
There, too, were games of chance
With chances for none;
But oh! Girl-of-the-Tank, at last!
Gleaming Girl, how intimately pure and free

The gaze you send the crowd,
As though you know the dearth of beauty
In its sordid life.
We need you—my Limousine-Lady,
The bull-necked man and I.
Seeing you here brave and water-clean,
Leaven for the heavy ones of earth,
I am swift to feel that what makes
The plodder glad is good; and
Whatever is good is God.
The wonder is that you are here;
I have seen the queer in queer places,
But never before a heaven-fed
Naiad of the Carnival-Tank!
Little Diver, Destiny for you,
Like as for me, is shod in silence;
Years may seep into your soul
The bacilli of the usual and the expedient;
I implore Neptune to claim his child-to-day!

Sadie and Maud

Gwendolyn Brooks | *United States*

Maud went to college.
Sadie stayed at home.
Sadie scraped life
With a fine-tooth comb.

She didn't leave a tangle in.
Her comb found every strand.
Sadie was one of the livingest chits
In all the land.

Sadie bore two babies
Under her maiden name.
Maud and Ma and Papa
Nearly died of shame.

When Sadie said her last so-long
Her girls struck out from home.
(Sadie had left as heritage
Her fine-tooth comb.)

Maud who went to college,
Is a thin brown mouse.
She is living all alone
In this old house.

To Be Born
Miriam Alves | *Brazil*

Translated by Carolyn Richardson Durham

I was born
    from the ancient face a wrinkle vanished
I was born
    adorned skin on skin with the night.
I was born caressed in the   cradle of the star's
                                         infinite brilliance

I was born
    a flash of lightning begat me.

it's not so good to be born a girl/sometimes.
Ntozake Shange | *United States*

that's why society usedta throw us away/ or sell us/ or
play with our vaginas/ cuz that's all girls were good for. at
least women cd carry things & cook/ but to be born a girl
is not good sometimes/ some places/ such abominable
things cd happen to us. i wish it waz gd to be born a girl
everywhere/ then I wd know for sure that no one wd be
infibulated/ that's a word no one wants us to know.
infibulation is sewing our vaginas up with cat-gut or
weeds or nylon thread to insure our virginity. virginity
insurance equals infibulation. that can also make it
impossible for us to live thru labor/ make it impossible for
the baby to live thru labor. infibulation lets us get
infections that we can't mention/ cuz disease in the ovaries
is a sign that we're dirty anyway/ so wash yrself/ cuz once
infibulated we have to be cut open to have/ you know
what/ the joy of the phallus/ that we may know nothing
about/ ever/ especially if something else not good that
happens to little girls happens: if we've been excised. had
our labia removed with glass or scissors. If we've lost our
clitoris because our pleasure is profane & the presence of
our naturally evolved clitoris wd disrupt the very
unnatural dynamic of polygamy. So with no clitoris/ no
labia & infibulation/ we're sewn-up/ cut-up/ pared down
& sore if not dead/ & oozing pus/ if not terrified that so
much of our body waz wrong & did not belong on earth.
such thoughts lead to silence/ that hangs behind veils &
straightjackets/ it really is not good to be born a girl
when we have to be infibulated, excised, clitorectomized
& STILL be afraid to walk the streets or stay home at
night. i'm so saddened that being born a girl makes it
dangerous to attend midnight mass unescorted. some
places if we're born girls & someone else who's very sick
& weak & cruel/ attacks us & breaks our hymen/ we have
to be killed/ sent away from our families/ forbidden to
touch our children. these strange people who wound little

girls are known as attackers/ molesters & rapists. they are
known all over the world & are proliferating at a rapid
rate. to be born a girl who will always have to worry not
only about molesters/ the attackers & rapists/ but
also abt their peculiarities: does he stab too/ or shoot?
does he carry an axe? does he spit on you? does he know
if he doesnt drop sperm we cant prove we've been
violated? these subtleties make being a girl too complex/
for some of us & we go crazy/ or never go anyplace. some
of us never had an open window or walk alone, but
sometimes our homes are not safe for us either. rapists &
attackers & molesters are not strangers to everyone/ they
are related to somebody/ & some of them like raping &
molesting their family members better than a girl-child
they don't know yet. this is called incest, & girl children
are discouraged from revealing attacks from uncle or
daddy/ cuz what wd mommy do? after all/ daddy may
have seen to it that abortions were outlawed in his state/
so that mommy might have too many children to care abt
some "fun" daddy might be having with the 2-yr-old/
she's a girl after all/ we have to get used to it. but
infibulation, excision, clitorectomies, rape & incest are
irrevocable life-deniers/ life stranglers & disrespectful of
natural elements. i wish these wdnt happen
anywhere anymore/ then i cd say it waz gd to be born a
girl everywhere. even though gender is not destiny/ right
now being born a girl is to be born threatened; i want
being born a girl to be a cause for celebration/ cause for
protection & nourishment of our birthright/ to live freely
with passion/ knowing no fear that our species waz
somehow incorrect. & we are now plagued with rapists &
clitorectomies. we pay for being born girls/ but we owe no
one anything/ not our labia, not our clitoris, nor our lives.
we are born girls to live to be women who live our own
lives/ to live our lives. to have/ our lives/ to live. we are
born girls/ to live to be women . . .

In Naivete
Manjushree S. Kumar | *India*

The Minute,
The amniotic fluid dripped off me,
All Transience began.
Shriveled up, folds and creases
Marked my passage
Through the eternal doorway.
Passages, passages galore!
Labyrinthine meanings, interpretations
Swathed in sheaths of innocence,
Wrapped in Mystic knowledge,
Cradled in the
Music of my mother's murmurings
Limbs thrashing the ensconced space.
All was embraced—
Yes all of it.
I had folded them to my heart,
Flitting butterflies of cheer
Stoic, strong russet leaves
Floating down the brown,
Plucked from their bed of thought:
A long deep hush
On their ripeness and fall.
All was embraced
In paroxysms, I'd learnt
What dissolved
And flowed mutely through my arteries
my veins.

The Black Pearl

Constance E. Berkley | *United States*

The black pearl of a girl,
Cropped hair caught in cap,
Unfurled her awkward charms
Thurst slender arms skyward,
Pitched herself face first
Into the pool's cold embrace.

She laughter-lept up through the blue waves,
And placing one armstroke before the other
She pranced like a ballerina upon a stage,
Then clambered out onto the pool's edge.
The water falling from her angular curves
Transformed her into a tropic waterfall.

She stood ashiver-pores glistening,
Beneath moving droplets of moisture.

The eager sun swept prismic tints
Glinting through her lustrous color.
Her ebon glow at the water's edge
Cast a pall over the pool's onlookers.

Shafts of sunglow, blue halo of her hue,
Shot shadows across the silent poolside,
Struck secret chords, where rancor rose
Then crept quick across the summer breeze –

Abruptly the black child's joy subsided
Beneath the stare of discreet white wives
Focusing eyes upon her unique blackness,
Dare she intrude upon their country play,
Conjuring visions of other black children
Equally eager to barefoot leap through waves.

Girlhood

Like the comet fallen from orbit
The black pearl of a girl faltered.
Pride stood at the brink of peril,
Silent fear poised her for flight
Away from the oppressive whiteness,
Her eyes sought sanctuary in smile.

My eyes held her youthful tremors tight,
Apprehension braced black mother for battle.
Then as though sprung from steel trap
Defiance tilted her child-lips up,
Rebellion swelled her secret precipices
Where self stood sheltered from stranger.

Suddenly she sprang like a startled fawn,
To the forefront of her fairer companions;
Like young antelopes they went loping away,
Across the hot concrete to soft-grass play.
My eyes followed her frolicking form
Then shifted in gaze to the blue waves –
Where the black pearl had emerged
Like a blue moon over desert sands.

The Little Girl Like Me Killed Twice
Tara Betts | *United States*

Before the chubby-cheeked age of ten
I knew death could breathe on you early.
Another little girl spelled her name
same as me was found in a drainage ditch.
A predator bled a life out of her.
I never forgot same age, same name.

Twenty years later, I am watching
television with my mother in bed.
The same teenager, now a man set free
finds a tow-headed boy a few blocks
from the drainage ditch years past,
then loses him, the boy just a body
when found.

His elementary picture blazes innocent
across the screen, but the local paper
front page imprints plaits,
twisted black cotton candy
wrapped in pairs of purple plastic
bubbles, square teeth smiling
singed to ash, semen traced
on what's left. Brown skin
turned ash and bone.

She could have been me walking
to the library, the man slowing
down, with a tattered green wad,
sweating and asking my price.

Instead, she was untelevised,
at least she was fit to print,
unworthy of prime time news.
Does it matter
in name or face, when
you've been killed twice?

Only Child
Phebus Etienne | *Haiti/United States*

As we folded garments warm from the dryer,
we smiled at a golden brown toddler roaming around the table.
My mother reminisced about lamvéritab cooking on charcoal,
the mulatto complexion of her lost girl, and concluded
¿Li ta plis belle passé ou.¿

Early memory etched in me, an afternoon
soon after Valerie was buried. Our mother
searched a patch of blue beyond the lemon tree.
When I draped myself across her knees,
she pushed me to the speckled tile.

I have imagined an opposite of me, the daughter
who didn't sweat with exertion,
whose hair was not forced to submission with a hotcomb,
who could remain dainty all day in Easter lace,
who walked in summer not tanning darker
than a light brown paper bag.

Some children are made to become
replicas of their parents. Our mother could not
see us breathing like the butterfly leaves on a ginkgo tree,
stemming separately from a single limb,
but blossoming the same. She re-lived her grief
in the presence of newborns,
measured combination tones of my skin,
saw the nose which she wanted straighter,
and found me too much like the husband she had to leave.

lamvéritab ¿ breadfruit
¿Li ta plis belle passé ou.¿ ¿ She would have been prettier than you.

When is it clean?
Evie Shockley | *United States*

when your mother can rise from her place
on the pew during the early service,

so early that the sun barely fills the sky
with its weak straw, though row after row

in the auditorium is flush with folks who want
to be home before the football game gets underway

or hate the slower pace the later service takes
but still *got* to get their god on

before starting a new week: when she can rise
and tip down the aisle, three-inch heels

pointing a warning at hell through the plush
mauve carpet, smile and nod at the preacher,

who is sitting on the pulpit's little throne
with his bible beneath his palm, a man thick-chested

and stout-bellied with moral authority, whose face
gleams with crushing benevolent power:

when she can give him a pleasant nod,
and circle around behind the microphone standing

like a thin silver trophy between the heavenly
floral arrangements, give a firm tug

to the hem of her suit jacket, and lean over
the dimpled nob, the ribbons encircling the crown

Girlhood

of her broad-brimmed hat quivering with each
breath, the crisp white paper in her hands

held out at arm's length from her customary squint,
her eyes scooting back and forth

between this document and the village of worshippers
fanning themselves and waiting on her voice:

when she can stand there and coo *good morning,*
praise the lord and introduce her reading

as a poem by my daughter, with a quick look
at your beaming father, then take your words

between her lightly pinked lips and raise each one
to the light, before god and these witnesses,

enunciating the way she learned from the fourth-
grade primer in her schoolhouse's single room,

sending a sound through the vowels
like a bell: when she can do this—can rise and walk

and smile and read and have the church say *amen*—
then you can safely declare: it is clean.

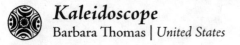

Kaleidoscope
Barbara Thomas | *United States*

A little Black girl in a slack cotton dress with faded colors

twirling and dancing

Looking into her mother's eyes for drops of sunshine
she sees only veiled clouds

she twirls and twirls

She looks, from across the room, at her father
her inside music stops her feet won't move

Slowly she turns and begins again to spin
Maybe if she turns fast enough the once-was-fertile
shade of green in her dress
will meld into the yesterday yellow, bursting into kaleidoscope colors that
envelope and comfort her

chasing away the colorless fear from inside

rescuing her from the 400 year old storm in her house

she twirls and twirls

Beatrice's Neck
Ann T. Greene | *United States*

My mother was
is
the darling of her hometown.
She and Miriam
her girlfriend then
laughed in the pews at Mt. Zion.
Their silky brown
in summer auburn heads bent
shoulders heaving
tongues battling illicit giggles
incited by another look at Beatrice.

Beatrice with her skinny neck
sitting a pew (or two)
in front of Mother and Miriam
whose curly locks freed from the
paper bag knots of the night before
danced.

Two colored Shirleys
Shirley Temples
with their saucy curls
unneeding heat.
Blessed brown girls of natural beauty
brown curled daughters
of the colored gentry
finger the lace hankies
Aunt Mamie starched and pressed
into their expectant hands.

Hankies full of pennies
copper pennies for Sunday collection at
Mt. Zion Church of God

where they would see Beatrice's neck
black
snow-capped by a pimple on the leathered skin
made by the tracks of Sun's rays
on her cotton picking back.

Oh how their eyes traveled
the creases of Beatrice's neck.
Oh how they filled with mirth
having seen the tell tale scars
the meniscus of pinked underskin at the hairline's edge
where Beatrice had touched up her naps.

Miriam laughed (between the Psalms)
and my mother hit her, their heads bounced together
colliding stars
these colored Shirleys
Shirley Temples
beloved daughters of the negro gentry
pretty girls with good hair
disturbing knotted hankies
of copper pennies
sated with the knowledge of Beatrice's shame.

My mother darling
of her hometown married my father.
It was spite
she confessed as she furrowed my scalp.
She gave him four children
nappyheaded every one.
She sighed as if to say
do I deserve this?
Four?

She followed me around the kitchen
we waltzed across the living room
the hot comb in her hand.

Girlhood

The smoke swirled leaving behind
the stink of my hair my burned ear.
All it took was that first touch
when
after she had sipped from her glass of gin
gin like heavy water where I glared distorted
half-done
one side in plaits
still throbbing from their shackling
the other oiled
aroused upright before being rolled in
paper strips and tied down
with a scarf of romping deer.
Then tied in a nylon net
and forbidden
although there was still
Saturday's light
to go outside.
Forbidden to play
almost to breathe
admonished to keep still sleep tight.

She sipped her gin and arched that red hot comb
before my eyes
I saw the burning before I felt it
and I ran half-crazed
half-done
away from her kitchen through the house
everywhere.
I was so ugly anyway
what difference did it make?

My mother
darling of her hometown
followed my father
before he was my father
out of Carolina and colored doorways.

And away from Mt. Zion
to the passionless droning of white
psalmody
where I and my brothers would be made to sit
with my father every Sunday morning.
He glistened with sweat and we
his copper pennies wrapped in the starch of
our mother's fury
buttoned and laced into silence we would sit
visible as all Hell
absent as nothingness
and my brothers with their shaven scalps
would point to me
my burns the pinked rims of my tender ears
slathered with Vaseline and radiating blood
for anyone to see.
My brothers would
heads together
sparks flying
from the friction of their hairs
blow snot between their fingers and choke into their palms
as their eyes slid sideways to look at me.
My father, whom I was made of,
could hear their laughter
and feel my eyes beg for sanctuary.
Oh Daddy please make them stop.
It's not my fault.

But he was quiet.
My Father said little to anyone, ever.
He had not spoken to my mother since my youngest brother
came who was not black like the rest of us.
He looked unlike my father and had my mother's hair.

So that she loved him more than life itself
she told me
and it was with him to him

that her unginned attention went.
It was his head not mine
not Daddy's
which lay between her milkless breasts and
her steady hand would walk through his scalp
and she would sing to him
my baby
my pretty baby.

In the summer it was that one
her favorite her curly-headed darling
that went home with her to Mama's house
and stayed inside
so as not to get darker
while I stayed behind reluctantly growing up
to starch and iron my father's shirts
and cook his pork chops which he ate in silence
with no grace.
Until the moment
the only moment we had together he took me in his
green De Soto to the beauty parlor
and stepped inside with his hat in hand.
Into the women's lair
with their nakedheads prior to perfection.
(Before beauty, absolution.)
And he said to the beautician,
brownskinned, with Spanish curles divining her face,
Can you do something with it?

The beautician took my motherless hair
unwashed
unpressed
in one hand.
Dismay darkened her pretty face and she told my
father
This will take a while.
And he nodded, releaved that it was not too late

after all.
She took me in the back and pushed me in a chair
and said
Velma see if you can do something with this girl's hair.

So that when my father arrived
(the setting sun backlighting his return)
and saw what Velma had done for me
he almost smiled.
He walked around my slatted body
he stood behind me in a mirror
and gave Velma a handful of dollars.
He offered me his arm and I
the woman to the green De Soto strolled
towards home.

Morena Mariposa
Jessenya Y. Hernandez | *El Salvador/United States*

My fourth grade hands
nag mi mama
while she cooks her enchiladas
>   *no se leer en ingles*
>   *se ríen de mi*

My sixth grade crushes bleed
when my dream boy labels me
albondiga con patas
colors my legs caca brown
so I ask mi papà
>   *porqué no eres blanco como mami*

My eighth grade muscles cringe
when mi abuelita picks me up
merengue música louder
than her muffler scraping the road
she sees me run to her car
lowers the volume
doesn't want me to get teased again

But my fine high school eyes
watch all who used to mop the ground
with my self-esteem
look stunned as I emerge from the cocoon
they all crave to taste my cinnamon brown skin
caress my winged thighs
as I fly fly past them
pretend they're not alive

When dream boy musters the courage
to take his foot out his mouth
and finally ask me to go out with him

TEMBA TUPU!

my butterfly reply

perdón
pendejo
no hablo ingles

Taproot I
Virginia K. Lee | *United States*

then no more talk
just mama's cries
and the whirling sound
of hot desert air rushing
through the front door
that makes a loud click
when daddy leaves

the aroma of his
Old Spice After Shave
and ribbons of white smoke
from his King Edward Cigar

reached behind the nubby
teddy bear brown couch
like long fingers
that tickle my nose
as I eavesdrop
on adult conversation

my six year old ears
hear daddy's words
tumble from his tongue
like large bricks that
shake the stucco walls
of our El Centro home

I want out
Let's quit this
We need to separate
he tells my mom

the cement of his words

weigh me down
can't move my legs
can't breathe

that night   in my bed
I wet a pool of anger

If You Black Get Back
Cheryl Clarke | *United States*

Vashti
with her one brown
and one hazel eye
was an ugly and dirty little black girl
whose nappy hair could not hold a curl
whose name nobody even wanted to say
much less to play
with her
so in awe of browns and tans we were.

Vashti
with her hard hazel eye
was dull in school
but broke no rule.
Teachers laughed openly at her stutter,
frequently calling upon her to read aloud.
Cowed, her face swelling like an udder,
she would rise to the effort
and the humiliation.

Vashti's hair was never straightened.
To be black was bad enough.
To be black and have nappy hair
was just plain rough.
Boys terrorized her.
Girls scorned her.
Adults walked the other way
to avoid the play
of Vashti's eyes
marking their cruelty.

So black she could stand out in a coal bin.
So black she was most nearly blue.

So black it was a sin.
So black she could stop the dew.
Vashti learned to live
and love with pain.
Wore it like a coat of armor
rather resembling an armadillo.

Red Clay
Oktavi Allison | *United States*

each rainy season
the grandmothers
in collusion
see to
it

a horrific
rite of passage

squatting tsungas
pour sand
raze labial lips
screams sewn shut
inside weltering vulvas

earthen floor
makeshift
carving board for
callow virgins

Pretty Girls Just Are
Bunmi Ogunsiji | *England*

Pretty girls don't talk.
They don't have opinions,
Nor do they indulge
In intellectual conversation.
Pretty girls don't think.
They never bother to delve
Beneath the surface of insincere words spoken.
Pretty girls don't care.
They close their eyes to everything ugly,
And never dabble in such trivia as politics.
Pretty girls merely look.
Pretty girls just are.

Poem for Flora
Nikki Giovanni | *United States*

when she was little
and colored and ugly with short
straightened hair
and a very pretty smile
she went to sunday school to hear
'bout nebuchadnezzar the king
of the jews

and she would listen

shadrach, meshach and abednego in the fire

and she would learn
how god was neither north
nor south east or west
with no color but all
she remembered was that
Sheba was Black and comely

and she would think

i want to be
like that

Nikki – Rosa
Nikki Giovanni | *United States*

childhood memories are always a drag
if you're Black
you always remember things like living in Woodlawn
with no inside toilet
and if you become famous or something
they never talk about how happy you were to have your
mother all to yourself and
how good the water felt when you got your bath
from one of those
big tubs that folk in Chicago barbecue in
and somehow when you talk about home
it never gets across how much you
understood their feelings
as the whole family attended meetings about Hollydale
and even though you remember
your biographers never understand
your father's pain as he sells his stock
and another dream goes
And though you're poor it isn't poverty that
concerns you
and though they fought a lot
it isn't your father's drinking that makes any difference
but only that everybody is together and you
and your sister have happy birthdays and very good
Christmases
and I really hope no white person ever has cause
to write about me
because they'll never understand
Black love is Black wealth
and they'll
probably talk about my hard childhood
and never understand that
all the while I was quite happy

She *Kadambini, immortalised by Tagore*
Bashabi Fraser | *Scotland*

Is Everywoman.
She is conceived without hankering
Grows without being wanted
And screaming she thrusts forward
To find her shrill note mingling
With the groans of a disapproving family
And a faltering mother's furtive care.

Her little hands learn to fetch and carry
Her father's newspaper and slippers
And balance his morning cup of tea
On a tipsy, crazy saucer, as her feet
Teach themselves not to go too fast
And spill or too slow to irritate.

She becomes a quick learner and a
Swift worker, swirling bedclothes to make
Beds that are tossed into shape and
Tucked into place with the
Hey presto magic of a Wallace and Gromit
Precision-filled, mechanical world ...
Only, in hers, she is the machine—
Efficient, obedient, immaculate.

Her brothers know that they can
Bring home football soiled
Strips, mud-splattered trainers
And line the house floor
With socks and their rucksacks
For her to gather and rub clean
Tumble-wash, unpack and reassemble
Today, for their next game tomorrow.

She can make her wants simple
Her appetite small
Bypass the nourishment
And wait in the stalls
Mixing abilities in tired
Schoolrooms; saying cheers
To her brothers who gleam
Amongst blazered peers.

She has a few choices—
Of love and a cradle
Of demanding attention
And a lifetime of Babel—
Or marriage and drawn dreams,
Of shopping and mopping
Of lost sleep and long hours
Youth giving at its seams—

...Or if she can scrape through
To grab one last space
In the ruthless rat-race
Of Uni and grade grind
She might just make do
To become the smart
Role model for young ones
With swelling breasts
Bursting with ambitions—
She'll have gusto in her speech rhythms
A swing to her hipline
Shadows under eye makeup
Holding back the brine.

She'll be the wizard cook
The bewitching wife
The mum of the dark ages
Who has forgotten a good life.
She will become the
Middle-aged embarrassment
Of her teenage entourage
And a perfect ensemble

Girlhood

Of a modern collage...
    Still running errands for her father
    Surreptitiously tidying
    Her mother's grey hair;
    Standing proxy for her
    Brother as a niece weds in time
    For the baby nearly there.
And if she is lucky
Her pressure may rise
To make her heart burst
And then all around her
Will recognise her at last
As the woman who sustained
Them, and feel bereaved
Of one who remained
Alive for the living—
Unwanted, unnoticed
Unidentified till dead—
Like Tagore's Kadambini.

Labyrinth Poem
Jadi Omowale | *United States*

At nine, I like old people.
Like a loyal dog, I follow them.
I am good company.
A congenial, obedient listener.

I sit on Mrs. Madelyn's sofa,
eat stale sugar cookies, drink hot tea.
She shows me her blue ribbons.
Pale hands press photos of her garden.

Old Mrs. Smith is baking biscuits.
She says, come taste the honey butter warmth.
My eyes do not reach above the stove,
I am happy and loved like a puppy.

Outside the over heated rooms of the aged,
I am a ghost child. A good girl
in the harsh yellow lit rooms
where too many bodies move.

Where the good mother is too busy to see me,
except when my hands are razors
I use to cut through all that movement
to a still, silent space of my own.

I dream of honey sweet child falling from her lips,
she is too busy moving among all those bodies.
There is no time for honey sweet girl.
There is only time for slap or strap.

I am the good girl dog. I follow the old ladies
in the quiet sanctuaries of their coming deaths.
I am made warm and visible in their kitchens.

From "The Iconography of Childhood"
Sherley Anne Williams | *United States*

II.

These are tales told in darkness
in the quiet at the ends
of the day's heat, surprised in
the shadowed rooms of houses
drowsing in the evening sun.

In this one there is music
and three women; some child is
messing with the Victrola.
Before Miss Irma can speak
Ray Charles does of "The Nighttime"
and *Awww* it Is the fabled

music *yo'alls* seldom given
air play in those Valley towns
heard mostly in the juke-joints
we'd been toold About; and so
longed for in those first years in
the Valley it had come to

seem almost illicit to
us. But the women pay us
no mind. We settle in the
wonder of the music and
their softly lit faces listening
at the songs of our grown.

III.

Summer mornings we
rose early to go

and rob the trees
bringing home the
blossoms we were told
were like a white girl's
skin. And we believed
this as though we'd
never seen a white
girl except in
movies and magazines.

We handled the
flowers roughly
sticking them in oily
braids or behind
dirty ears laughing
as we preened ourselves;
savoring the brown
of the magnolias'
aging as though our color
had rubbed off
on the petals' creamy
flesh transforming some
white girl's face into
ornaments for our
rough unruly heads.

V.

The buildings of the
Projects were arrayed
like barracks in
uniform rows we
called regulation
ugly, the World in
less than one square block.
What dreams our people
had dreamed there seemed to

us just like the Valley
so much heat and dust.

Home training was
measured by the day's
light in scolds and
ironing cords; we
slipped away from chores
and errands from
orders to stay in
call to tarry in
the streets: gon learn what
downhome didn't teach.

And
Sundown didn't hold us
long. Yet even then
some grown-up sat still
and shadowed waiting
for us as the sky
above the Valley

              dimmed.

VI.

Showfare cost a lot
but we ran the
movies every chance
we got, mostly grade
B musicals that
became the language
of our dreams. Baby
Lois sang in the
rain for the hell of
it; Helen was a
vamp. Ruise was the
blood-red rose of

Texas, her skin as
smooth and dark as a
bud with just a hint
of red.
Sweating and
slightly shamefaced, we
danced our own routines
seeing our futures
in gestures from some
half remembered films.
We danced crystal
sidewalks thrilled in the
arms of neighborhood
boys and beheld our
selves as we could be
beyond the Projects:
the nine and ten year
old stars of stage and
screen and black men's hearts.

Rites of Passages
Jane Alberdeston | *Puerto Rico/United States*

I.

Abuela says in the old days
when there was nothing,
there was always crab,
chased in the sandy backyards of Anasco
still ringing with the night's areyto.

With tongs and spoons, shoe heels and hangers,
she snatched them as the crabs skittered away.
Uphill, downhill, through bruja brush
and mimosa patch, she scooped them into buckets,
straw garden hats, potato sacks.

Abuela says kept them under her Papa's criollo
sun, muddy-blue cangrejos crawling
over each other in big plastic paint drums.
She fattened them like they were prize chickens,
tossing in leftover pegao and bread,
corn off the old cob and fresh coconut.

II.

I watch them under the bucket's lid,
find a crab legless, defeated,
macho against macho.
Ignoring the riot around him,
another pinches grains of rice, as if
contemplating life's meaning.

Careful not to fall in, I smell their sweat:
a Junco dirt road, cleavage in a cook's dress.
In a few hours, Abuela will shoo me away
and begin to hose them down,
whispering in her hill-Spanish.

Abuela teaches me at five
how to eat crab: her fingers pop their eyes,
peel back the belly's lid like small jewelry
boxes. They snap open, reveal steaming meat,
sunny-white and velvet, humming with sweetness.

All afternoon, my sister and I,
stick figures, stand at the stove,
listening to the cauldron's boil,
the cacophony of bubble and whistle,
their hairy legs and ours,
a Loiza sapphire, a Fajardo sunset.

The men of the house— turned ghosts,
drowned out by our girl din. Eight hands
doing work: granddaughter, daughter, grandmother
cracking, plucking, sucking juice
from the dead.

By dusk, our lips are swollen,
red as the honey inside
of the crab girl's abdomen.
Busy with my fingers, I forget to wonder
if I am just as coral. Shell shards cling
to our cheeks, sting our uncombed hair.
We lean in to one another. We sweat,
slip straps fall off shoulders.

Childhood
Grace Nichols | *Guyana/England*

My childhood
was a watershed of sunlight
and strange recurring mysteries

the fishes before a drought
came in droves
floundering at our backdoors

saltwater drove them in
moving groggy shadows
beneth the mirror surfacing

sunfish/patwa/butterfish
half stunned I watched
bare hand I gripped

at Sunday school
we didn't learn to pray
for the dying freshwater souls of fish

Angel
Venus Thrash | *United States*

I am seven
I want to be an angel
in the second grade Christmas pageant
because I have never been an angel.

Angels are hushed and still.
Loud as bare feet on a mound of cotton.
Fluttery as leaves on a breezeless night.
I want to be an angel.

I must not bat an eye.
I must stop chasing boys in the hall.
To be in the second grade Christmas pageant
I must act like a lady.

I have never acted like a lady.
I have never been an angel.
I steal my brothers' cars and trucks.
I pop off the heads of my dolls.

Angels are hushed and still.
I am loud and fluttery.
I have demanded to be called Vince.
I am only seven.

I want the boys to wrestle me not run from me.
I want to peck the cheeks of giggly little girls
I want to be in the second grade Christmas pageant.
I want to be an angel

because I have never been an angel.
I tear from Auntie's hand sewn dresses.
My hair sits in a ratty mess by midday

Girlhood

after Mama made it so pretty for me.

Because Mama has said I am her angel.
Daddy loves every loud-laughing, tree-climbing part of me.
Made me too strong to be bound by pink ribbons and bows.
I am seven.

I want to be an angel.

Mother and Me
Mamta G. Sagar | *India*

I'm exactly like my mother
—thin body, bony fingers,
dark circles below the eyes;
within, a heavy heart
loaded with cares; a mind
beset with thoughts it can't
quite carry; and on the surface,
a smooth smile.

I'm like my mother exactly;
her tears flow in my eyes.

Gardening and Growing Up
Ebony Golden | *United States*

mama says
sit lady like
cross legs at ankles
squeeze knees tight
enough to press
the creases out
daddy's sunday church
going slacks

but i ain't

i sit with my legs wide
even wearing skirts
hemmed above the knee
at mid thigh

and my pussy perfumes
the stale masculine air

i sit with my legs wide
pastel moths
kiss vulva
lick excretions
become iridescent
float on pheromones

i don't wear panties
in summer
and juices dance
trickle down
the back of my thighs
fertilize the earth beneath me

i leave flowers where ever i go

Girl at the Window
Pinkie Gordon Lane | *United States*

She sits there
hand on cheek, head
turned towards the open window
where shadows pulsate
like quivering beasts

Summer and autumn
contend in blue skies
and spiraling air —
ghosts and green light
a mere breath touching

A golden animal streaks
across space
and lavender hills outline
the rim

Will they tell
the level of seasons?
Will they fly home
to the sky?

Her skin is copper-toned
and eyes the nests
of birds   She
dreams of Nairobi
and wildebeests

the equator a blue line slung in midair

Journal at Sixteen
Joy Gonsalves | United States

Yesterday, I lost my virginity.
I waited for the cab at the curb
of the elementary school
up the street, out of his mom's sight
if she drove past. Outside,
the clouds rolled their bellies
across the sky in fits.
Inside, the janitor wheeled his trash.

I miss my boyfriend, still inside
the basement of his house.
He must be putting
something else in his mouth
—ice cream this time—
and then, he'll go back to his video games.

It was Valentine's Day, so
I saved the half-eaten heart I gave him.
What else? I wore green velvet leggings
and the pink cotton panties
he wants me to grow out of.

My crotch still kind of hurts,
and I keep thinking about Mom,
how she doesn't know
I didn't catch the bus today, either.
And Dad's face, when I had
my first period: You're a lady now.

Four-something, and I heard the wind
howling at me. The backseat
of the cab was ripped and it smelled
like a dirty house. They all do.
The rides are long and all the drivers
are strange men. But he knows
I'll do anything for him. He knows,
even after a good cry, I'll do it again.

Guinea Hen
Olive Senior | *Jamaica/Canada*

in Granny's eyes, our foremost barnyard warrior is not
    after all our fierce Rooster or surly Turkey Gobbler
but mild Guinea Hen, her badge of office her spotted
    feathers. She stands on guard at that barrier they
    call
Reputation. For Granny explicating the difference
    between Good Girls and Bad always ends her homily
with warning as fact: *Seven year not enough*
    to wash speckle off Guinea Hen back

When Granny holds up Guinea Hen as the symbol
    of girls' ruin, we study her pattern and interpret
Granny's warning to mean: *Not that you can't do so.*
    Just don't let the world know.
    Never let the spots show.

American Pie
Nagueyalti Warren | *United States*

I'm seven in the porch swing
looking up at a periwinkle sky—
tiny cotton-wool clouds
floating so like a turtle
I can see how the world turns—
It's not fast, but slower than the butterfly's
wing fanning our honeysuckle bush.
I'm in shorts, halter-top, blue tennis,
daydreaming I'm a movie star,
when four boys on Schwinn Stingray bikes
petal past our wide front porch.

I smile and wave, they yell,
"nigger bitch!"
fast riding down the long street.

Acts of Power
Sharan Strange | United States

At 8,
the magnets of my fickle thoughts
were three; school, boys & play.
They gave me furlough from home's cell.
At school, I pleased benevolent wardens
with mathematical & verbal skill.

                              Boys
were mine to climb trees with, hunt
blackberries & plums, plot strategy
in simulated war. One boy, my brother,
tirelessly taunted me in games of tag.
He'd let me come *this close* before
springing out of reach...

                              Play
went on mostly inside my head. I
devised a life that appeased some inner
god, that plucked a wire in me to sound
I AM & released me from the stasis
of numb things. It spun me out like a top,
dancing to the world's bright limits; then,
responding to a rhythm arbitrary & true,
arced me back to the axis, communal core.

                              I sat
in a field among tall green reeds whose
cayenne-colored tips waved like anemone.
We'd suck the salty juices from the stalks –
taste of our thirsting bodies, taste of
the source of life, the sea.

                              Drunk
on their tears, I ran toward home
and in the road between collided
with the sudden car. Rebellious brakes
halted it –no, I! It sent me hurtling,
a sprung torpedo singing home. The machine
acceded to a force more delicate
& braver than its own.

Sins of the Fathers
Jacqueline Johnson | *United States*

A nine year old dressed in black keds,
red striped shirt and shorts.
I rode your bike to see Uncle E.
You Skip, my only escort.
Some six feet tall, acrid smell
of animal on your sweaty, yellow skin.

You stop near a highway ravine.
How the earth lost its sound.
I saw my death in your eyes
like all the young dogs and cats
that mysteriously disappeared in your care.
Brown girl long neck, long waist,
trapped among deep green of trees.
Flashes of whiteness, blueness of sky
as you stood like a shadow over me.

On the day you tried to kill me
all my ancestors entered
a great swoosh pushing your hands
off my nine year old neck.
I became wind, and bird.
My screams a mother wail
that did not stop for years,
until I traveled south became
my grandmother's daughter.

I remember your father's shouts
                    shaking of his body
                    as he beat you to the ground.

Little Black Girls, The Original Eve
Karen Williams | *United States*

A
Bodacious
  Black
  Bad
    Beautiful
      Beguiling celebration
of verve, curves
raw naked nerve
spreads her
    beautiful
     black
      strong
on the cutting edge legs
and breathes, heaves
clutches the heavens
and gives birth to
    beautiful
     brown seeds
of ingenuity
each time
she gives birth to
   Black
    Beautiful
     Female
     Me

     The Original Eve

destined to spring
from her
  Beautiful

  Black
  loins
to incubate
  give birth
    to more of her
    Beautiful
    Black
      seed

Little Black Girls
One of the true joys of motherhood

Morning Ritual of Protest
DeLana Dameron | *United States*

I demand more moments of sleep, now,
after rejecting the necessity of nighttime hours.

Mama dresses me like display-case doll,
cures slobber-ash with quick slick saliva
thumb brush, smoothes out, flattens,
shapes my nose and chin; molds a sculpture.

Mama made sure to measure my naps
in perfect quarters on head, twisted and
clasped with matching barrettes, my hair
pulled tight till my eyes welled hatred
for the rites of girlhood.

Mama would later learn that her tomboy of a girl
with neatly parted hair, dress with ruffles forever,
ankle-cuff socks and patent-leather shoes,
wouldn't last past recess and mudpies,
or naptime fumbles to loosen mama's expectations.

Illusion
Colleen J. McElroy | *United States*

I hate wide mouth black girls
with their loud walnut faces.
I hate their bright white eyes
and evil tongues,

their hen cackle laughs
that startle birds
roosting in trees miles away.
I hate their graceful jungle steps,
the steps they fall into too easily,
a downbeat only they can hear.

They stir cities,
cause concrete to tremble.
I hate the way their backs
taper into a narrow base
before spreading, graceful
round and proud as a peacock's.

Their firm black legs
insult me with swift movements,
feet in tempo even as they walk
to pick up the evening paper;
turning pages noisily to find
comic strips, the rustle of paper
paced with the pop of many sticks
of Juicy Fruit.

I hate the popping fingers,
the soft flash of color
turning like butterscotch buds
in a field of wind wild
dandelion greens.

Girlhood

I turn away from high cheek bones
and wide spread mocha nostrils
finely honed to catch the scent
of paddy-rollers or pig faced sheriffs.

This country has made them
sassyfaced.
They sneer at mousey mongoloid blondes
who move coolly blind
through a forest of suburbs,
lisping about posh uptown hotels.

I hate the pain that makes them
bulldog their way through
downtown crowds,
makes them nurture dead minds
and naturally accent cheap clothes
with finely curved licorice colored shoulders.

They bury Nerfertiti charms
under outstretched lips,
grow older under frowns
and a hurricane of bad manners;

they grow barbed, cold,
these Sapphires and Mabel Sues
from ebony to dusky brown,
from creme and rust to lemon yellow.

They are my sisters
and we sit in a barracks of noise,
trading screams with wandering
no-caring   louder   brothers.

Stoplight Politics
Ruth Forman | *United States*

check out
sista
on de corner
bar-b-q Fritos Fanta soda
dookie braids
knee-high boots
Raiders jacket
gold tooth
talkin shit

she embarrass you huh

go head sista
roll on by
you
rollin somewhere
you
gon conquer the nation
worl in yo hand
wich yo education

you
better den sista
on de corner
thank god
you never
did hang wit de brothas
goin nowhere
talking shit
waitin for de light to turn green

go head
turn yo head

Girlhood

look straight ahead
n roll that Lexus home
to yo fifty g man hundred g crib

pray for de light ta turn green
befo you look back ova
one more time
n realize
you both de same thang
hopin on de same thang

you jus got a car

The Crazy Girl
Sharan Strange | *Germany/ United States*

She was given to fits,
so was her brother.
There was a category
for him. *Retarded*, they said.
Something nearer to sin named her.

Oh, the family claimed
its share of deviance —inbreeding,
generation after generation
of drunks, rootworkers, thieves,
feuds carried on with
the extravagant viciousness of kin.

But hers was an unpredictable
violence —more disturbing because
she wasn't a man, besides
being a child. So they settled
on puberty —the mysterious workings
of female hormones —until she
outgrew it and the moniker stuck.

It accounted for the rage
worn on her face, tight as
a fist, fear and restlessness in eyes
like July 4th's slaughtered pig.
Rebellious, wooly hair only
partly tamed by braids, she often
inflicted pain during play.
Boys her favorite victims,
she tore clothes, skin,
marked virgin expanses of face, neck, arms
with scratches like filigreed monograms.

Girlhood

Her notoriety was assured when,
at 16, she disappeared, leaving
rumor to satisfy the family's need
to understand, giving context to
her uncle's slow slide into madness,
her sullen body bruised by constant
scratching, as if she could
somehow remove his touch.

Girl Talk
Monique Griffiths | *England*

Cha, me tired of men whistling at me
when I walking the government street.
And why the knowing glances and stares
when our eyes accidentally meet?
I'm fed up of being furtively fondled
without my knowledge or consent.
Wonder if those loving words
were contrived or lovingly meant?
If you're black and on the game
who can you really tell?
Who wants to hear from a commodity
that we never ever sell?
And if you've had an abortion
does even your best friend know?
Or did you tell your boyfriend
you had a particularly heavy flow?
God, when I start to think of it
I feel my head gon bus
We must write it all down
cos is who we can really cuss?
Black child, be strong out there
Cos sometimes you can't let it out
but the rest of us keeping silent
we still know what ya talking bout.

High School
C heryl Clarke | *United States*

Sister Elise Marie.
Ah, Daughter of Charity (of St. Vincent de Paul).
Vigilant and volumptuous in her habit.

The girls wore lipstick
the wrong color sweater
the wrong length of sock
hems too short
hair too long
too much jewelry
just to be told by Sister
to take it off
tie it back
roll em down
wash it off
to be kept after school
to clap her erasers
to discover her in the
cloakroom adorning her cinched
waist with some errant scarlet scarf
slipped from its hanger
to the floor.

Rigorous in the classroom as St. Ignatius
in a den of apostates
was Sister Elise Marie
and charismatic:

    'Girls, the serpent pride,
    the apple arrogance,
    the banishment punishment,
    the knowing of sin.'

Loved poetry. Hated Aquinas.
Quoted *Fleurs du Mal* regularly and languidly
for the wearing of perfume:

> 'And from her clothes, of
> muslin or velvet,
> All redolent of her youth's purity
> There emanated the odor of furs . . . .
> Ah, girls, What the devil does,
> he does well.'

Then chastening herself after the vagaries
of poetry with lessons in Rome's manifest
destiny:

> 'Naked in the main
> the natives of La Côte d'Ivoire.
> Private parts exposed . . .
> First the Church gave them clothes . . .'

On All Saints' Day
recounting the 400-year history
of her order,
evangelical was Sister Elise Marie:

> 'Girls, though we were Vincent's idea,
> Louise, scrupulous widow, had a vision of us,
> trained and bound us
> to good works
> for the poor
> to charity
> humility
> later chastity . . .'

Fondling her bodice, smoothing her skirt,
Sister Elise Marie
transfigured:

Girlhood

'Girls, the many-layered gabardine
and its undercloth
of
muslin
screening out lustful stares.
This mountainous cornette, white,
guides my gaze heavenward
longing for sight of the beatific vision,
never to pander vain stares . . .
Girls, uncross your knees and close your legs.'

'She'
Sista Roots | *England*

Born a girl child
Into this world
    Wild
Appearing as a flower
More beautiful
By the hour
Mummy's little pearl
And Daddy's little girl

Forwarding bolder
As she gets older
Learning the tricks
Flashing her eyes
With surprise
No more toys
Attention on boys
And false love's Joys

Time has flown
Now she's full grown
Colour telly
Big belly
She's feeling sick
'im fly her two lick

She choke up
    Inside
She ain't
    His bride
She ain't
    His wife
Let's look at her life

Worryin''bout
That speck of dust
Clean it

Girlhood

Or he'll make
A fuss.

Wash the clothes
Cook the food
Hurry or else
He'll be in a mood

Never has time
To think
For herself
Priority being
What's cheap
On the shelf

On the bed
With one eye shut
Trying to avoid
That pain
In her gut

Just as she fall
The baby start bawl
She cover her ears
And fight back
The tears

Shut in a box
Did she
Iron his socks

Just like
She granny
And she mother
        Unlike
She father
And she brother

This can't be life
There must be another!

Home Girl Talks Girlhood
Allison Joseph | *United States*

Remember that longing for hips
and breasts, the rising curves
of womanhood? Honey, I was
so skilled at wishing
for a body I didn't know
what the hell to do with:

round, proud, everything
high and firm, long legs
curved just so, a dancer's

bearing. Just who I was
going to lure with all this,
I didn't know—all I did know

was that I quaked, afraid
each time I had to pass
those boys on the corner,

their eyes inspecting me,
finding what wasn't there,
calling after me—*you ugly,*

too skinny, for real.
How much time did I waste
longing to be a woman,

fooling around in Mother's
make-up—slashes of red vivid
against my lips, loose powder

freed on her dresser top.
I'd forage among bottles

Girlhood

of perfume, spray myself

with musk's dark odor,
fingers stained by mascara,
rouge. And when she'd find

me, she'd demand *just what
you think you doing, you
no damn woman yet*, and I'd
wait again, hoping my body
would begin, hoping to be
like her—all business,

all woman as she wiped
the paint from my face,
smoothing on cream to clean

my skin, bringing me back
to my ashy girlhood self,
muted child of color.

You Are 12
Trapeta B. Mayson | *Liberia/United States*

You are 12 and your mother is crazy.
You don't know what it all means but you scared.
You hear her answering herself, you see
her shaving her head bald and drawing blood
You feel her moving in the night while you
hold your breath in the dark. She different now.
She mean and you believe that she hates you.
It's bad enough you dark and african,
nappy and flat chested in the 80s.
Now yall the neighborhood joke, not quite as
bad as Poo and them whose father killed his
own brother over porkchops one Sunday,
but yall up there/top of the line misfits.
It's a small block and yall are too well known.
They whisper about your family and
they greet the police cars weekly after
her latest outburst. Philadelphia's
finest drag your crazy mama somewhere
looking like a big deflating rag doll.
Their eyes say they sorry for you but you
know better. They are satisfied. *Yeah them*
uppity african niggas who thought
they was so much better done fell on they
face. You lose your father to shame and your
brother to the streets. Your sisters become
your children. Problems weigh your ass way down.
You the woman of the house. You are 12.

For Paula Cooper (*The 18 year old who waits on death row*)
Jackie Warren-Moore | *United States*

Paula of the trembling brown cheeks and silent tears
I see you struggling and stumbling
day leaning into day.
Seasons and years measured by the shadows on the walls and the
metal clang of lockup,
Death and fifteen years of abuse bearing down on you.
Hungry and wanting you plunged the knife.
Like a sacrificial lamb, did you think her blood would wash clean
the misery of your life?
33 times you twisted and plunged into another's life.
Still the freedom did not come. The pain did not end.
Only the time of waiting continues.
Waiting for a kind word. Waiting for the abuse to end. Waiting to
be wanted. Waiting to be loved. Waiting for a time there will be
no waiting. Waiting to die convulsing in the electric chair.
Paula of the soft brown cheeks and silent tears,
Wishing you laughter and 18 year old joy.
Wishing you a decision no harder than what dress to wear to the Prom.
Hungry and wanting.
I see you on streetcorners throughout the country. The same soft
brown cheeks and silent tears.
I see you in the faces of a generation left waiting.
Like a sacrificial lamb, I see you
Silent silver streaks flowing down baby brown cheeks.
Waiting.

An Anointing
Thylias Moss | *United States*

*Boys have to slash their fingers to become brothers. Girls trade
their Kotex, me and Molly do in the mall's public facility.*

*Me and Molly never remember each other's birthdays. On purpose.
We don't like scores of any kind. We don't wear watches or weigh
ourselves.*

*Me and Molly have tasted beer. We drank our shampoo. We went
to the doctor together and lifted our specimen cups in a toast. We
didn't drink that stuff. We just gargled.*

*When me and Molly get the urge, we are careful to put it back
exactly as we found it. It looks untouched.*

Between the two of us, me and Molly have 20/20 vision

*Me and Molly are in eighth grade for good. We like it there. We
adore the view. We looked both ways and decided not to cross the
street. Others who'd been to the other side didn't return. It was a trap.*

*Me and Molly don't double date. We don't multiply anything. We
don't know our multiplication tables from a coffee table. We'll never
be decent waitresses, indecent ones maybe.*

*Me and Molly don't believe in going ape or going bananas or
going Dutch. We go as who we are. We go as what we are.*

*Me and Molly have wiped each other's asses with ferns. Made
emergency tampons of our fingers. Me and Molly made do with what
we have.*

*Me and Molly are in love with wiping the blackboard with each
other's hair. The chalk gives me and Molly an idea of what old age*

Girlhood

is like; it is dusty and makes us sneeze. We are allergic to it.

Me and Molly, that's M and M, melt in your mouth.

What are we doing in your mouth? Me and Molly bet you'll never guess. Not in a million years. We plan to be around that long. Together that long. Even if we must freeze the moment and treat the photograph like the real thing.

Me and Molly don't care what people think. We're just glad that they do.

Me and Molly lick the dew off the morning grasses but taste no honey until we lick each other's tongues.

We wear full maternity sails. We boat upon my broken water. The katabatic action begins, Molly down my canal binnacle first, her water breaking in me like an anointing.

Primer
Rita Dove | *United States*

In the sixth grade I was chased home by
the Gatlin kids, three skinny sisters
in rolled-down bobby socks. Hissing
Brainiac! and *Mrs. Stringbean!*, they trod my heel.
I knew my body was no big deal
but never thought to retort: who's
calling *who* skinny? (Besides, I knew
they'd beat me up.) I survived
their shoves across the schoolyard
because my five-foot-zero mother drove up
in her Caddie to shake them down to size.
Nothing could get me into that car.
I took the long way home, swore
I'd show them all: I would grow up.

Excerpt from **When Chicken Heads Come To Roost**
Joan Morgan | *United States*

On our quest to create ourselves
we brown girls play dress up.
What is most fascinating about this
ritual of imitation is what we choose to mimic—
what we reach for in our mothers' closets.
We move right on past the unglamorous
garb of our mothers' day-to-day realities-
the worn housedresses or beat-up slipper—and
reach instead for the intimates. Slip our sassy
little selves into their dressiest of dresses and
sexiest of lingerie like being grown is like
Christmas or Kwanzaa and can't come fast enough.

Then we practice the deadly art of attitude—
rollin' eyes, necks, and hips in mesmerizing
synchronization, takin' out imaginary violators
with razor-sharp tongues. Perhaps to our
ingenuous eyes transforming ourselves into
invincible Miss Thangs is the black woman's
only armature against the evils of the world.

Interestingly enough, we do not imitate our mothers
at their weakest most vulnerable, shedding
silent midnight tears, alone and afraid. That we
don't do until much later, when we are fully grown,
occasionally trippin' and oblivious to our behavior's
origins.

As Black women, we face the world in our mothers' clothes.[*]

---

[*] Italics represent my paraphrase of Morgan's concluding paragraph.

WOMANHOOD

Identity

Ain't I a Woman?

Sojourner Truth | *United States*

Adapted by Nagueyalti Warren

That man over there say
a woman needs to be helped
into carriages and lifted over ditches
and to have the best place everywhere.
Nobody ever helped me into carriages
or over mud puddles
or gives me a best place.

And ain't I a woman?

Look at me!
Look at my arm!
I have plowed and planted
and gathered into barns
and no man could head me.

And ain't I a woman?

I could work as much
and eat as much as a man,
when I could get to it,
and bear the lash as well.

And ain't I a woman?

I have born children: Thirteen!
and seen most all sold to slavery,
and when I cried out a mother's grief
none but Jesus heard me.

And ain't I a woman?

That little man in black there say
a woman can't have as much rights as a man
cause Christ wasn't a woman.
Where did your Christ come from?
From God and a woman!
Man had nothing to do with him!

The Sorrows of Yamba
From the *Universal Magazine* for July, 1797

COME, kind death, and give me rest;
Yamba hath no friend but thee;
Thou canst ease my throbbing breast,
Thou canst set a pris'ner free.

In St Lucia's distant isle,
Still with Afric's love I burn;
Parted many a thousand mile,
Never, never to return.

Down my cheeks the tears are dripping;
Broken is my heart with grief,
Mangled is my flesh with whipping,
Come, kind death, and give relief.

Born on Afric's golden coast,
Once I was as blest as you;
Parents tender I could boast,
Husband dear and children too.

Wily man! he came from far,
Sailing o'er the briny flood;
Who with the help of British tar,
Buys up human flesh and blood.

With my baby at my breast,
(Other two were sleeping by)
In my hut I sat at rest,
With no thought of danger nigh.

From the bush, at even tide,
Rush'd the fierce man-stealing crew,
Seiz'd the baby by my side,
Seiz'd the wretched Yamba too.

Then, for cursed thirst of gold,
Strait they bore me to the sea;
Cramm'd me down a slave ship's hold,
Where were hundreds stow'd with me.

Naked on the platform lying,
Now we cross the tumbling wave;
Shrieking, sick'ning, fainting, dying!
Deed of shame for Britons brave!

At the savage captain's beck,
Now like brutes they make us prance,
Smack the whip about the deck,
And in scorn they bid us dance.

In groaning there I pass'd the night,
And did roll my aching head;
At the break of morning light,
My poor child was cold and dead.

Happy, happy, there she lies!
Thou shalt feel the lash no more,
Thus full many a negro dies,
Ere he reach the destin'd shore.

Drove like cattle to a fair,
See they sell them young and old;
Child from mother too they tear,
All for cursed thirst of gold.

I was sold to master hard,
Some have masters kind and good;
And again my back was scarr'd;
Bad and stinted was my food.

Poor and wounded, faint and sick,
All expos'd to burning sky;

Master makes me grass to pick,
And I now am near to die.

What! and if to death he send me,
Savage murder tho' it be;
British laws will ne'er befriend me,
They protect not slaves like me.

Mourning thus my friendless state,
Ne'er may I forget the day,
That in dusk of even late,
Far from home I dar'd to stray.

Dar'd, alas! with impious haste,
Toward the roaring sea to fly;
Death itself I long'd to taste,
Long'd to cast me in and die.

But tho' death this hour I find,
Still with Afric's love I burn;
Where I left a spouse behind,
Still to Afric's land I turn.

And when Yamba sinks in death,
This her latest pray'r may be;
While she yields her parting breath,
O! may Afric's land be free.

Ye that boast to rule the waves,
Bid no slave ship sail the sea:
Ye that never will be slaves,
Bid poor Afric's land be free.

Thus, where Yamba's native home,
Humble hut of rushes stood,
Her happy sons again may roam,
And Britons seek not for their blood.

E. S. J.

Black is Fancy
Una Marson | *Jamaica*

I Am very black,
I look in the mirror,
My eyes are bright,
And my teeth,
They are very white.

There is a picture in my room,
It is a picture
Of a beautiful white lady,
I used to think her sweet,
But now I think
She lacks something.

I used to feel
I was so ugly
Because I am black,
But now I am glad I am black,
There is something about me
That has a dash in it
Especially when I put on
My bandana.

Since Aunt Liza gave me
This nice looking glass
I begin to be real proud
Of my own self.
I think I will take down
This white lady's picture,
It used to make me ashamed,
And all black folk
Seemed ugly.

But I don't know,

This white lady is sweet,
But she is too white,
Besides, she is not my friend,
She is my mistress.
I think she is too white.
Maybe I will be more proud
Of my black skin, if I don't see her,
I will remove her picture.

The Black Finger
Angelina Weld Grimké | *United States*

I have just seen a most beautiful thing:
      Slim and still,
Against a gold, gold sky,
     A straight, black cypress
   Sensitive
   Exquisite
A black finger
Pointing upwards.
Why, beautiful still finger, are you black?
And why are you pointing upwards?

Black Faces
Anita Scott Coleman | *United States*

I love black faces:
They are full of smoldering fire,
And Negro eyes...white...with white desire,
And Negro lips so soft and thick,
Like rich velvet within fine jewelry cases.
I love black faces.

America Negra
Anita Scott Coleman | *United States*

I am Indian;
I am grown old
Huddled beside sand dunes
Cradled in the lap of a plateau.
Cacti my shade,
Sky and land,
Land and sky,
The sky is clear as a mirror,
But the land is a painted desert;
Many the pictures I see there.
I am weary of seeing them ...
Mirages of misery.

I am Irish and Scotch and Welsh,
Islands of rock,
Islands alone in the ocean,
Waves of the ocean bombarding;
Inflowing tides wash my shores,
Tides ebbing wash my shores clean,
Wash, wash mighty waters.
Is not England and France,
Germany and Spain,
Singapore and Shanghai in my veins?

Yes......
I am Africa.
Africa stealing forth to meet
A lover in the everglades,
Chief Heartache,
Parleying with famine and sorrow
With never a war whoop.
Africa,
Singing the Irish caoine

Bewailing in accents of Scotland;
Mute are the harps;
Why are they voiceless?
Silent the bagpipes—
There was no victory.

I am Africa,
Africa the maiden;
My breasts are sweet apples;
My limbs are the flowering
Limbs of the fruit tree.
My body is fertile oasis
Alone in the barren desert,
Ever green in the sands of the desert.

In my veins the blood of all nations,
In my hands the jewels of all nations,
In my being the wisdoms and the passions of all
nations.

I am Africa
Rooted in America,
Africa the maiden,
Africa the conquered and the conqueror;
Beat, beat my heart
To the sound of the tom-toms;
Throb, throb my heart
To the roll of the drums.
Transplanted from Africa,
Nurtured in America,
Son of many races,
Fathered by many,
I am become
Man universal.

The Heart of a Woman
Georgia Douglas Johnson | *United States*

The heart of a woman goes forth with the dawn,
As a lone bird, soft winging, so restlessly on,
Afar o'er life's turrets and vales does it roam
In the wake of those echoes the heart calls home.

The heart of a woman falls back with the night,
And enters some alien cage in its plight,
And tries to forget it has dreamed of the stars,
While it breaks, breaks, breaks on the sheltering bars.

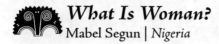

What Is Woman?
Mabel Segun | *Nigeria*

A woman is a person
Especially when she chairs
A committee of women.

Crazy Black Luce
Sylvia Hamilton | *Nova Scotia*

Here she comes
jingling, jangling
slapping her
worn-out tambourine
Crazy Luce.

Coloured ribbons
floating from her hair.
Round rainbow disks
growing from her dress.
High button, once shiny shoes.

Sundays
were her days,
special days.
Church service through,
Luce making music
along the dirt road.
Kicking up dust,
making kids laugh tears.

Others said she was crazy.
Keep away from her.
Look at her dress:
covered with shiny
rainbow rounds,
coloured ribbons
floating from her hair,
high boots and full skirts.
Never without her tambourine.

Crazy Luce.
Sang

when no one else would
sing.
Made music
when there was
no music to be made.

Made kids laugh tears
when they thought
they couldn't

Crazy
Black
Luce.

black ooman
Ahdri Zhina Mandiela | *Jamaica/Canada*

black ooman rebellin
black ooman ah stawt tellin
ah tellin tings
whe mek yuh kwivvah
ah chat deepah dan silent rivvah

if evvy day pure strife
only bring more wrawt
like a shawp blade knife
ah cut inna wih awt
always ah struggle fih wih life

evvy jook
mek it wuss
like a sore
full ah pus
but wih will kill too
if wih mus
suh jus

back awff

black ooman rebellin
black ooman ah stap sellin
ah stap sellin
inna dih maakit
ah stap ah troddin
wid ovah-loaded baaskit

awfta all dem miles
wih foot dem ah bun
wih spirits ah bwile
wih language ah tun

fram rank to vile

naw rant naw cuss
cause wih nuh really
want nuh fuss
but wih bile bag ah buss
suh jus

back awff

Ellease
Ellease Southerland | *United States*

I am a Nigerian whisper
between the lioness
and the wrinkled rose
the quick steps of a dance
between the bland sun rising over Spain
and the red sun
      set in the Oklahoma sky.

I am a collection of moments,
brief tones of an evening song.

My soul is smooth sand spread
beneath the sun burning colors.
I am the blue sound of oceans
and the quiet of night.

Bass Line *for Patrice*
Robin Caudell | *United States*

I know the rock
From which you were carved
The archangel harping
Round your base

Fire in your obsidian eyes
Stoke a passion, a potential so
Magnificent
I hold my breath
Fall through your eyes
To God, oh, god, oh
Lord Jesus

A dusk daughter
Knows a master's son
Even when he thumps bass
Know by the curve of my back
The arch of my brow
My palms are as purple
I sit where clouds split
Carve my daughter from basalt
Eddy round her base

CarthageTimbuktuBealeStreet
CarthageTimbuktuBealeStreet
CarthageTimbuktuBeale Street
SonghaySonghaySonghay

I know rock.
Waters.

Nanny

Lorna Goodison | *Jamaica/Canada*

My womb was sealed
with the molten wax
of killer bees
for nothing should enter
nothing should leave
the state of perpetual siege
the condition of the warrior.

From then my whole body would quicken
at the birth of every one of my people's children.
I was schooled in the green-giving ways
of the roots and vines
made accomplice to the healing acts
of Chainey root, fever grass & vervain.

My breasts flattened
settled unmoving against my chest
my movements ran equal
to the rhythms of the forest.

I could sense and sift
the footfall of men
from the animals
and smell danger
death's odor
in the wind's shift.

When my eyes rendered
light from the dark
my battle song opened
into a solitaire's moan
I became most knowing
and forever alone.

And when my training was over
they circled my waist with pumpkin seeds
and dried okra, a traveler's jigida,
and sold me to the traders
all my weapons within me.
I was sent, tell that to history.

When your sorrow obscures the skies
other women like me will rise.

Granny Speaks on Loretta Aiken
Toni Asante Lightfoot | *United States*

Loretta was born with a joke
in her tears. The first star
she pointed out was the North.
Then would laughed a dirty laugh
when splaining Venus stayd out
from twilight o tdayclean.
She knew all kinds of things

She tried to be a good girl
But this town ain't got much
Sympathy for an orphan.
Mother of two.
At 11 she come home bloodied
tween her legs. Last blood she saw
for 9 months. What her pa supposed to do
but make sure the man who ruint her
made her an honest woman?
My son ain't know he gonna be
burnt to ashes before his grandson born.
Left Loretta in old miserable hands.

Left her alone mostly and a woman child
ain't safe on mountain roads.
So when the sheriff find her walking
home he snatch her and again
sweet Loretta's blood stopped till
a wet full head of hair burst through
just to be taken away. Her momma,
a burro of a woman, was walking prayer.
Still we cried for her soul when
Christmas morning service
ended with her mangled under a truck.
A present for God by nighttime.

When the troubles come on some folks
they don't leave till there ain't no more
pain left to feel. Time turned each one
of Loretta's shames into jabs and each pain
into side splitting tears, Loretta Aiken

into Jackie Mabley. That girl knew life
was a bunch of overripe bananas. You can
throw them away or turn them into sweet
pudding or add nuts and make some bread.

I—Woman

Conceicão Evaristo | *Brazil*

Translated by Carolyn Richardson Durham

A drop of milk
runs down between my breasts.
A stain of blood
adorns me between my legs.
Half a word choked off
blazes from my mouth.
Vague desires insinuate hopes.

I—woman in red rivers
inaugurate life.
In a low voice
I rape the eardrums of the world.
I foresee
I anticipate
I live beforehand.
Before—now—what is to come.
I, the female matrix
I, the motive power
I—woman
shelter of the seed
continual motion
of the world.

Ancient Roots
Stella Abasa Dadzie | *England*

I am an ancient oak
twisted, gnarled, permanent
indifferent to the passage
of time

I am amber and gold
russet and sage
bone-white
blood-redmoss-green
I am rain-blanched and sun-
bleached
and where once I was scorched
by lightening
I am an angry charcoal black
with keloid scars

solid and thick-girthed
my thighs can resist
the fury of the elements
yet remain vulnerable
to the footfalls
of passing strangers
they twist and turn
charting new paths
into the rich dark earth that
nurtures me
they burrow deep
seeking life's sustenance
and other treasures

My skin is rough and weather-beaten
rain-lashed
yet wind-smoothed

so that others
may grow to touch
the sky
where shy, itinerant seeds
once took root
and burst forth in celebration
of reckless beauty
dark, barren places
where I was once torn
limb from limb
and nothing more can grow

I was once a sappling
exploding with energy
and purpose
I chose to make my home
by the river
where her calm, impassive face
could mirror my growth
her music a soft, sighing lullaby
soothing me as I sleep

when the sun parches the earth
sapping my strength
she revives me with cool water
from her own abundant store
her gentle waves
caressing my aching feet

Her gift is an orchestra
with many players
drums and violins
a choir of joyful singers

and there are many unexplored
places secret nooks
colonized by teeming armies
whole cities that thrive
beneath its protective bark
hidden crannies
will prevail

And if by chance
an axe should fell me
should I succumb
to the vengeance of the hurricane
or the slow, creeping stealth
of nature's wrath
I shall sink gratefully into the earth
that has sustained me
through the centuries
returning my gifts

rousing me from my slumber
as they herald the dawn
of each new day

Time is my armory now
scudding clouds keep their watch
as the changing seasons
offer new possibilities
healing wounds
and renewing old paths

Tomorrow I shall be here still
wiser and sturdier than before
for I have withstood the fury of
thunder
the rage of forest fires
I know
my life-force

Black Woman

Shayna Israel | *Belize/United States*

Black Woman
there's power in your beauty
that's more than your duty,
that's why you're here, so school me.

Black Woman
you're the first and the highest
they disguise their lust
can't deny us, or try us,
we marvelous.

Black Woman
you are truly a queen
but not second to a king
how can a woman be second when life is birthed from her being?
Sometimes it hurts to be seeing
Black Women
in the conditions that we are
when we can lift ourselves from our own constructed bars.

Black Woman
you traveled through enough space and time
to understand that freedom is just a state of mind
so state to your mind that you will be free
and your Consciousness will return to its infinity.

Black Woman
your beauty last infinitely
it doesn't fade
it's just expressed differently
and from what I can see
you are the beautiful being that you were meant to be.

Black Woman
I'm thankful that you sent for me
and my love for you goes past the sensory.

Black Woman
all the colors of the night sky's in your skin
open your senses to the Queendom within
begin seeing this truth through your third eye
that's all I ask of you my, my, my.

I/Too/Am the Fair Sex

Beverly A. Russell | *United States*

I/too/am the fair sex
but no frogs I kissed
turned in to handsome princes
and no knights in shining armor
     rescued me
from the clutches of the fiery dragon
nor did I marry a handsome prince
and live happily ever after

     instead
I was fair game for anyone
to be bought   beaten
and bruised at will
my virginity was taken violently from me
I was forced to work until my hands bled
even when with child I was valued
          as a breeder

I fought back my tears
as I saw my man
lynched and castrated

I have borne my pain well—
my pain has made me strong
and I too am the fair sex

(but I did not marry a handsome prince
     and live happily ever after)

     instead
my life has been one
long-fine-slender-thread tied
to pain and suffering—
     I /too/am the fair sex

I Come from a Long Line
Beverly A. Russell | *United States*

I come from a long line
of   hot/black/mamas
who knew a lot
        of secrets
secrets of the red earth
and   the blue-black Nile
secrets of the low-down blues
and   about payin' some dues
they be knowin' deep
dark   mysterious secrets
        real secrets
        ethereal secrets
yeah   I come from a long line
of   hot/black/mamas
        down right foxes
and I know
        a lot of secrets
my lineage includes Nefertiti
        Harriet Tubman/Sojourner Truth
        Bessie Smith/Nina Simone...
and   the list goes on
                and on
for   I come from a long line
                a long line
of   hot/ black/mamas
and I know...
        a lot of secrets

Ana Red
Tchise | *United States*

"I will know what the water says
when it covers my mouth,
fills me with stories
drying on the sand.
It comes with the ivory teeth
of dead Africans floating
off shore across pieces of eight.
It comes with a chained walk
into the arms of* Asesu;
the road of the waters that whispers
into the ocean's lap crick, crack,
crick, crack."

Ana Red is seaweed now,
black daughter of Arab horsemen
the water sings her litany,
her resurrection,
says it will find her a name
build it out of drying clamshells
and orange chevrons,
twist it into the broad khaki leaves
of the water grass

whales sleep in her throat
teaching her silent laughter
she remembers the white man
staggering jagged Portuguese
lousy keys
a conglomeration of bones
sealed in a sack
without a soul
and wakes in church
looking up at the bishop's staff

the lunar disk that pretends
to be the body of a lamb
whose name she has forgotten
she remembers
what the water reveals
with its sharpened coral
 she remembers
kabob with rice and flatbread
kora music
rippling through the air
straightening out the edges of night

his lace frightens her
with its holes
fits and starts
in flowered patterns
the civilized mask of a brutal culture
a sleeve covering the hilt of a sword
webbing of pure deception
noblewoman
with indigo eyes
Ana nods over her handiwork
 like a fish making its own net
trying to remember where she began
the song that was playing
when they tricked her away

trying to call up the time
before the water said her name
before she bore the half-caste children
of a man whom her father
would have executed
before lunch

The water says it will remind her
stay with her
fill her with names

It says women own the river,
It says blood is mightier than time
says time circles the moon like a
wedding band
says sing and she opens her mouth
to find whale music
muscular and round
pulling her lungs down into
an understanding of things that are not heard

* The "road" of Yemanja (Ocean Goddess) said to be the messenger of Olokun, the
  (god) who rules the depths of the Oceans.

I Thought You Was Black
Digna | *Honduras*

I thought you was black,
That's what I was always told.
You don't even look Spanish.
Again they were bold:
Say something in Spanish and prove it to me.
Then I would say in my normal English voice,
Why, you don't believe me stupidy?

Then they would ask if I'm West Indian.
I said, *We don't all come from there you know.*
If you want to know where I'm from just ask me and I'll tell you.
Soy de Honduras. Naci alli y creci aqui.

I enter a store owned by Latinos,
Can I help you?
No thank you. I know where it is.
Oye, cuida esta morena que no robe nada.
Yes, some of us steal, but some of us don't.

Cuanto es la cuenta? I ask in Spanish.
Oh, tu hablas espanol?
Que te importa? Que es la cuents?
$2.23, señorita.

Pues tengo suficiente dinero pero no le voy a pagar.
Tiene que tener cuidado como hablar al frente de la gente
porque soy morena pero soy hispana. Primero soy una persona.

The people judge me and accuse me because of my skin color.
People like me for being Spanish not because I'm black.
Then they like me because I'm black not because I'm Spanish.
Unos me quieren porque soy hispana no es porque soy morena
y otros me quieren porque soy morena no es porque soy hispana.
Cuando me van a aceptar por mi?
When will they accept me for me?

Look at Her
Tureeda Mikell, Story Medicine Woman | *United States*

Bantu tongue
Ripped
Into a thousand pieces
Babbling on and on

Eyes
Disguised by Euro lies
Colonized visions
Break her looking glass
Scatters her soul
In thunder's search for light
Circle broken
Her token
Blows in
in-no-sense
As she
Walks and prays
In displays of
"Being Saved"
Holy Anvil
Cripples her feet
Hobbling through his-story.

Evil womb-man!!
Vultures fiend to
Pick clean her truth
As a missed-tree bleeds
Millenniums sanctioned memory

Honors sentenced to die
No questions why
Stolen from
Heavens' Earth
Immortal birth
Sacred worth

She flies blind
In constant search of rights

Womanhood: Identity

Convinced by
I—dolls of sacrifice
A victim to another's gods'
Senseless rules
She plays the fool.

Hear, See and speak no evil
Judge not
She falls into a bottomless pit
Without a floor or rug
Deemed a lunatic

Drugged by a world
Of hidden tricks
Turned inside out
Upside down
Wrong made right
Sold by the pound
She hemorrhages
Unseen
In dreams and
Screams
Where no one listens
In Babylon

In Babylon
Babbling on and on

Tongues in My Mouth
Demetrice A. Worley | *United States*

Tired of waiting for me,
my ancestors' spirits are lifting
my heavy tongue, forming
words in my mouth.

Sa koon ain je gun,[1] my maternal
great-great grandmother's Blackfeet voice,
the light of her soul, locates my words.

*Tuwa wasteicillia maka kin lecela
tehan yunkelo*,[2] my paternal
great-great grandmother's Sioux voice,
guides me beyond concern for self.

*Asiyefunzwa na mamye hufunzwa
na ulimwengu*,[3] my foremothers'
Swahili voices, tell me listen,
hear the wisdom.

My ancestors are making me
practice my languages,
forcing me to make foreign sounds,
to turn new words over,
until the tongues in my mouth
speak in a single voice,
until the tongues in my mouth,
speak the truth that no one wants to hear.

1. Bright-white flamed instrument.
2. Whoever considers themselves beautiful, on earth, only endures.
3. The child, who is not taught by her mother, will be taught by the world.

Paint Me Like I Am *for Dorothy, Annie, and Tina*
Joyce Carol Thomas | *United States*

Why don't you paint me
Like I am?
Laughing and dancing and
Smiling a lot
Running with the children
With the sun in my face
Why don't you paint me
Like I am?

Paint me nappy headed
And curly haired and walking
With that amazing grace
Paint me happy
And shouting in the temple

Paint me balancing dream
Baskets of passion fruit
On my head
Paint me with the elegance
I had when I taught the
Chamber maid how
To adorn herself and how
To be a woman

Paint me when I remember that I
Am the daughter of Limpopo legends
Of brooks and streams
And growing green things

Paint me without the tears
And the bowed down expression
Paint me without the ropes
For I am unchained

Can't you hear it
In my voice
How some wish
They could sing
Like me
Paint me precious
Paint me star-bright
Paint me free

Miss Virginia
Joyce E. Young | *United States*

She cried as she sat on the back steps
for hours, rocking herself
and rubbing her hands.

When she did that we knew
she'd be going to Kings County* again.
Miss Virginia, hair barely covering her head,
black-rimmed glasses sitting on her nose,
eyes that saw more than she spoke of,
worried tone always in her voice.

She had to clean her husband Hilton's
greasy mechanic's overalls, listen
to his slurred words and drunken belches.
Wash her fast-talking son's dirty,
sweaty tee shirts. Know that he
tongue-kissed a woman in the front yard
as my mother watched from the porch.

How did she live with them?

She called her only daughter Honey Bunny
the sweetness in her life of sullen roomers
and haughty neighbors on our block of row houses,
sandwiched between red brick apartment buildings.

If she'd had another way, would she have danced,
carved something out of wood, shaped a life for herself from clay, traveled
to another state,
spoken with ancestors who could have
taken her by the hand and held her up?

*Kings County Hospital, Brooklyn, New York

Ransom

Alzira Rufino | *Brazil*

Translated by Carolyn Richardson Durham

I am a black woman   period
return my identity to me
tear up my birth certificate
I am a black woman without ellipses
without commas, and without anything missing
I no longer want in-betweens
I am a black woman "cannon ball"
I am a black night weariness
I am a black woman   period

Truthful

Alzira Rufino | *Brazil*

Translated by Carolyn Richardson Durham

I am a decent Creole woman
I am not vile
I'm on tight
balanced strings
of Brazil.
My color frightens
"this race offends" I heard it said
it isn't in the black man's teeth
it isn't in the black man's sex
it is the black man's art of
living
or better said
surviving
with this thing that he drags
the shackles that they try to hide
but these shackles exist
in living together.
The shackles are in the favela.
I see shackles in the alley
in the fetid dwellings
in the hopeless skins
in the torrents of no's.
In this powerful checkers-and-chess
I got lost
on the routes of razors
in the prison cells and the lures
black bobbin of a mess
they want to make a
Creole marginal world.

Ancestor Reflections (I AM)
Tamboura A. Parks | *United States*

I am!

I am the very reason my ancestors ever existed;

I am the sole reason they survived their circumstances.

I am the spirit that grew under oppression.

I am the courage that raised her mulatto head.

I am the wisdom of herbs and balms that cured whipped backs.

I am the woman that cried freedom, and bought it!

I am the girl sold from my mother, at birth.

I am the daughter whose eyes my father never knew.

I am the seed that grew in the womb of my barren ancestors.

I am the product of countless rapes of little slave girls,

I am the hope they saved in the back of their minds;

I am the song they sang in the hot noon day;

I am the force that pushed them on in the struggle.

I am the mighty blow they struck at injustice,

I am the poison that killed ole mistress!

I am the joy that filled their hearts;

I am the tears that stood in eyes too angry to cry.

I am the jubilee following the emancipation proclamation!

I am the bitterness of that promise long denied.

I am the hope of moving into a better land.

I am!

I am!

I am!

Caledonia
Colleen J. McElroy | *United States*

Caledonia, Caledonia
What makes your big head so hard ....

The way I hear tell aunt jennie
tapdanced on the hood of her husband's
car because she heard he *might*
have smiled at miz dora emma's daughter
Brand new ford baby pink it was
and a convertible right out of days
full of white buck shoes sock hops
and little richard wailing over the local
disc jockey all night party station
Neighbors whooped and laughed seeing her
fly straight out the front door swearing
that man would never live another day
seeing mama running down the block
just in time to catch her falling
butt first into the gutter
But mama wouldn't laugh because jennie
knew who had not accidentally put too much
red pepper in daddy's beans and rice
that night he came home smelling
of southern comfort and blue grass
neither of which mama ever touched
And who bought a one way ticket home
for uncle brother's first wife
stuck up and full of airs
just because she came *from* california
in the '40s before it was fashionable

Mama and aunt jennie both hardheaded
and lean on words
inhaling and saying humph and um-um-um

to a chorus of head wagging un-huh's
whenever they hear tell I'm having female
problems full of husband troubles
They have been married for as long
as anyone can remember and now so dependent
on their husbands and each other and husbands
on them and the other there's no telling
where one begins and ends
or which sister has religiously whipped
the other into shape
until I've learned that love, like hate
is always acted out

The Scream
May Miller | *United States*

I am a woman controlled.
Remember this: I never scream.
Yet I stood a form apart
Watching my other frenzied self
Beaten by words and wounds
Make in silence a mighty scream —
A scream that the wind took up
And thrust through the bars of night
Beyond all reason's final rim.

Out where the sea's last murmur dies
And the gull's cry has no sound,
Out where city voices fade,
Stilled in a lyric sleep
Where silence is its own design,
My scream hovered a ghost denied
Wanting the shape of lips.

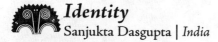

Identity
Sanjukta Dasgupta | *India*

I am a flying kite
Not a doormat.

I am a bird in a bush
Not the one in hand.

I am a river in full spate
Not a dripping faucet.

I am the forest fire
Not a kitchen burner

I am a skylark
Can't sing to another's tune.

I am the Mother-provider of every root
Not just a delving earthworm.

I am *sangam* and *shakti*
Power of fire, water, air and earth

Bursts out of every pore
Charges down every vein

I am torn to bits
I am nuclear fission

I am rebel atom
I am fearless and proud

I am archer, warrior *Chitrangada*
Not a user-friendly doormat, mate!

Iris
Phebus Etienne | *United States*

A driver caught her smile,
envying the night-tinted gauze clinging
to the globes above her waist.
He christened her spring blossom
ready to be picked, his overtures
promised to keep her flourishing
ankles deep in sapphire water.
She had not seen herself as bouquet

or garden since that warm autumn
which brought weekenders and foreigners
to relics and basilicas,
leaving no affordable vacancies in Rome.
Shelter came with a guide
who spoke of Athena's temple
in temperate tones, pointed out
pagan stones in the Vatican's dome,
his eyes never straying
below the curve of her jaw.
In his spare room, she slept
dreamless and serene as the Tiber
on a moonless night.

An elbow across her throat
jerked her awake. She wanted
composure, to be
the actress in a tidy screenplay,
appeasing her assailant with gestures
of consent while drawing
a stiletto concealed in a boot,
transformation, at least, into elegant filament,
ancient rose root, quaking
but not uprooting in hurricane winds.

He had smiled exiting her body, satisfied
with blood which would not stain her wedding bed.
She saw herself reflected,
haggard with fear, in those eyes.

She would ignore appraisals of her legs,
trip into silence when girlfriends
touted conquests and pursuits,
evade questions about her solitude.
Bruised pistil, unreceptive stamen,

she repeated compliments from a flirt
as she roamed crowded piazzas
for mosaics, not of nameless wildflowers,
but framed posy most like her,
cloaked even at the peak of its blooming,
iridescent in daylight, calyx joined
like black palms meeting in prayer,
secrets melting into the lifelines.

Frances Michael
Cheryl Clarke | *United States*

Sister Frances Michael was a black nun,
a black nun in a white order.
Not a missionary order or a cloistered
order but a teaching order.
When she wasn't teaching science
she coached basketball.
(Easier since shedding the habit.
Never regained her peripheral vision,
though. But compensation is a nun's way.)

When she wasn't in the gym
or wasn't in the lab,
Frances Michael roamed the halls
with a wide-legged gait and a chip
on her shoulder.
Only sister Alphonsus, the choir
directress, was bold enough to counsel
Frances Michael to tread more straightly
and narrowly, to act less arrogantly.
Mother Superior kept to her office
whenever she heard Frances Michael's
brown laughter.

Brainy, brawny, brash Sister Frances Michael.
The white flight girls with their make-up
and hair spray called her the *Ace of Spades*.
The model black girls who integrated the school
proffered the affectionate ridicule of *Mike*.
The rowdy, truant girls—a mixed, rag-tag bunch,
whose cigarettes and adult books she always took—
called Frances Michael *Dyke*.

Sometimes as Women Only
Gloria Gayles | United States

we know the hard heavy pull of
weights riveted to our dreams
and yet
sometimes as women only
do we gasp in narrow spaces
and remain locked behind walls
too rough for etchings from our soul

we are new queens of ebony
celebrating ourselves in
diadems of natural beauty
feeling the swing of large gold hoops
around our tight-skinned smoothness
walking a regal dance and singing the music
of a clear struggle that names us well

but
as women
we are sometimes marked beyond adornment
for we have seen white lines run
east west north south cracking on our flesh
like earthquakes that no longer tremor
and we have felt the pressure of rigid staves
peaking breasts grown limp from the pull
of hungry mouths we alone can feed
we
are
fragile figurines
whose neurosis comes and goes
with the pull of the moon

black sturdy shoulders
we are monuments that refuse to crumble

Womanhood: Identity

deep-rooted oaks from which the generations
like thick-leaved branches grow and thrive
we are the strong ones
having balanced the weight of the tribe
having made our planting as deep as any man's

 and yet
as women
we have known only meager harvests
we sing strong songs
and the world hums a sweet lullaby
we write rich poems
and the world offers muted applause
for a jingling rhyme

sometimes
as women only
do we weep
we are taught to whisper
when we wish to scream
assent
when we wish to defy
dance pretty
        (on tiptoe)
when we would raise circles of dust
before the charge

Untitled (or What I said as a Child)
Angela Jackson | *United States*

What I said as a child I say
as a woman:
>There is romance in common
> movement
>of sound and sand.
>   Religion of a
>   kind. is
>   true, affirmed.
>Our is the worn water and ripe fire, leaves
>that burn alongside the road
>into
>smoke
>thick as Nigerian oil. A cover
>for and skill
>We balanced a house of extended families
>   atop our heads.
>The music drifted down
>   around our faces.
>Wind crossed our cheeks
>   in scarifications.
>Spirits feathered around our waists
>and fell to our knees;
>a dance
>of prayers that I said as a child
I say again:
>We walked in the air of the ancestors,
>hot, and tight   like
>the space between two breasts. A crossing
>of tongues
>in the middle of an African night
>The future is a quiet bed, a spread
>   of hunger, and fallenwish
>   is mystery to divine:

a drum technique
　　　　hidden in a man's hands.
　　We sit on the edge of our own echo, and craft.
What I said as a child I say as a woman:
We are from a house of balance and control.
The road ahead is burning smoke and oils.
What comes after is an act of will.

The Lost and Found

Riua Akinshegun | *United States*

I hunt for decayed wood
Objects to rescue
Trampled thoughts lost on drugs
My lessons are taught through
borrowed sounds in walls

I sit with children no one sees
anymore
I talk to children whose mouths
have been painted out
I know their names

I found bicycle parts
An old love
A torn finger nail
Telephone wires
Ancestral memories

I have recycled flawed dreams
A cracked window pane
And the sun

I am not a parasite
I am the glue that could hold you
together
A scavenger

She Learns to Become Quiet
Donkia Ross | *United States*

In the early spring
of her body, her back smears the wall
and her legs close like eyes at the blunt,
sweat smell. They grind thickly in the stale
room, and she is afraid of splintering
as her release ebbs weakly against her
thin sheets. Last night
she dreamed she sat atop her lover's breast, tore
her lover's face until it was pure.
Until they both were. Instead, she is in a room
heavy with the absence of smoke, and her voice
is like breathing against the scent.

>She clears her throat
>for a cigarette, calls for her father; he is already
>returning
>to his tea and Kafka in the next room.

II
A woman lives like a field,
rows trickling like hips into waist.
It is all rocks and trees
to her; she knows nothing of milled
stone or polished wood. She bears the seasons
of clotted boots and metal. Leaves rustle
at her like clothes in the dark, and pieces of her sift
away on their sound.

>She has been fallow
>for a season. Soon the men will return
>to cleave her flesh.

III
She doesn't sleep on her back now.
Her lungs no longer work

that way, and she is tired of names clouding
her face the way suburban housewives eclipse
their yard boys, bodies sharpened with salt
and moon in the deepening light.
She is ignorant of the ways of skin,
of resurrection. The body has found her.
She wonders at the pieces floating by.

IV.
Lost in the pilings of autumn—
earth hulled and scraped of
seed and rind—she winds against the fog,
returns to the dim, unremembered weight of her flesh.
She tears the shroud in silence.
She muffles the earth in her arms.

Uterus Root
Michelle T. Clinton | *United States*

"this class i took in santa cruz
in women's studies
was my first real woman identified experience
my first long straight look
at the big & wonderful & historically relevant
vagina, the pussy, the mother cunt
& how every body comes through the womb
& how the white boy existentialists
a dying breed say:
you are born alone
& we know better
we know your momma was right there
right from between her legs
 your first home
the sound of your first heart beat
set your ass up for the drum
& dancing & fucking & everything that is a natural rhythm

it was the feminists first
hipped me to the root
the uterus root
see boys make their seed
they just mix it up on a regular basis
on a day to day basis
on a minute to minute basis
& discharge it
their bodies expel those seeds
into the indifferent night
nocturnal ejaculation
when they can't find nothing
to catch that nut
for them straight girls
& they boyfriends

honey, he's probably fixing some up
right now, something hot & sweet
he want to let loose in you
someplace, tonight

but girls, see
we was born w/ every egg we'll ever have
we made every one while we was growing
inside the womb of the mother
so my momma made the first molecule of me
inside the belly of the grandmother
& the grandmother held the first
biochemical trace of my ass
& pass me inside the belly of my mother
& my mother walked around close to twenty years
w/ me inside her ovaries
& she guarded me against venereal disease
& technology
& i set up inside her
w/ all the other eggs
floating in the blood of her emotion
& the father came along & touched her
& i commenced to grow"

Woman Poem
Nikki Giovanni | *United States*

you see, my whole life
is tied up
to unhappiness
it's father cooking breakfast
and me getting fat as a hog
or having no food
at all and father proving
his incompetence
again
i wish i knew how it would feel
to be free

it's having a job
they won't let you work
or no work at all
castrating me
(yes it happens to women too)

it's a sex object if you're pretty
and no love
or love and no sex if you're fat
get back fat black woman be a mother
grandmother strong thing but not woman
gameswoman romantic woman love needer
man seeker dick eater sweat getter
fuck needing love seeking woman

it's a hole in your shoe
and buying lil sis a dress
and her saying you shouldn't
when you know
all too well—that you shouldn't

but smiles are only something we give
to properly dressed social workers
not each other
only smiles of i know
your game sister
which isn't really
a smile

joy is finding a pregnant roach
and squashing it
not finding someone to hold
let go get off get back don't turn
me on you black dog
how dare you care
about me
you ain't got no good sense
cause i ain't shit you must be lower
than that to care

it's a filthy house
with yesterday's watermelon
and monday's tears
cause true ladies don't
know how to clean

it's intellectual devastation
of everybody
to avoid emotional commitment
"yeah honey i would've married
him but he didn't have no degree"

it's knock-kneed mini-skirted
wig wearing died blond mamma's scar
born dead my scorn your whore
rough heeled broken nailed powdered
face me
whose whole life is tied

up to unhappiness
cause it's the only
for real thing
i
know

I Am a Black Woman
Mari Evans | *United States*

I am a black woman
the music of my song
some sweet arpeggio of tears
is written in a minor key
and I
can be heard humming in the night
Can be heard
        humming
in the night.

I saw my mate leap screaming to the sea
and I/with these hands/cupped the lifebreath
from my issue in the canebrake
I lost Nat's swinging body in a rain of tears
and heard my son scream all the way from Anzio
for Peace he never knew I
learned Da Nang and Pork Chop Hill
in anguish
Now my nostrils know the gas
and these trigger tire/d fingers
seek the softness in my warrior's beard

I
am a black woman
tall as a cypress
strong
beyond all definition still
defying place
and time
and circumstance
    assailed
        impervious
            indestructible
Look
    on me and be
renewed

Present

Sonia Sanchez | *United States*

this woman vomiten her
  hunger over the world
this melancholy woman forgotten
before memory came
  this yellow movement bursten forth like
Coltrane's melodies all mouth
  buttocks moven like palm trees,
this honeycoatedalabamianwoman
raining rhythms of blue / blk / smiles
this yellow woman carryen beneath her breasts
  pleasures without tongues
  this woman whose body weaves
  desert patterns,
this woman, wet with wanderen,
reviven the beauty of forests and winds
is tellen u secrets
gather up yo odors and listen
as she sings the mold from memory

    there is no place
for soft / blk / woman.
there is no smile green enough or
summertime words warm enough to allow my growth
and in my head
i see my history
standen like a shy child
and i chant lullabies
as i ride my past on horseback
tasten the thirst of yesterday tribes
hearen the ancient / blk / woman
should be like:
me, singen   hay-hay-
hay-hay-hay-ya-ya-ya

hay-hay-hay
-hay-ya-ya-ya

like a slow scent
beneath the sun
        and i dance my
creation and my grandmothers gathering
from my bones like great wooden birds
spread their wings
while their long / legged / laughter
stretches the night.
and i taste the
seasons of my birth. mangoes, papayas
drink my woman / coconut / milks
stalk the ancient grandfathers
sippen on proud afternoons
walk with a song round my waist
tremble like a new / born / child troubled
with new breaths
    and my singing
becomes the only sound of a
blue / blk / magical / woman. walking.
womb ripe. walken. loud with mornings. walking
maken pilgrimage to herself. walking.

Women
Alice Walker | *United States*

They were women then
My mama's generation
Husky of voice – Stout of
Step
With fists as well as
Hands
How they battered down
Doors
And ironed
Starched white
Shirts
How they led
Armies
Headragged Generals
Across mined
Fields
Booby-trapped
Ditches
To discover books
Desks
A place for us
How they knew what we
Must know
Without knowing a page
Of it
Themselves.

poem in praise of menstruation
lucille clifton | *United States*

if there is a river
more beautiful than this
bright as the blood
red edge of the moon if
there is a river
more faithful than this
returning each month
to the same delta if there

is a river
braver than this
coming and coming in a surge
of passion, of pain if there is

a river
more ancient than this
daughter of eve
mother of cain and of abel if there is in

the universe such a river if
there is some where water
more powerful that this wild
water

pray that it flows also
through animals
beautiful and faithful and ancient
and female and brave

A Runaway Lil Bit Poem
June Jordan | *United States*

Sometimes DeLiza get so crazy she omit
the bebop from the concrete she intimidate
the music she excruciate the whiskey she
obliterate the blow she sneeze
hypothetical at sex

Sometimes DeLiza get so crazy she abstruse
about a bar-be-cue ribs wonder-white-bread
sandwich in the car with hot sauce
make the eyes roll right to where you are
fastidious among the fried-up chicken wings

Sometimes DeLiza get so crazy she exasperate
on do they hook it up they being Ingrid
Bergman and some paranoid schizophrenic Mister
Gregory Peck-peck: Do
they hook it up?

Sometimes DeLiza get so crazy she drive
right across the water flying champagne bottles
from the bridge she last drink to close the bars she
holler kissey lips she laugh she let
you walk yourself away:

Sometimes DeLiza get so crazy!

Middle Passage Blues
Jacqueline Johnson | *United States*

In the still of a Dominican night
eighty-six left home
paid four hundred and fifty dollars each
to steal away to Puerto Rico.

You all share reconstructed freedom dream:
more work, opportunity and yes,
swift passage to America.
Or was it early dawn when you left your baby.

In the beginning no one noticed
or cared about your breasts leaking for want of suck.
No one noticed your pain,
blouse sticky with dripping milk.

Men calculate time in their own terms.
Said bring food for two and half days.

No one was prepared for an engine breakdown.
Your captain with a boat so badly made it had no radio.
No way to put on a life preserver, swim to shore.
Not one dingy to detach and row back home.

Candy, sardines and soda gone.
Men and women sick from drinking sea water.
Like being in the bottom of slave boat's hull.
Stench of dysentery, and the body's business,

lips cracked, breasts still leaking,
a rosary between them gathering heat in the sun.
Within a day the old ones begin to die.
The young throw themselves into ocean.

Womanhood: Identity

Two of you have left your four and six month babies.
One of you just nineteen bares her breasts
becoming a Madonna to strangers.
Men kneel like sinners to drink baby's milk.

Another nurses so many the life force leaves her
a woman marked by teeth and hunger.
You refuse to give suck to grown man lips.
Your blouse wet with milk and defiance.

Perhaps it was the misery of a stalled boat,
cruelty of a missing captain safe on a different vessel,
that inspired three men to ambush and
throw you into the Caribbean sea.

The women left become unwilling conspirators,
forced to give suck and feed.
They become part nymph, part human.

Their brown body's sacrifice
site of a new
and different middle passage.

In This Century of Pain
Eliana Potiguara | *Brazil*

Translated by Carolyn Richardson Durham

In this century of pain we will no longer have pussies
Because to be a mother in this century of death
Is to be in a fever in order to sub-exist
And to be a female in pain
Plundered as a woman.

I repeat
That in this century we will no longer have sex
It matters little to me that they understand
They may only be able to understand in another stupid
century.

We no longer have vaginas, we don't procreate any more
Our husbands died.
And to give birth to sick children
For them to kill our sons
And throw them in common graves
On the somber roads of life
In this world without people
One boss is enough.

In this century we will no longer have breasts
Resentments, eyes, mouths, or ears
Never mind pussies or ears
Principles, morals, prejudices, or defects
I no longer want the agony of centuries

In this century we will no longer manage
Antics, beauty, love, or money
In this century, oh God!
We will no longer be manageable.

Hemispheres of the Mind
Stephanie Pruitt | *United States*

I made pie. Have some. Would you
like a drink? Put up your feet. Let's
listen to Sade. Do you dance? There's leftover light
beers from a party. Yahtzee? Checkers? I'll show you
my old scrapbook. Thirsty? A lemon
pie is in the icebox. I have movies. We could paint
our toes. *The Color Purple?* Look
at that new Sanchez poem on the
table. *Lady Sings the Blues?* Did you hear
what they're saying about Halle? *Hollywood
Shuffle?* Try this on. Red is your color. I just got my heat
fixed. Are you cool? The new
Essence came yesterday, read your horoscope. I have to cut
the caffeine. A drink? I'll slice
that pie.

Do not leave me all alone.
There's a crazy woman here.
She's in a cutting mood
and my wrists are ripe.

Bitterness

Alzira Rufino | *Brazil*

Translated by Carolyn Richardson Durham

I am the knot on wood
something the axe
insists on
something that the blade resists against
cries
because
it is going to cut me.

Mawu of the Waters
Abena Busia | Ghana

I am Mawu of the Waters.
   With mountains as my footstool
and stars in my curls
I reach down to reap the waters with my fingers
   and look, I cup lakes in my palms.
   I fling oceans around me like a shawl
and am transformed
      into a waterfall.
Springs flow through me
and spill rivers at my feet
                     as fresh streams surge
                  to make seas.

I Be
Audrey Tolliver | *United States*

I be mean
I be strong
I be bad
I be wrong
I be single
I be poor
I be fertile
I be whore

Say my neck roll with a snap
Say that sisters don't take no crap

Say I be tough and I don't cry
Well it's time you stopped the lie

Cause when I forget what I'm sposed to be
I've even managed to be me

You So Woman *for Anya*
Ruth Forman | *United States*

lady
when ya purple heels hit concrete
afros swing
cool jazz hot baby
strollin by cry amen

so holy
preachas stutta
thighs so righteous
pews jump up n catch the spirit n
hymns speak in tongues

so sweet
bees leave the daffodils behind
for honey you make table sugar taste sour n
Mrs. Butterworth sho can't find a damn thing to say
when you aroun

lookin so good
cockroaches ask you to step on em
 sos they can see heaven
befo
and after they die n

you love ya people so much
if you was on pilgrimage
the Sahara Desert would run to the Atlantic
jus to make sure you don't get thirsty n
camels would kiss you for choosin they back

but Africa don't got you
we do n glad too

so girl
you jus keep on
makin the sunset procastinate n
givin the rainbows a complex
you a silk earthquake

you a velvet hurricane
n girl you so woman
i be damn
if you don't put a full moon to shame.

Just Because
Nicole Shields | *United States*

Just because
I like to wear my hair cut
short and natural

Just because
I don't have a boyfriend
and don't foresee having
one in the near future

Just because
I am very private and
like to do things by myself

Just because
I have not made passionate
love in a long time

Does not make me a lesbian!

Deliverance
Tchise | United States

We have come through the water
with bells singing over the thunder within us
We have come through the water
with bells singing over the thunder within us
We have come through the water
with bells singing over the thunder within us
we are delivered through the spray of the ocean
we are delivered through the spreading fingers
of our grandmothers and the roots of their stories
we come through the heat of the asphalt
we are the streamlined daughters of steel
girders and brick-masons with eyes
more honest than Sunday rain
simple as straight whiskey
in the kitchen after church
We are the sons of silver service for ten
day-workers in candlelight and black aprons
leaning over the bread and olives
we are delivered like chilled orchids in winter
we are delivered by the doctor
by ourselves in the new grass
behind the barns
beneath the alters
and shotgun wielding grandfathers
we are walking histories lined with shelves
for the storage of wide banded truth and jagged rage
we are delivered by lightning and the flast
in the blood of time spinning
on its knees to look for its glasses
in the darkened portal of the universe
we are stepping down from heaven
into pools of laughter
descending in the boat of Ra

Womanhood: Identity

and calling out across the ocean
with arrows of rubies and goose-stepping destiny
Blame no one when you choke
on jasmine beneath the pall of worms

let the dusk cease its conversation
when your eyes settle on its purple rings

deliver your age into the red season
of prayer and glass
let the beasts speak within your blood stream
about what you must do
and do all that the giants have carved for you
across the mouth of the mountains
read the text within your palms
and come down speaking slowly
to the deaf about what it means
to be delivered
slipped into the darkness
between the worlds like a sealed envelope
rushed through the magnificent hips
of the last two-headed woman
with yellow moccasins outside her door
Let mama speak into your ear
And she will tell you
we are delivered through music and water
we are delivered through light and sound
we are delivered by strength
and that strength is folded
into the warp of our lives
we are delivered by strong thread
and common sense
we are delivered by amazement
we are delivered through the water
with bells singing over the thunder within us.

Womanspeak
Amelia Blossom Pegram | *South Africa/England*

tearing my skirts
jumping the hedgerows
racing barefoot through
the brush
ribboned ponytails flapping in the chase
swinging exhausted through the gate
flopping on the porch
to catch a breath

Those were girl-days

Now I have tamed my hair
closecrop
Thirty-six ceed my breasts
Ensheathed hips in pencil-slim skirt
Step sedate
feet imprisoned
in stiletto pumps

And you come by say
Girl, looking mighty fine.
What's happening, Girl?

Five-foot-two frame stretched tall
I heave my breasts
toss my head
"Did I hear you call me, GIRL?"

I Am the Creativity

Alexis De Veaux | *United States*

I am the dance step
of the paintbrush singing
I am the sculpture
of the song
the flame breath
of words
giving new life to paper
yes, I am the creativity
that never dies
I am the creativity
keeping my people alive

Raised by Women
Kelly Norman Ellis | *United States*

I was raised by
Chitterling eating
Vegetarian cooking
Cornbread so good you want to lay
Down and die baking
"Go on baby, get yo'self a plate"
Kind of Women.

Some thick haired
Angela Davis afro styling
"Girl, lay back
And let me scratch yo head!"
Sorta Women.

Some big legged
High yellow, mocha brown
Hip shaking
Miniskirt wearing
Hip huggers hugging
Daring debutantes
Grooving
"I know I look good"
Type of Women.

Some tea sipping
White glove wearing
Got married too soon
Divorced in just the nick of time
"Better say yes ma'am to me"
Type of Sisters.

Some fingerpopping
Boogaloo dancing

Womanhood: Identity

Say it loud
I'm black and I'm proud
James Brown listening
"Go on girl shake that thing"
Kind of Sisters.

Some face slapping
Hands on hips
Don't mess with me
"Pack your bags
And get the hell out of my house"
Sort of Women.

Some Ph.D. toting
Poetry writing
Portrait painting
"I'll see you in court"
World traveling
"Stand back, I'm creating"
Type of Queens

I was raised by
Women.

A Godiva
Thylias Moss | United States

Myself, I always thought it
a throwback revealing primate roots
I'd as soon forget. Oh but what

would I do without that stuff
softer than a hand, a spool
unwound on my head and gold
already, before

the weaver comes with that talent
I share; my one-word name
rivals the best of them:
Rumplestiltskin, God.

My calling came and went public as
a hedge on horseback in Coventry, the
sun fermenting the color of my hair
into grog that will not

lay wasted. *Eat, drink, be merry*
those aren't nude words. I put it all
on the table for surgery, not feast.
I want to be cut through to my

black woman's heart. She had one
in 1057 as well as a continent
that had not been reconciled nor
clothed. Breasts hanging as fruit

should, unpicked sculpture on a
tree, museum pieces. She is
something good for you that is not
medicine. And I

am her transmitted, no longer
literal, needful of reasons
to take off clothes that don't explain
living, and distort everything God

gave us, while trying to be
metaphors for the gifts. If I succeed
there is a tax that will die. I ride
like a morbid Midas, my lips

and fingers coax their love objects
into the most golden silence of them all.
The usual death rider got time off
for good behavior. I just worry

that I might like this, that I'll take
my heart out of the black woman and
put it in a dead thing.

So you think I'm a Mule?
Jackie Kay | *Scotland*

"Where do you come from?"
'I'm from Glasgow.'
"Glasgow?"
"Uh huh. Glasgow."
The white face hesitates
the eyebrows raise
the mouth opens
then snaps shut
incredulous
yet too polite to say outright
liar
she tries another manoeuvre
"And your parents?"
'Glasgow and Fife.'
"Oh?"
'Yes. Oh.'
Snookered she wonders where she should go
from here—
"Ah, but you're not pure"
'Pure? Pure what.
Pure white? Ugh. What a plight
Pure? Sure I'm pure
I'm rare . . .'
"Well, that's not exactly what I mean,
I mean . . . you're a mulatto, just look at . . .'
'Listen. My original father was Nigerian
to help with your confusion
But hold on right there
If you Dare mutter mulatto
hover around hybrid
hobble on half-caste
and intellectualize on the
"mixed race problem",

I have to tell you:
take your beady eyes offa my skin;
don't concern yourself with
the "dialectics of mixtures";
don't pull that strange blood crap
on me Great White Mother.
Say, I'm no mating of a
she-ass and a stallion
no half of this and half of that
to put it plainly purely
I am Black
My blood flows evenly, powerfully
and when they shout "Nigger"
and you shout "Shame"
ain't nobody debating my blackness.
You see that fine African nose of mine,
my lips, my hair, You see lady
I'm not mixed up about it.
So take your questions, your interest
your patronage. Run along.
Just leave me.
I'm going to my Black sisters
to women who nourish each other
on belonging
There's a lot of us
Black women struggling to define
just who we are
where we belong
and if we know no home
we know one thing:
we are Black
we're at home with that.'
"Well, that's all very well, but . . ."
'I know it's very well.
No But. Good bye.'

In Service
Maxine Tynes | Canada

This poem is dedicated to the generations of Black women who sustained life and survival for their families by bending low in labour in generations of white kitchens.

Saturday morning armies
of Black women
young
and old
and, young and old at the same time
in the same face
in the same care and time and work-worn hands
you rise with the dawn
leaving home and brown babies
behind you, in the day's early light
pulling coat and scarf close
avoiding the mirror
shrinking from the cold morning of
bus ride
to prestigious street corner.

you are not alone
you are with your sisters in this
Northend-to Southend
Jane Finch-to Rosedale
Montreal-to Outremont
Harlem-to Scarsdale
wearing head-rag
carrying dust-mop, scrub-bucket
in-service three days a week march in the dawn.

you possess a key, cherished girl (never woman) of this house
you tap and scuffle and wipe feet at the back
and enter the world of
day's

day's
day's work in service
taking your place in that army of
round and strong and weary backs
moving with grace and sure familiar stride
from your kitchen
your babies
your own forgotten morning at home
to this
three days-a-week armies of Black women
in service.

Blackgertrude

Cynthia Parker Ohene | *United States*

peanuts and indigo clocks latimer used comforters coverings enclosed
watermelons patched as being being-as indigo peanuts on pennsylvania
ave near-ly a-rab horses

carting ohinches plums peeeeeeee chez & she be understanding bes
understanding black handed times five dem belly hot with she under-
standing of ways gospel.

Blues in Arpeggio
Cynthia Parker Ohene | *United States*

                  Refashioned in yemonja
conduit mermaids come ashore
on the lament of nine muses
                           levitating

and we'll understand it better bye and bye

mz cinda's slipper room
affixed along a tripod
of plants that "grow up
with no masters"
halts desert affinities
blooms willow womanness

mz cinda custodian of mountain water
slips of pods, tree products from
virginia's guitar hills prizes
buffalo clover and latticed rootings
a skein of peruvian fairies and tulip pinks sprawl yon
and gilt the overlays of vine and verbena

mae lays mz cinda's braids to fan across the small of her
working back twists an orange coil at the tips
dried from peeled oranges it scents the darkened room
she smells the seeds that sowed them and directs mae to
add chandeliers of bloodgrass

elijah's wife comes by to bring patterned shells for mz cinda
to paint by the numbers
elijah's wife an apostle like the santero women of her clan
removes from her sack a burnished oil to unrankle the skin about
mz cinda's eyes

mz cinda whistles as she moors her feet deeper into the clay floor
whistles deeper as her song meanders about
her jesus in the sweet bye and bye

By hand
Cynthia Parker Ohene | *United States*

mz cinda's washboard packed with
bea's bestowments of mande figurines
cast from broken windows

below arched constrictions:
a makeshift corset hobbled prosthetics
ceremonial pots with kasai velvet

her deeded quillwork
of cree
and illicit notions eulogized by the abandoned
necklace cimarron horses

mz cinda raised her best: "sharecrop the sacred
no shrouded offers from alabaster carpetbaggers
only bridles from buffalo soldiers"

Cat Tales
Carmen Gillespie | *United States*

Every morning before sun claimed
full Alabama power,
before it rose to arrogant apex,
she stole the eggs from
the hens for his breakfast
with soft and clucking
apology.

When the skillet was hot
with leftover bacon fat,
she would crack the eggs
into the black iron, their gelatinous
clarity turning white.

The smell always aroused him.
She could not remember the eggs
without recalling the feel
of his unvarying, unimaginative hands.

He always waited
while she broke the yolks
and started the grits, the angle
of light heating the kitchen.
He would go to the back while
she stirred in the honey and butter.

Afterwards,
walking home beside the creek,
her cattail legs cut through
the grass like machetes,
small cuts slicing her skin
like an initiation.
There, sun surrendered

to crickets and shades.

Mama slapped her
when she told about the
trips with the tray to the back room
each morning.

Mama slapped, averting eyes
from her daughter's swelling belly
inevitable and temporary as the handprint
rising on the girl's still unblemished face.

She ran to her place in the cool dark
under the house with the cats,
also dark and forgotten, seeking
shelter from the unrelenting heat.

There among the glass pickle jars
sticky with leftover liquor
she remembered the story
overheard of the slave mothers'
secrets unsuspected.

Through the dawn darkness
she shielded the slivers, secret
and shining in morning moonlight
trying not to betray them
with nervous slip—
        first coup,
                eggs, bacon,
and then the grits
with a little extra mixed in with
the honey and butter.

Before the baby came,
his insides were shredded
like the downy guts of the brown

cattails by the creek.

That morning she found him
in the backroom,
dead and unsuspecting,
  and ran to tell his neighbors
        Mr. Pitts had passed.

We the Women

Grace Nichols | *Guyana/UK*

We the women who toil
unadorn
heads tie with cheap
cotton

We the women who cut
clear fetch dig sing

We the women making
something from this
ache-and-pain-a-me
back-o-hardness

Yet we the women
who praises go unsung
who voices go unheard
who deaths they sweep
aside
as easy as dead leaves

Have you ever been convicted of a felony?
If so, explain *for Ruby*
Amanda Johnston | *United States*

Fighting devils ain't new to me. Hell, I've been fighting them since I was born.

They always come looking like men I love. Mama showed me how to cradle
their fire until the heat no longer singed my arms. We learned to swallow our
salt and peppered tongues with ease. One will sacrifice everything in hell's
kitchen, but not my babies. I always fed them something sweeter, saving
the brine and rinds for myself.

I like to bake. Even know how to make most stuff from scratch. I can dice,
julienne, and score an apple pie crust like in Woman's Day Magazine.
Didn't mean to make his face flower like that, forgot I was even holding the
knife. Boom, Boom, Boom, ever heard the devil beating at your front door
hungry and clawing for neck bones? Forgot exactly how the blood spilled, tried
to tell the police that.

I like to bake. My babies need to eat. For years I cooked for other inmates.
Guess you could say I'm experienced. Let me show you. I promise I'll do
a good job.

this here aint a allen ginsberg poem!
Cynthia Parker Ohone| *United States*

for the bondswoman at the corner of 138th and willis ave. who begins
each day with lord please don't let me haveta who raises 9 kids and 4
grands without leave who prone begs prison guards to release her sanitary
pads who as mule of the world makes a drop to cop who makes change
at any laundromat & any cafeteria who leaves the light on & hopes her
sons will not be stopped by 5 0 who quotes malcolm in howard beach
who reminds me where i came from & why i will return whose lyricism
is memoried in muh dear's back who reads by remembering the shapes
who writes by tracing them who makes biscuits with lard & buttermilk
who swells from diabetic sores who on sundays wears a peacock feather
in her crown who is blinded by ms. justice flinging her headlong through
steel scales leaving tattoos of the **TRIANGULAR TRADE** who collects
bottles of love and acid & sells them side by side whose still van der zee is
hottentot & maisha around the way whose gaze leaves that well of loneli-
ness who be badu but cries like nina who wakes up on the 9th month of
mother's day & burns his shit whose beloved mama is etched in stone who
bleeds without cycle & drinks straight no chaser when she conjures bessie
& gets brittney whose genesis is her exodus who binds meatloaf with utz
potato chips who buys pickled pig's feet pickled eggs & lil' debbies @
the bodega for a dollar who at jesus will save you church of god in christ
pledges her allegiance to the holy ghost whose power is living in spite
of who goes where everyone is her friend but noone is my poem bes a
bluespoem for the sistahs at the corner of ahunnard and thirtyeighth and
will/is.

Rag Dolls
Ayanna Black | *Jamaica/Canada*

I see you women
trudging down spadina
at six in the morning
your babies go to day care
you to the sweat shops
some dressed in black
some in bright colours
mauve
purple
red
some perfumed in garlic
some in *cus-cus*

I see you women
being mangled
your screams
lost in the machines
can't afford to bleed
the machine
you are the machine
a voice yells
faster
faster
tomorrow you're replaced

i see you women
being raped
in dark stairwells
and behind closed doors

frozen with shock
a week later:
rag dolls on the psycho ward
Diagnosis: Paranoid Schizophrenia

208

Domestic Work, 1937
Natasha Trethewey | *United States*

All week she's cleaned
someone else's house,
stared down her own face
in the shine of copper-
bottomed pots, polished
wood, toilets she'd pull
the lid to—that look saying

Let's make a change, girl.

But Sunday mornings are hers—
church clothes starched
and hanging, a record spinning
on the console, the whole house
dancing. She raises the shades,
washes the rooms in light,
buckets of water, Octagon soap.

Cleanliness is next to godliness . . .

Windows and doors flung wide,
curtains two-stepping
forward and back, neck bones
bumping in the pot, a choir
of clothes clapping on the line.

Nearer my God to thee . . .

She beats time on the rugs,
blows dust from the broom
like dandelion spores, each one
a wish for something better.

Frailty Is Not My Name

Maureen Ismay | *Jamaica/England*

Frailty is not my name
            yet,
On the other hand,
I'm not a big strong, black woman
iron hard and carrying
all the sorrows of the world on my back.

My breasts large and hard as boxes
My eyes big and bulging
My skin, black and shiny and greasy

I'm not big and strong
and keeping a man underneath my tail
able to take all that garbage
                'Here dawg take that'

        I'm no mythology
        shaking the earth
        and freaking out the leaves.

I'm not a strong black woman
admirable and brawd

ten children at my breast
all at the same time
while cooking and cleaning
and singing and fixing up
my man . . .
with beads in my hair
and camel on my skin.

On the other hand
        Don't call me frailty!

SRAM: Ground Zero
Robin Caudell | *United States*

Alcohol-soaked cotton cloth
Cools my latexed fingers
Cleaning missile's guidance plate.
Its shiny steel blurs
Beneath globs of silicone gel
Viscosity of Dippity-Do x 4.
I slather gel, not for
God, Reagan or Bush
But my daughter in Florida
With her father who left
Us to find him/self.
Grandmom:
"Find himself? What kind of mess is that?
He's in his skin, ain't he?"

George, the shop chief, stops me
Calls the bone crew to No. 11449922.
Before he slides the silicone cover
Over the plate, he writes:
"Fuck you Khaddafi!!!!!"
In gel with short, broad
Kansas-red fingers.
My comrades laugh, slap high-fives
Before torquing screws I bury
Beneath pucky, fluffy
As Grandmom's meringue,
That dries hard as Master Sgt.'s
Basalt balls.

Before we're off Alert
We hear we SRAMmed
Khaddafi's granddaughter
To Allah.

Her blood veils
My hands arthritic
From wiping missiles
On marrow-cold
Days beneath earth
Mounds glowing now
Like Tut's tomb.

*SRAM is the acronym for Short-Range Attack Missile

WOMANHOOD

Physical Appearance

Beauty: When the Other Dancer is the Self
     —Alice Walker, From *In Search of Our Mother's Gardens*

Kinky Hair Blues
Una Marson | *Jamaica*

Gwine find a beauty shop
Cause I ain't a belle.
Gwine find a beauty shop
Cause I ain't a lovely belle.
The boys pass me by,
They say I's not so swell.

See oder young gals
So slick and smart.
See those oder young gals
So slick and smart.
I jes gwine die on de shelf
If I don't mek a start.

I hate dat ironed hair
And dat bleaching skin.
Hate dat ironed hair
And dat bleaching skin.
But I'll be all alone
If I don't fall in.

Lord 'tis you did gie me
All dis kinky hair.
'Tis you did gie me
All dis kinky hair,
And I don't envy gals
What got dose locks so fair.

I like me black face
And me kinky hair.
I like me black face
And me kinky hair.
But nobody loves dem,
I jes don't tink it's fair.

Womanhood: Physical Appearance

Now I's gwine press me hair
And bleach me skin.
I's gwine press me hair
And bleach me skin.
What won't a gal do
Some kind a man to win.

Ay, Ay, Ay of the Kinky-Haired Negress
Julia DeBurgos | *Puerto Rico*

Ay, ay, ay, that am kinky-haired and pure black;
kinks in my hair, Kafir in my lips;
and my flat nose Mozambiques.

Black of pure tint, I cry and laugh
the vibration of being a black statue;
a chunk of night, in which my white
teeth are lightning;
and to be a black vine
which entwines in the black
and curves the black nest
in which the raven lies.
Black chunk of black in which I sculpt myself,
ay, ay, ay, my statue is all black.

They tell me that my grandfather was the slave
for whom the master paid thirty coins.
Ay, ay, ay, that the slave was my grandfather
is my sadness, is my sadness.
If he had been the master
it would be my shame:
that in men, as in nations,
if being the slave is having no rights
being the master is having no conscience.

Ay, ay, ay, wash the sins of the white King
in forgiveness black Queen.

Ay, ay, ay, the race escapes me
and buzzes and flies toward the white race,
to sink in its clear water;
or perhaps the white will be shadowed in the black.

Ay, ay, ay, my black race flees
and with the white runs to become bronzed;
to be one for the future,
fraternity of America!

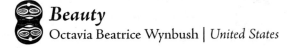

Beauty
Octavia Beatrice Wynbush | *United States*

'Tis wondrous strange in what things men find beauty.
One sees it in the sun kissing the sleeping hills awake;
Another in the moon, trailing paths to fairy-land across the
  slow-moving water.
This man finds beauty in first youth; his friend, in mature
  woman.
But beauty lurks for me in black, knotted hands,
Hands consecrated to toil that those who come
Behind them may have tender, shapely hands;
And beautiful are shoulders with bearing heavy burdens stooped
That younger shoulders may grow straight and proud.
And faces, dark, sad faces, too, are beautiful—
The patient, wistful faces of the many
Who have viewed their lands of promise from afar,
Turned from the mountain to the lonely path
Of sober duty, and gazed on
The promised land no more.
'Tis wondrous strange
In what things men find beauty.

Venus' Complaint
Shanta Archaya | *United Kingdom*

I would never wish to be a shadow of myself,
a speck of a ghost flickering across
the lower chin of the sun.
Call that a beauty spot –
barely visible to the naked eye,
indistinguishable from other dots
dissolving in the galaxies?

I am the goddess of love and beauty –
identified with Aphrodite, emblem of fecundity,
invoked to turn the hearts
of women to virtue and chastity –
sprung from the foam of the sea,
daughter of Jupiter, wife of Vulcan.
With the mighty Mars,
gods and demigods have I had affairs;
Cupid and Aeneas I count among my sons.

I am Hesperus, the evening star –
the second planet from the sun.
I am the spark that inspires wonder,
not this darkness; from my bright centre,
I survey luminous skies; the horizon
mere limitation of human perception.

Nothing in this dream existence of ours
can move too close or too far
from its given place in the universe.
Then must I learn to align myself every
few hundred years for this ceremony –

Let my dark image be observed
by half the earth's population

that cannot breathe in my atmosphere?

Placed as I am, there is no option,
no choice to figure out what goes on
in the universe except what I have been
chosen to bring to the party –
laughter, music, dance, pleasure, poetry…

Roots
Donnie N. Belcher | United States

My edges were straight
But I had nappy roots.
American culture
Devours individuality
Like vultures on prey.
Making you believe
Your physical appearance
Isn't okay.

        So like
        If I don't like
        Have like
        Long, silky straight hair
        Then that makes me like
        Not pretty, like right?

I can perm my hair
And perm my hair
But every six weeks
Reality grows there.
The dark came to the light
When I needed a touch up,
But it was actually a touch down
And my self-esteem was the underdog
And that game was lost.
Torturing my head was imitation
And imitation was my initiation
Into being accepted.
My edges were straight
But I was on the edge of insanity
Being someone that wasn't me.
I was on the edge of a cliff
And if European beauty jumped,
Maybe, just maybe, I would have jumped too.

I've got black woman lips,
Black woman hips,
And sun-kissed skin.
Not to mention a black woman attitude.
I left the B.S. institute
And started to home school.
My edges were straight
But I had nappy roots.
No matter how tall the tree
It always has roots
And without roots
The tree dies
And I was on the route
To self-hate.
My tree wasn't bearing any fruit.
If you plant apples, you don't get oranges.
So where did I get the crazy idea
That nappy was not right?

                      Can't go nowhere
                      Cause hair ain't combed.
                      Can't let nobody see me like this
                      See me at my essence
                      Vulnerable and pure
                      Confident and true
                      Rather have chemically damaged hair
                      Than outcast nappy hair.

By American standards
My hair is all the way bad.
It's dreadlocked
And I dread the fact that
Some people don't love themselves enough
To be natural.
I dread the fact that
Some people have to be filled with artificial flavors
To taste good.
I dread the fact that
My people don't love themselves.

I'm locked within my reality
And on the edge of myself.
I dread jumping into your mentality.
My edges are now nappy
And I've now got nappy roots.
I am beautiful and beauty is
Truth.

Spread Out
Metta Sama | *United States*

(Look)
My spread is red, frog
red, poison. My spread is wide-
legged, I mean, this spread
is soft, store-bought,
patternless, clean. I should
feel blessed. I sleep beneath a poison-
dart spread. I don't feel
free. I don't
float.
I wonder about my great grandmother,
about her blood, where
her blood spread when she birthed
my grandmother, Lila Lee,
Lila with the steel gray hair,
so straight down her back
I always wanted to touch it. Lila
Lee wasn't weaved soft but industrial
steel cold. She had a silver comb &
brush on a silver tray, a mirror
with a silver back, a silver back,
hers. Steel cold, my grandma.
I longed to touch Lila's silver strands,
feel my way past the metal of her;
she had a concrete tongue, I never
heard her speak, so I'd stare
at her ravished/ravenous braids, and
Scuse me Grandma, but could I
unbraid your hair, please ma'am?
Will you teach me to plait?
And she'd set her grey eyes on
my momma
who wasn't born on a spread;

my grandma spread her legs
on a floor and spit my momma out,
way out, black bottom out, down
South where black folks don't appreciate
thin hair, treat thin hair like thin ice, fearing
a river quivers beneath the surface.
My momma's hair birthed complex;
hair like a quilt; piece here: nappy,
scrap here: silk, a swatch not unlike cotton; piece,
scrap, swatch: summer, crackling
leaves, tree bark; her hair springs forth
my hair
my hair is springy, springy
clingy hair, black black black black
hair. Thicker than my momma's,
dark as my father, strong and anguished,
sensitive to the scalp, my hair
(but a warrior sleeps in there),
no silver comb could glide on a slide
through my hair. Anyone could lay down
in the spread of my hair, quilt
a family history.
I wish I never had to sleep
under a store-bought spread
because my momma knows how to quilt
in her head. I'm missing something.
I've never seen my great grandmother.
Was she a woman of patchwork love,
sometimey, cut from cloth love?
Did she save strands of her husband's
hair, her babies' hair, sisters', mother's,
father's, brother's? Did she thread
their hair and wrap her man in its love?
I need one memory of love, stitched,
a spread out nappy red black kinky
thin love, I'll take poisonous love
if that's the only kind out there.

No, hair
sometimes lies, but I want it
straight: a family quilt,
scratchy, a quilt thick with sweat,
thick with guilt quilt, with babies' blood.
I want to bury my body in a nipple
dripping milk, my great granddaddy's
arm vined with hair,
laid bare across his woman's belly,
where my grandma curls
her finger round the promise
of black hair, quick & tricky as love.

That's What I Hear
Jacqueline Johnson | *United States*

I.

I remember me and Denny, darkest kids
on the block. Ugly. Scorned, teased, envied.
Being seen and invisible at the same time.

I hear now that he is grown Denny
is so black and so beautiful
he looks like black Jesus or someone.

II.

It wasn't until I cut all my hair off
bought earrings three times the size
of my wrists that men from Ibadan, Benin

Jamaica zoom in. Who is that woman
with the big head? Who is that beauty?
That's what I hear.

Borrowed Beauty
Maxine Tynes | *Canada*

we've come full circle
from turban/headed women (hiding cornrows)
in servitude; cooking
suckling
cleaning
everlasting   cleaning
cooking
suckling
cleaning
from turban-headed women (hiding cornrows)
to precious, time-driven 'dos
to free-form Afros
nocturnal braids escaping into
beautiful, magical,
free-flying cloud Afros at
dawn, dusk, midnight
to our cornrows earning some woman named "10"
magic money in flickers of
light and colour.

Do you know, Africa's child, woman,
black brown tan;
with our corn rows?
you are nobody's beauty but our own
and named Sahara, Zaire, Zimbabwe, Cairo
Nefertiti, Cleopatra or Nigeria.

this is no borrowed beauty,
this is home.

Say That I Am
Paulette Childress | *United States*

Say that I am beautiful.
Say that I am
because my face is ebony
of an African tree
and queenly Benin bronze,
yet by rift of time
and fire of slavery,
distinctly mine.

Say that I am
because my body,
bold and still strong,
blossoming sweet
with secret promises
or fulfilled and swollen
with life,
is Mother of the Earth

and my legs,
like sleek flamingoes on the Nile,
strut straight and proud
against cold Western winds;

because I love a man
and mother children
in a world that has denied me—
tried to strip me bare
and take my love away.

Say that I am
because I keep the song
and dance
the smile

eternally.

Because my soul is constant source,
Sun-giving warmth
and light
and life,

say that I am beautiful.
Say that I am!

Wooly Metal Hair
Ella Turenne | United States

My wooly metal hair,
why you painin' me . . .
That's what hype lil' black girls
think when they go get relaxed.
They don't sing accolades,
Don't shout testaments,
Don't take care, admit
That you are beauty,
Natural, Afrikan—
To the root—
Well you are
But let's face it,
these roots are not always comely.
They get tangled,
Knotted,
Uh-huh . . .
They get nappy, too.
My wooly metal hair,
we sometimes pain you so.
We should
love the full body of
trillions of tiny tendrils,
love the rich deep light/dark
hues of black/brown color,
love the way you change
With your lock/twist/braids
yet are still the same wild/natural/unruly miracle.
We should
love the way you come
bouncing back
love the way you are strong
like the people you represent
'cause you do represent.

And me?
I love the way I can call you my unique
An element of me forever like soul.
My wooly metal hair,
Ancestors passed down your secrets/allure/power.
You are sacred. . . timeless.
You should be worshipped,
not fried/died/dechemicalized to death.
That be bad for brain cells,
causin' patches of nothingness leadin' to insanity . . .
My wooly metal hair,
I'll give you your due props,
'cause after 400 years,
there's still not much I can call mine,
'cept you of course.

Don't Tell Me to Relax My Hair

Javacia Harris | *United States*

One day I realized
My curls were not uptight
Just poised
That's the day my scalp
Always itching for attention
Decided to chill out
My ends that had split up
Decided to work things out
So I decided to let them reach for each other
Reach for my waist
While I danced in the rain
No umbrella
Glory running wet down my back

There's History in My Hair

Karen Williams | *United States*

I once read a poem
about the politics of hair
then afterwards looked in the mirror
and wondered when I was little
in my coal colored halo of kink and frizzle
did a prevailing stick straight world
see a nappy, ugly me

I mean could they see all the way to Africa in my eyes
my nakedness, my culture exposed enough for them
to wish they had a missionary at hand
to civilize, sanctify me
a little girl who proudly wielded a pink ace comb
and volunteered at school
to comb their naturally silky hair

I was young
called it playing beauty shop
only realizing years later
even then, how beautiful I was
with my tawny skin unlike crushed pearls
my mahogany eyes more deep, sparkling
than those blue as cerulean skies
where across flew the bird of privilege, paradise

I was young, then
a fledgling phoenix still waiting to be born
and to think all this came
from reading a poem
from examining the politics
of my skin and hair
and realizing
even as a happy, nappy little girl

how phenomenal
how compelling
how infinite
my beauty was
and still is

the blond on his arm *after reading* US Weekly
Teri Ellen Cross | *United States*

there's no comparing to her lithe figure
wonder if she works out all day
if *he* pays for her trainer
if she even has a job
then she is blond which is a different
category than white   blond has its own
story   its own golden fabric of myth
add blond to white and automatically
he is out of my league   always
no matter how much I scrub
in the morning showers
 the dark patches on elbows
and knees won't go away
only red replaces them
raw after disgust has its turn
black is my soul they say
black is my skin they say
brown is my skin I say
and the only color my soul knows
is longing the weight of
its opaque density

"Ten"
Naomi Long Madgett | *United States*

I have become
a sixteenth century
Italian sculpture
in blackface
with hips too broad
and belly corn-
bread-ample, ham-
hock happy

Nobody idolizes
me
anymore
singing me lovingly
lustily (like Sterling)
"sweet-hipted mama
sweet-hipted Mame"

I have
not so simply
grown bountiful and
sometimes wiser than
brothers
chasing illusions
of frail, pale African
queens
with lisping voices
and platinum
corn-rowed hair.

Bo Derrick, the Caucasian star of the motion picture *Ten*, was erroneously credited by the media with inventing the hairstyle (Cornrows) that is traditionally African. Also see Maxine Tynes' poem "Borrowed Beauty."

about our hips
Harriet Jacobs | *United States*

our hips,
they a poem to pulchritude
they sing anthems to negritude,
our hips   they smooth and sweet
as candied yams, and fine as grandma's
home cured ham
they beauty—it was not designed
to be restrained by calvin klein
they smile and giggle, they laugh out loud
they free and full, they strong and proud
our hips hold secrets from the past,
and hold our future in their grasp
our hips got motions known to tease
made james brown sing
some please please please
our hips,
make brother thank the lord above
they got sweet hips like ours
to love

That Black Ass
Tara Betts | *United States*

Loud with primal curves,
her posterior must be
some trait for adaptation
or mating. Clothes cannot
contain such an oddity. Let's
pay so we can stare, for centuries.
Her daughters will be paid to shake
for music. Send her dead ass back
to Africa after we've put her labia
in formaldehyde and we've counted
our money. Ass is all that's worth
seeing here. This mark of the whore,
savage sex caught in a labyrinth
of steatopygia. I want to keep
looking at this zoo on two legs.

Hummers
Deb Parks-Satterfield | *United States*
Thanks to Carol B.

SIDE A

because we're black, because we're women
because you're beautiful and so am i
we don't speak
we
hum

hands on cats-in-a-bag hips, necks on ball bearings
lips curled back in derision
acknowledgement loaded with contempt . . . yo' hair, yo' clothes
yo' everything
stripped mashed onto a slide shoved under a microscope thick
with who the fuck do you think you are or could be?

i won't tell you yo' slip's showin' or there's lipstick on yo'
teeth or even that yo' woman is sleepin' with me
no
i won't tell you you 'bout to lose yo' job or yo' boy is sellin'
crack at school
no
i'll just hum

SIDE B

black women's eyes
molten chocolate eyes unite with mine

submerging
we nod smile

that deep secret smile we know something you don't

we know how we came to be in this moment
our contact speaks worlds centuries of understanding cuts
through class and the darkness or lightness of skin
i know you know no matter what facade i've chosen to
help me survive this day
and the days to come that we are exactly the same
when we stop to talk our voices slide into a familiar silky
rollercoaster cadence. "girrrl puhleeze no you didn't!"
we surface
too brief, not enough
black women's eyes

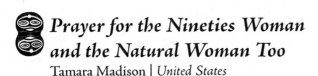

Prayer for the Nineties Woman and the Natural Woman Too

Tamara Madison | *United States*

These iron-pumping, track-jogging, Jazzercise-stepping, food-starved, anorexia-nervous, bulimia-bitten, thyroid-thumped, lipo-sucked, cosmetically-cut, electrolycized, bikini-clad women with their cropped-shoulders, propped balloon-breast and stiffly-starched spines can kiss my café au lait, never-girdled, swivel-hipped, untamed behind that rumbles with its own rhythm, five foot eight, 200 pound, stretch mark-strumming, AAA grade, no artificial flavors, sweeteners, or preservatives, 100% natural woman entire ass.

Amen.

she daydreams:
Teri Ellen Cross | *United States*

freckles everywhere, no, no freckles
green eyes though—the ones 'dat turn blue in 'de light
yeah and skin, caramel-colored like a sugar daddy, no, no toffee

no lightskinned, like Jennifer Beals or Halle Berry
yeah that, coffee with three creams color and the nose
would have to be just a little bit skinner, right

and the hair long definitely, long—like Indian down ya' back long
but honey-brown 'dough and wavy, like mixed-girl wavy
kinda like white people hair but thicker

then the body—no stretch marks anywhere
no pimples on my butt either wid' skin just as smooth as, as
that sugar daddy after it's been in my mouth for too long

and elbows and knees 'da same color as 'da rest of me
no dark spots, no skinned-knee or skinned elbow scars
and long legs too, wid' no scars—nowhere

(like the one I got on my leg from when it got tow' up
 when i was riding on the back of Teresa's bike)

and no black spots on my legs either like the ones I got from shaving so much
and the bikini line, ohmigod, the bikini line is like the white girls at the beach
no ingrown hairs nowhere and i can shave it into shapes and stuff with no
bumps!

even throw in a tan line, yeah cus I would be 'dat light
and keep my curves, you know keep my butt and my boobs but my nipples see
'dey would be lighter since I'm lighter, jus' not brown

and then all 'de boys will be like, who dat? cus I'd be so fine I'll stand out then
and 'dey all would be jocking me, likin' on me cus' I'll be black 'cept pretty now

Nocturne
Naomi Long Madgett | *United States*

See how dark the night settles on my face,
How deep the rivers of my soul
Flow imperturbable and strong.

Rhythms of unremembered jungles
Pulse through the untamed shadows of my song,
And my cry is the dusky accent of secret midnight birds.

Above the sable valleys of my sorrow
My swarthy hands have fashioned
Pyramids of virgin joy.

See how tenderly God pulls His blanket of blackness over
the earth.
You think I am not beautiful?
You lie!

To Those of My Sisters Who Kept Their Naturals
Gwendolyn Brooks | *United States*

Never to look
a hot comb in the teeth

       Sisters!
       I love you.
       Because you love you.
Because you are erect.
Because you are also bent.
In season, stern, kind.
Crisp, soft—in season.
And you withhold.
And you extend.
And you Step out.
And you go back.
And you extend again.
Your eyes, loud-soft, with crying and
     with smiles,
are older than a million years.
And they are young.
You reach, in season.
You subside, in season.
And All
below the richrough righttime of your hair.
You have not bought Blondine.
You have not hailed the hot-comb recently.
You never worshiped Marilyn Monroe.
You say: Farrah's hair is hers.
You have not wanted to be white.
Nor have you testified to adoration of that
     state
with the advertisement of imitation
(*never* successful because the hot-comb is
     laughing too.)

But oh the rough dark Other music!
the Real,
the Right.
The natural Respect of Self and Seal!
        Sisters!
Your hair is Celebration in the world!

For Muh' Dear
Carolyn M. Rodgers | *United States*

        today Blackness
     lay backin
& rootin

told my sweet mama
to leave me alone
about my wild free knotty and nappy
hair
cause i was gon lay back
   and let it grow so high
     it could reroute its roots
        and highjack the sky!

she sd. why don't you let it grow
right on down to the ground honey chile,
grow yo'self a coat of hair fuh winter
matter fact you so BLACK now, huh!
why don't you jest throw
a fit
of BLACK lay backin & rootin.

Hot Comb
Natasha Trethewey | *United States*

Halfway through an afternoon
of coca cola bottles sweating rings
on veneered tabletops and the steel drone
of window fans above the silence
in each darkened room, I open a stiff drawer
and find the old hot combs, black
with grease, the teeth still pungent
as burning hair. One is small, fine toothed
as if for a child. Holding it,
I think of my mother's slender wrist,
the curve of her neck as she leaned over
the stove, her eyes shut as she pulled
the wooden handle and laid flat the wisps
at her temples. The heat in our kitchen
made her glow that morning I watched her
wincing, the hot comb singeing her brow,
sweat glistening above her lips,
her face made strangely beautiful
as only suffering can do.

Naola Beauty Academy New Orleans, Louisiana, 1943

Natasha Trethewey | *United States*

Made hair? The girls here
put a press on your head
last two weeks. No naps.

They learning. See the basins?
This where we wash. Yeah,
it's hot. July jam.

Stove always on. Keep the combs
hot. Lee and Ida bumping hair
right now. Best two.

Ida got a natural touch.
Don't burn nobody.
Her own's a righteous mass.

Lee, now she used to sew.
Her fingers steady
from them tiny needles.

She can fix some bad hair.
Look how she lay them waves.
Light, slight and polite.

Not a one out of place.

hair: a narrative
Cheryl Clarke | *United States*

it is passing strange to be in the company
of black women
and be the only one who does not worry about
not being with a man
and even more passing strange
is to be among black women
and be the only one wearing her hair natural
or be the only one who has used a straightening
iron

An early childhood memory:

me: sitting in the kitchen
holding down onto my chair
shoulders hunching
toes curling in my sneakers.

my mother: standing behind me
bracing herself against the stove
greasing the edges of my scalp
and the roots of my hair violently
heating the straightening comb alternately
and asking between jerking and pulling:
    "why couldn't you have *good* hair?"
by the time mother finished pressing my virgin wool
to patent leather,
I was asking why I had to have hair at all.

(the first time I heard a straightening iron crackle
through my greased kitchen, I thought a rattlesnake
had got loose in the room.)

so much pain to be black, heterosexual, and female

to be trained for some *Ebony* Magazine mail order man
wanting a woman with long hair, big legs, and able
to bear him five sons.
hardly any man came to be worth the risk of nappy edges.

the straightening iron: sado-masochistic artifact
salvaged from some chamber of the Inquisition
and given new purpose in the new world.

what was there
about straight hair
that made me want to suffer
the mythical anguish of hell
to have it?
made me a recluse
on any rainy, snowy, windy, hot, or humid day,
away from any activity that produced the least
moisture to the scalp.
most of all sex.
(keeping the moisture from my scalp
always meant more to me
than fucking some dude.)
there was not
a bergamot
or a plastic cap
that could stop
water
from undoing
in a matter of minutes
what it had taken hours of torture
to almost perfect.
I learned to hate water.

I am virgo and pragmatic
at fifteen I made up my mind
if I had to sweat my hair back with anyone
it would be my beautician.

she made the pretense bearable.

once a month I would wait several hours
in that realm of intimacy
for my turn in her magical chair
for my four vigorous shampoos
for her nimble fingers to massage
my hair follicles to arousal
for her full bosom to embrace
my willing head
against the war of tangles
against the burning metamorphosis
she touched me naked
taught me art
gave me good advice
gave me language
made me love something bout myself.
Willie Mays' wife thought integration
meant she could get a permanent in a
white woman's beauty salon.
and my beautician telling me to love myself
applying the chemical
careful of the time
soothing me with endearments
and cool water to stop the burning
then the bristle rollers
to let me dry forever
under stacks of *Jet, Tan,* and *Sepia.*
and then the magnificence of the comb-out.

'au naturel' and the promise of
black revolutionary cock a la fanon
made our relationship suspect.
I asked for tight curls.
my beautician gave me a pick
and told me no cock was worth so drastic a change.
I struggled to be liberated from the supremacy

of straight hair,
stopped hating water
gave up the desire for the convertible sports coup
and applied the lessons of my beautician
who never agreed with my choice
and who nevertheless still gives me language, art,
intimacy, good advice,
and four vigorous shampoos per visit.

Phenomenal Woman
Maya Angelou | *United States*

Pretty women wonder where my secret lies.
I'm not cute or built to suit a fashion model's size
But when I start to tell them,
They think I'm telling lies.
I say,
It's in the reach of my arms,
The span of my hips,
The stride of my step,
The curl of my lips.
I'm a woman
Phenomenally.
Phenomenal woman,
That's me.

I walk into a room
Just as cool as you please,
And to a man,
The fellows stand or
Fall down on their knees.
Then they swarm around me,
A hive of honey bees.
I say,
It's the fire in my eyes,
And the flash of my teeth,
The swing in my waist,
And the joy in my feet.
I'm a woman
Phenomenally.
Phenomenal woman,
That's me.

Men themselves have wondered
What they see in me.

They try so much
But they can't touch
My inner mystery.
When I try to show them,
They say they still can't see.
I say,
It's in the arch of my back,
The sun of my smile,
The ride of my breasts,
The grace of my style.
I'm a woman
Phenomenally.
Phenomenal woman,
That's me.

Now you understand
Just why my head's not bowed.
I don't shout or jump about
Or have to talk real loud.
When you see me passing,
It ought to make you proud.
I say,
It's in the click of my heels,
The bend of my hair,
the palm of my hand,
The need of my care.
'Cause I'm a woman
Phenomenally.
Phenomenal woman,
That's me.

MOTHERHOOD

MOMMA MOMMA MOMMA/*momma momma momma*/*mammy*/
nanny/*granny*

—June Jordan, From "Getting Down to Get Over"

The Slave Mother
Frances E. W. Harper | *United States*

Heard you that shriek? It rose
　　So wildly on the air,
It seemed as if a burden'd heart
　　Was breaking in despair.

Saw you those hands so sadly clasped—
　　The bowed and feeble hand—
The shuddering of that fragile form—
　　That look of grief and dread?

Saw you the sad, imploring eye?
　　Its every glance was pain,
As if a storm of agony
　　Were sweeping through the brain.

She is a mother, pale with fear,
　　Her boy clings to her side,
And in her kirtle vainly tries
　　His trembling form to hide.

He is not hers, although she bore
　　For him a mother's pains;
He is not hers, although her blood
　　Is coursing through his veins!

He is not hers, for cruel hands
　　May rudely tear apart
The only wreath of household love
　　That binds her breaking heart.

His love has been a joyous light
　　That o'er her pathway smiled,
A fountain gushing ever new,
　　Amid life's desert wild.

Motherhood

His lightest word has been a tone
    Of music round her heart,
Their lives a streamlet blent in one—
    Oh, Father! must they part?

They tear him from her circling arms,
    Her last and fond embrace.
Oh! never more may her sad eyes
    Gaze on his mournful face.

No marvel, then, these bitter shrieks
    Disturb the listening air;
She is a mother, and her heart
    Is breaking in despair.

She's Free!
Frances E. W. Harper | *United States*

How say that by law we may torture and chase
A woman whose crime is the hue of her face?
With her step on the ice, and her arm on her child,
The danger was fearful, the pathway was wild .
But she's free! yes, free from the land where the slave,
From the hand of oppression, must rest in the grave;
Where bondage and blood, where scourges and chains,
Have placed on our banner indelible stains .
The bloodhounds have miss'd the scent of her way,
The hunter is rifled and foiled of his prey,
The cursing of men and clanking of chains
Make sound of strange discord on Liberty's plains . . .
Oh! poverty, danger and death she can brave,
For the child of her love is no longer a slave.

from Poem to her Daughter
Mwana Kupona binti Msham | *Kenya*

Daughter, take this amulet
tie it with cord and caring
I'll make you a chain of coral and pearl
to glow on your neck. I'll dress you nobly.
A gold clasp too- fine, without flaw
to keep with you always.
When you bathe, sprinkle perfume, and weave your hair in braids
string jasmine for the counterpane.
Wear your clothes like a bride,
for your feet anklets, bracelets for your arms...
Don't forget rosewater,
don't forget henna for the palms of your hands...

Motherhood

Georgia Douglas Johnson | *United States*

Don't knock at my door, little child,
  I cannot let you in,
You know not what a world this is
  Of cruelty and sin.
Wait in the still eternity
  Until I come to you,
The world is cruel, cruel, child,
  I cannot let you in!

Don't knock at my door, little one,
  I cannot bear the pain
Of turning deaf-ear to your call
  Time and time again!
You do not know the monster men
  Inhabiting the earth,
Be still, be still, my precious child,
  I must not give you birth!

Lineage
Margaret Walker | *United States*

My grandmothers were strong.
They followed plows and bent to toil.
They moved through fields sowing seed.
They touched earth and grain grew.
They were full of sturdiness and singing.
My grandmothers were strong.

My grandmothers are full of memories
Smelling of soap and onions and wet clay
With veins rolling roughly over quick hands
They have many clean words to say.
My grandmothers were strong.
Why am I not as they?

Our Grandmothers
Maya Angelou | *United States*

She lay, skin down in the moist dirt,
the canebrake rustling
with the whispers of leaves, and
loud longing of hounds and
the ransack of hunters crackling the near branches.

She muttered, lifting her head a nod toward freedom,
I shall not, I shall not be moved.

She gathered her babies,
their tears slick as oil on black faces,
their young eyes canvassing mornings of madness.
Momma, is Master going to sell you
from us tomorrow?

Yes.
Unless you keep walking more
and talking less.
Yes.
Unless the keeper of our lives
releases me from all commandments.
Yes.
And your lives,
never mine to live,
will be executed upon the killing floor of innocents.
Unless you match my heart and words,
saying with me,

I shall not be moved.

In Virginia tobacco fields,
leaning into the curve
of Steinway

pianos, along Arkansas roads,
in the red hills of Georgia,
into the palms of her chained hands, she
cried against calamity,
You have tried to destroy me
and though I perish daily,

I shall not be moved.

Her universe, often
summarized into one black body
falling finally from the tree to her feet,
made her cry each time in a new voice,
All my past hastens to defeat,
and strangers claim the glory of my love,
Iniquity has bound me to his bed,

yet, I must not be moved.

She heard the names,
swirling ribbons in the wind of history:
nigger, nigger bitch, heifer,
mammy, property, creature, ape, baboon,
whore, hot tail, thing, it.
She said, But my description cannot
fit your tongue, for
I have a certain way of being in this world,

and I shall not, I shall not be moved.

No angel stretched protecting wings
above the heads of her children,
fluttering and urging the winds of reason
into the confusion of their lives.
The sprouted like young weeds,
but she could not shield their growth
from the grinding blades of ignorance, nor

shape them into symbolic topiaries.
She sent them away,
underground, overland, in coaches and
shoeless.

When you learn, teach.
When you get, give.
As for me,

I shall not be moved.

She stood in midocean, seeking dry land.
She searched God's face.
Assured,
she placed her fire of service
on the altar, and though
clothed in the finery of faith,
when she appeared at the temple door,
no sign welcomed
Black Grandmother. Enter here.

Into the crashing sound,
into wickedness, she cried,
No one, no, nor no one million
ones dare deny me God. I go forth
alone, and stand as ten thousand.

The Divine upon my right
impels me to pull forever
at the latch on Freedom's gate.

The Holy Spirit upon my left leads my
feet without ceasing into the camp of the
righteous and into the tents of the free.

These momma faces, lemon-yellow, plum-purple,
honey-brown, have grimaced and twisted

down a pyramid of years.
She is Sheba and Sojourner,
    Harriet and Zora,
    Mary Bethune and Angela,
    Annie to Zenobia.

She stands
before the abortion clinic,
confounded by the lack of choices.
In the Welfare line,
reduced to the pity of handouts.
Ordained in the pulpit, shielded
by the mysteries.
In the operating room,
husbanding life.
In the choir loft,
holding God in her throat.
On lonely street corners,
hawking her body.
In the classroom, loving the
children to understanding.

Centered on the world's stage,
she sings to her loves and beloveds,
to her foes and detractors:
However I am perceived and deceived,
however my ignorance and conceits,
lay aside your fears that I will be undone,

for I shall not be moved.

Charleston Childhood Montage
Jacqueline Johnson | United States

Grandmother was seventy-five and I eleven
when she told me about her first baby.
A boy, who had only lived a few months.
Her memory meticulous with a will of its own.
As we sat in the dark den, air heavy with summer heat
smells of salt fish, eggs and coffee
she said, one day he got so ill I had
to take him to the hospital. A white nurse
made me sit outside in the waiting area for hours,
refused to let us see a doctor.

My grandmother barely 18, first baby in tow
asking for help for a small, tan baby boy
having to stare down a woman who took
race more seriously than her vocation.
I can almost hear sound of her refusal;
that flat eternal no.

Grandma's sepia face, tearless
and stark in morning light, her voice
drifting into hidden hills and valleys,
timbres only the soul knows
telling me how her baby died in her arms
how that white nurse never did a thing to save him.
She needs no pity, only that I listen;
know the world I have inherited.

Fishing Among the Learned
Nikky Finney | *United States*

On the banks of her butterfly pond
Grandmother would stand
as fluid as a waterfall
teaching with a Five and Dime pole in her hand

Be still and listen to that
She could be heard to say

She would make
more good decisions
lose more control
gain and relinquish power
care about more people
recycle more energy
discern more foolishness
in an afternoon of Fishing
than Congress ever could
be they every one
unanimous
all Democrat
all Republican

My first semesters ever were spent
staring up at this Human University
shifting my weight from leg to leg
waving first cowfly then firefly from off her apron dress
and listening to the sound around us
there was noise there was instruction
there was indeed a difference in the two

This kind of standing stare at still water
this speaking on the depths of a true life lived full
Sociology

footprints baked into the soft bank
Geography Advanced
these outdoor lessons could go on for days
as long as there was sun and bait
there was learning

To educate means to lead out
She told me on the road home
I had no idea what she was saying or why now
At well lit nightfall
in between the quiver of country bugs I'd wonder
why does she stand me there each morning
that pole in my hands
gripped as tight as teeth full born to a jaw insisting
Pond water is as good as any book

A good teacher can do more than talk about it
She'd already said to me in dreams
She can see it clear

There on that bank
Preparing me for giant Orcas
when she knew full well in those days
Bream and Mullet were all we had tugging our lines

You don't fish just to catch
you fish so you can keep
so you can put something back
the teacher taught
it has less to do with the fish
and more to do with your line in the water
your hand on the pole
with discerning rituals
with what you can figure out about yourself
while standing there
in between the bites
know what you will not let corrupt you

Motherhood

that you cannot be bought or sold
assume another will come after you have long gone
their pole tight in hand as well
hoping to catch something
Put something back whenever you can

Now that is something to keep

I left her hot iron gates ready for labor
and the unforeseen anything in between

With a plain cane pole
Grandmother given
and a plastic bobber found
these days
I cast out among the Learned
and teach to alter sleeping states
I stand before the University Pond
and fish for the living
who bubble among the Learned
who know
real life bestows no terminal degrees

We all dangle here
caterpillars and grub worms
twirling into this new year
preparing one day for silk jackets
or sheepskin shoes for things better and days
deeper reasons
we cast out our many different lines
the bait and the barely hooked
the new recruits watch
the old sentries look out silent
as we push away from shore calling our rolls
like salmon remembering the way
do or die

I return too
determined that this year
fishing is the key
to everything
that moves

A poet needs to flyfish
sometimes
in the middle of the bluest grass
in order to catch glimpses of privileged information
that there are too many meetings
and not enough conversation going on
and stand girded before the listening eyes
of those who pay their hard earned money
to wonder if I am teaching anything
that the world will later ask of them
to be sure and know

I must

A poet needs to hope beyond hope
inside the polished granite of Academe
that the newly arrived
with their canes dragging in the sands will help
that others who have been here all along have not given up
that we all will keep going to the bank Fishing
but this time throwing our prime catch back
to forego the weigh-in of the dying
the comparison of scales
but keep the feeling of casting out close

I am Fishing to know that the Learned
are really hearing the living inside the walls and out
and not spending so much time and talk
just on our brilliant selves

A fishy poet invited to cast out a line

Motherhood

has to cast out a cat gut cord
a thousand pound live wire
with hook enough for all
and reel in everything she sees
and speak of the good with the bad and hope for the best
do or die

And for nine month cycles stand with the rest
spinning for silk for sheepskin for sanity
for something higher more enduring than sweet tenure or paper trails
for the sake of the high and the honored art of teaching
of returning something real to the mental food chain
that of truthing to transform life

In the unnamed names of all the ghosted teacher women
soldiered around the edges of this pioneer groundscape
who for generations kept this place well oiled and honest
whose names go unexcavated still
I stand I cast I stare I feel I fish for what is true
so that the legacy of here is not what some of us believe
and others dare only whisper
that only men and horses and basketballs
make it to stone and get to last forever
that there is something here in these still waters
more powerful than we could ever imagine
it is something we have hooked but not yet pulled to surface
something we'll eternally feel on our lines but never lay our eyes upon
if we do not study the scholarship of Fishing

I am casting out a line to ensure
that our souls remain olive oiled and patient alive and able to hear
discern the noise from the instruction

A poetress sometimes must float in a beautiful man made pond
she must wade out among the Learned in order to learn
that none of us are casting far enough off shore
there in the dimpled uncharted waters

in the undiscovered raging sea
where more than what we expect always lives
and waits for the courageous to come and dip toe in
in the spirit of the old ones who would pull up anchor in a minute
and take their chances never worrying that all their eggs were in one
basket

We have barricaded ourselves away
from the scholarship of risk from all the elements
that first made us feel and fight and therefore freely birth
conversation

This beginning together again is sacred ritual
and we remember
"If we do what we've always done,
We're gonna get what we've always gotten."

Don't pull your line in too fast
Grandmother would say out the corner of her eye
Keep your gook in the water all the way to the edges
that's where the great tadpoles swim.

There are possibilities all the way until the end
Whatever you do take Fishing with you
The sound of air bubbles and that of lips
pursed just below the surface of an idea ready to bite
and the bobber being pulled down right then
and once airborne and arching the tiny mullet changing
to the giant Orca
right before our very Learned eyes

Now that is something to Keep

Mother
Nancy Morejón | *Cuba*

My mother had no patio garden
but rocky islands
floating in delicate corals
under the sun.
Her eyes mirrored no clear-edged branch
but countless garrottes.
What days, those days when she ran barefoot
over the whitewash of orphanages,
and didn't laugh
or even see the horizon.
She had no ivory-inlaid bedroom,
no drawing-room with wicker chairs,
and none of that hushed tropical stained-glass.
My mother had the handkerchief and the song
to cradle my body's deepest faith,
and hold her head high,
banished queen—
She gave us her hands, like precious stones,
before the cold remains of the enemy.

Soul Through a Licking Stick
Sarah Webster Fabio | *United States*

My
black Ma
sure knows
her thing;
her scar-face
spoon
is her
big, stick,
and with
this
wooden
sceptre
she rules
her world
with a lick.

In her
backyard
there's no
money tree,
to prune
her switches
from,
but she can
lay as good
a whipping
on your
behind
as if she'd
used
some
Georgia
pine.

Then,
she can
brush off
the bruises
and really
get Down
deep
into her
pot and
cook—
I mean
burn
a lot.

    She
whips up
the best
soul food
you've ever had
and her cakes,
pies, and
cobblers,
Man,
they're
really
bad!

Her Ma
and her
Ma's Ma
taught her
all she knows;
they got
their
nits and grits
from
down home

and it
shows.

Anyway
she wields
that stick—
loving like
or bold,
you're
going to
get from that
licking
stick
a whole
lot'sa
SOUL!

Beauty's Daughter
Linda Susan Jackson | *United States*

O, the rub of living with the sun
and being in darkness, through
the fog of rant and rules she hurls
at me since my father left.

She smells frantic,
asks me
Why are you still here?

Aching for the moment
I once pleased her,
learning to read beneath
the lines of mother and daughter,
slicing open the seams

of her abandoned beauty.
I wait until she sets down
dry and wrinkled,
over exposed

Discipline
Lauren K. Alleyne | *Trinidad and Tobago*

I reached out to smack her smart-talking mouth:
a warning to better mind her manners
in front of me—didn't give it a thought.
Except the blow never landed: she whirled
back, stayed my hand with a defiant grip;
her watchdog eyes daring me: *Just-You-Try-It*.
I reached for her again & hardly knew
what it is exactly I meant to do
besides teach her a lesson in respect.
Mosquito fists unrelenting, she kept
on coming—wild, breathless—my little girl
trying the weight of her *NO* in the world. . .

I didn't know whether I should be proud
Or knock her bony backside to the ground.

Night Song

Shirley Dougan King | *United States*

Much has been said about Black Mammy
but little about
Black Mother.
You remember her—the slave woman
who had to stand   silent
as she watched her children
being sold away   (silent)
as one would do a litter of pups;
        the one who gave
her life-milk to little "master"
while her child cried hungry and alone;
        the one who knew
freedom came too late for her
but   washed Miss Lucy's clothes
just so hers could buy those books
        for learning;
the one who watched her man hanging
from   that tree of sorrow
yet   (in the face of master)
                strong for her children.
Black mother—
The one who hates the hell hole
                she's living in.
but   scrubbing for her children
every Sunday for that bit of heaven
                Sunday morning services.

Black mother,
you remember her—
                the one who got all joy
                and pride from your successes,
the one who wore that old coat
so you could have a new one;

the one who taught you
what love—unselfish really meant;
      the one who volumes
      could be written about.

Gettin Down to Get Over *Dedicated to my mother*
June Jordan | *United States*

MOMMA MOMMA MOMMA
momma momma
mammy
nanny
granny
woman
mistress
sista

luv

blackgirl
slavegirl

gal

honeychile
sweetstuff
sugar
sweetheart
baby
Baby Baby
MOMMA MOMMA
Black Momma
Black bitch
Black pussy
piecea tail
nice piecea ass

hey daddy! hey
bro!
we walk together (an')
talk together (an')

dance and *do*
(together)
dance and do/hey!
daddy!
bro!
hey!
nina nikki nonni nommo nommo
momma Black
Momma

Black Woman
Black
Female Head of Household
Black Matriarchal Matriarchy
Black Statistical
Lowlife Lowlevel Lowdown
Lowdown and *up*
to be Low-down
Black Statistical
Low Factor
Factotem
Factitious Fictitious
Figment Figuring in Lowdown Lyin
Annual Reports

Black Woman/Black
Hallelujah Saintly
patient
smilin
humble
givin thanks
for
Annual Reports and
Monthly Dole
and
Friday night
and

Motherhood

(*good* God!)
Monday mornin: Black and Female
martyr masochist
(A BIG WHITE LIE)
Momma Momma

What does Mothafuckin mean?
WHO'S THE MOTHAFUCKA
FUCKED MY MOMMA
messed yours over
and right now
be trippin on my starveblack
female soul

a macktruck
mothafuck
the first primordial
the paradig/digmatic
dogmatistic mothafucka who
is he?
hey!
momma momma

dry eyes on the
shy/dark/hidden/cryin Black
face
of the loneliness
the rape
the brokeup mailbox
an' no western union roses
come inside the kitchen
and no poem
take you through the whole night
and no big
Black
burly
hand

be holdin yours
to have to hold onto
no
big Black burly hand
no nommo
no Black prince
come riding from the darkness
on a beautiful black horse
no bro
no daddy

"I was sixteen when I met my father.
In a bar.
In Baltimore.
He told me who he was
and what he does.
Paid for the drinks.
I looked.
I listened.
And I left him.

It was civil
perfectly
and absolute bull
shit.
The drinks was leakin waterweak
and never got down to my knees."

hey daddy
what they been and done to you
and what you been and done
to me
to momma
momma momma
hey
sugar daddy
big daddy

sweet daddy
Black Daddy
The Original Father Divine
the everlovin
deep
tall
bad
buck
jive
cold
strut
bop
split
tight
loose
close
hot
hot
hot
sweet SWEET DADDY
WHERE YOU BEEN AND
WHEN YOU COMIN BACK TO ME
HEY
WHEN YOU COMIN BACK
TO MOMMA
momma momma
And Suppose He Finally Say
"Look, Baby.
I Loves Me Some
Everything about You.
Let Me Be Your Man."
That reach around the hurtin
like a dream.
And I ain never wakin up
from that one.
momma momma
momma momma

II

Consider the Queen

hand on her hip
sweat restin from
the corn/bean/greens' field
steamy under the pale/sly
suffocatin sun

Consider the Queen

she fix the cufflinks
on his Sunday shirt
and fry some chicken
bake some cake
and tell the family
"Never mine about the bossman
don' know how a human
bein spozed to act. Jus'
never mind about him.
Wash your face.
Sit down. And let
the good Lord bless this table."

Consider the Queen

her babies pullin at the nipples
pullin at the momma milk

the infant fingers gingerly
approach caress the
soft/Black/swollen/momma breast

and there
inside the mommasoft
life-spillin treasure chest

Motherhood

the heart
breaks

rage by grief by sorrow
weary weary
breaks
breaks quiet
silently
the weary sorrow
quiet now the furious
the adamant the broken
busted beaten down and beaten up
the beaten beaten beaten
weary heart beats
tender-steady
and the babies suck/
the seed of blood
and love glows at the
soft/Black/swollen momma breast

Consider the Queen

she works when she works
in the laundry *in jail*
in the school house *in jail*
in the office *in jail*
on the soap box *in jail*
on the desk
on the floor
on the street
on the line
at the door
lookin fine
at the head of the line
steppin sharp from behind
in the light
with a song

wearing boots
or a belt
and a gun

drinkin wine when it's time
when the long week is done
but she works when she works
in the laundry in jail
she works when she works

Consider the Queen

she sleeps when she sleeps
with the king in the kingdom
she
sleeps when she sleeps
with the wall
with whatever it is who happens
to call
with me an with you
(to survive you make
do/you explore more and more)
so she sleeps when she sleeps
a really deep sleep

Consider the Queen

a full/Black/glorious/a purple rose
aroused by the tiger breathin
beside her
a shell with the moanin
of ages inside her
a hungry one feedin the folk
what they need

Consider the Queen.

III

MOMMA MOMMA
momma momma
family face
face of the family alive
momma
mammy
momma
woman
sista
baby
luv

the house on fire/
poison waters/
earthquake/
and the air a nightmare/
turn
turn
turn around the
national gross product
growin
really gross/turn
turn
turn the pestilence away
the miserable killers
and Canarsie
Alabama
people beggin to be people
warfare on the welfare
of the folk/
hey
turn
turn away
the trickbag university/the
trickbag propaganda/

trickbag
tricklins of prosperity/of
pseudo-"status"
lynchtree necklace
on the strong
round
neck of you
my momma
momma momma
turn away
the f.b.i./the state police/the cops/
the/everyone of the
infest/incestuous investigators
into you
and Daddy/into us

hey
turn
my mother
turn
the face of history
to your own
and please be smilin
if you can
be smilin
at the family

momma momma

let the funky forecast
be the last
one we will ever
want to listen to

And Daddy see
the stars fall down
and burn a light

Motherhood

into the singin
darkness of your eyes
my Daddy
my Blackman
you take my body in
your arms/you use
the oil of coconuts/of trees and
flowers/fish and new fruits
from the new world
to enflame me in this otherwise
cold place
please

meanwhile
momma
momma momma
teach me how to kiss
the king within the kingdom
teach me how to t.c.b./to make do
and be
like you
teach me to survive my
momma
teach me how to hold a new life
momma
help me
turn the face of history
to your face.

Round
Amanda Johnston | *United States*

I.

Belly,
you hold so much
have given so much
need so much work.

Belly,
scarred & cut
raw with each new birth.
Stretched into a new song?
blues. Why do I feel so low
when this body is singing
calling the same line out
from other bellies that want
to pick up the beat? Why
do I squelch my song
when the orchestra is tuned
and ready?

II.

You'd say it was
the phone company they'd hire anyone
and that's why you had so many
"friends" coming over
after union meetings
drinking beer and talking loud.
I remember men
who looked like women, women
who looked like men. Uncle Bubba
wearing your faux fur. I remember
the choo choo chooing down
the hall to your bedroom
toward your belly.

III.

Mother, our bellies
hold the same music.
Our rhythm? Morse Code
S-E-X

Nine Moons
Oktavi Allison | *United States*

Ruddy, white hands
slaps her
head rag sideways
yanks at
squalling ringlets
drags her to
straw dust floor

A breathless ride
sours yam supper
leaves her
scuffled in
sticky muslin
his sweat
licks the bruise

Nine moons pass
saffron crowns
mahogany labia
bluest eye souvenir

Melanin floats
infant dreams
baths the fright of
ungodly conception

Airport Scene After Her First Solo Visit
Toni Asante Lightfoot | *United States*

She wanted to fly like us, experience
peanuts and ginger ale at 35,000 feet.
Rent metal wings
and hurtle through the sky—
free to defy
Autism's gravity and simply be
the passenger in seat 13E.
She was coasting,
a look-ma-no-hands smile
resplendent on her face.

My fear
shortened her ride,
as I led her by the hand
to the front of the line,
telling the attendant
to keep watch
that she is *different*.

The disbelief in her embarrassed,
unblinking 21-year-old stare cut deep.
"Why?
Why did you do that to me?"

My hug had become
a vise—she needed
a ventilated love.

Bruised but standing, she turned
to exit through the gate—
her flight home
a lesser altitude.

Origin *For my mother*
Lauren K. Alleyne | *Trinidad and Tobago*

I.

What is the sea without us?
Those run-away-after-school days
bathing suits pressed secretly to our skins
the dash at the last bell for the gates
the ride never fast enough to the bay
where we'd shake the day's burdens
into a pile of purse and pumps
knee-socks knickers and white Keds
always careful with the fragile
creases of pleated skirts and collars
Me at six   ten   fourteen and growing
hormonal, heavier into my bones
but afloat in the water still light
enough to lift, your hands
wrapped around me you would laugh
at least I can always cradle you here

II.

Two men saw us once:
You filling the wide mouth
of a calabash, working
the stream of water over my head;
my eyes shut to its salty sting
– our bodies drifting
in the evening's easy repose.
Zami queens[1*], they called us
we who never speak of desire,
who have no language for longing.
We hung at the end of their pointing,
called into our bodies—named.

Motherhood

III.

I try to conceive you
before mother, before me
but I cannot imagine
you
a shining nude,
innocent, bride, open
and wanting—
split.
And from that—me,
whole

Yet, I am
here, your child,
borne by your body
hot and slick into this world,
its charged, different air.
Tell me,
what other longings called me
to you?

IV.

In my own woman-years
I am swimming out
I want to understand this body—
this spirit house, this bloom of flesh.

I think back to the sea,
(its endless depth
relentless and forgiving
its constant return)

imagine
I am floating
the sun on my face

my arms a one-sided embrace of the sky

I am carried
past shore and safety
I open my mouth and I am flooded,
claimed; I cannot speak.

V.

I want to find you here.

1.   Zami or Zami queen is the local term (derogatory) for lesbians.

Angel Babies
Virginia K. Lee | *United States*

more than once
pelvic area numbed
I lay listening
to soft hum of aspirator machine
that made a slurping sound
when fruit of my womb was sucked out

 couldn't wait to get back
into hip-hugging bell bottom jeans
and dance the Hustle

never dreamed I'd be haunted
by Roe v Wade
while I kept my uterine garden free
of blooming offspring

before the sun blushes peach in pre-dawn sky
I sometimes hear their laughter and giggles
a chorus singing
can't help wondering
if they're tormenting me for not giving them life

my angel babies lambent
round and about
invisible butterflies
little spirits protecting me
they even tickle my toes if uncovered
waking me in middle of the night

in the haze of gray blue evenings
tiny bright lights twinkle in the air
at 2 o'clock position
letting me know they're watching

I threw away all my chances
to be a natural mother
denied existence
to whole generations of my seed
I'm a hollow shell my soul echoes inside
my smile is a veil for a sad heart and nagging solitude
a tree that never blossomed

After Birth
Robin Caudell | *United States*

Blue Moon rises
paints
my daughter yellow
her plump lips purple
as Lady Slippers.
Remember her first birth
along the Nanticoke
beneath another Blue Moon.
Slavers hunted us
to bone
but the Conductor got us
over
the Delaware
out
Egypt Land
beyond moon-lit shadows
of glistening hounds.
Didn't look back
'til now.

Motherhood
Theresa Lewis | *Trinidad/Canada*

Her eyes were shining brightly
A glow was stretched
around her skin-tight face

She laughed out brashly
when they said
'You've had a boy'

A boy? she queried wildly—
(as though the species
had a dozen kinds)

A boy…a boy?
She laughed again in wonder

But when they placed him
in her arms
    she cried
    and cried
    and cried!

Voodoo

Miriam Alves | *Brazil*

Translated by Carolyn Richardson Durham

There's a road
sliding up the hill
  hidden
where a curve works overtime.

This road penetrates the wilderness
it runs back out
where the curve waves
  to hidden sadnesses
I buried there the Voodoo of uncertainties
stuck with pins
  of sorrows
in order to free my womb

The Mother
Gwendolyn Brooks | *United States*

Abortions will not let you forget.
You remember the children you got that you did not get,
The damp small pulps with a little or with no hair,
The singers and workers that never handled the air.
You will never neglect or beat
Them, or silence or buy with a sweet.
You will never wind up the sucking-thumb
Or scuttle off ghosts that come.
You will never leave them, controlling your luscious sigh,
Return for a snack of them, with gobbling mother-eye.

I have heard in the voices of the wind the voices of my dim killed
    children.
I have contracted. I have eased
My dim dears at the breasts they could never suck.
I have said, Sweets, if I sinned, if I seized
Your luck
And your lives from your unfinished reach,
If I stole your births and your names,
Your straight baby tears and your games,
Your stilted or lovely loves, your tumults, your
marriages, aches, and your deaths,
If I poisoned the beginnings of your breaths,
Believe that even in my deliberateness I was not deliberate.
Though why should I whine,
Whine that the crime was other than mine?—
Since anyhow you are dead.
Or rather, or instead
You were never made.
But that too, I am afraid,
Is faulty: oh, what shall I say, how is the truth to be said?
You were born, you had body, you died.
It is just that you never giggled or planned or cried.
Believe me, I loved you all.
Believe me, I knew you, though faintly, and I loved, I loved you
All.

Ala
Grace Nichols | *Guyana/UK*

Face up
they hold her naked body
to the ground
arms and legs spread-eagle
each tie with rope to stake

then they coat her in sweet
molasses and call us out
to see . . . the rebel woman

who with a pin
stick the soft mould
of her own child's head

sending the little new-born
soul winging its way back
to Africa-free

they call us out to see
the fate for all us rebel
women

the slow and painful
picking away of the flesh
by red and pitiless ants

but while the ants feed
and the sun blind her with
his fury
we the women sing and weep
as we work

O Ala

Uzo is due to join you
to return to the pocket
of your womb

Permit her remains to be
laid to rest—for she has
died a painful death
O Ala
Mother who gives and receives
again in death
Gracious one
have sympathy
let her enter
let her rest

Abortion
Vibha Chauhan | *India*

A tiny stirring of life
Breathing hard inside me
Struggling to survive,
Is shut out by the cistern
That dropt on it with a clang
When the fragile life
Holding it in balance
Was sliced off
By fine edged razors.

The tiny creature bawls
Showing its toothless gums
And screwing up flesh
Where eyes would have been.
Banging its jelly fists and feet
Against the metal that traps it,
In ceaseless, noiseless clamour
Unheard and unperceived.
But the loss of fresh air
Brings about its end.
The end of the creature
That few knew ever lived.

Mourning
Amanda Johnston| *United States*

Body, I hear you
mourning your lost inner child
with each blood prayer.

Issues

Ama Ata Aidoo | *Ghana*

We met
them
daily in the
queues:
the mother and the children
for whom she'd got
the best recipes for
cooking
stones.

Walls do not stare like
a brother's eyes.
One day,
mother shall raise
her head
face falling with
marvel
at what
forever-pregnant time
can
sometimes
deliver:

a three-legged lamb
or
human child,
who will come
teething
straight out of the labour-ward
at six in the morning:
slit itself open down the middle,
embalm
his own crevices with

diamonds
between
seven,

         and
eight,

         and at
nine,
from across the street
above the roar of the traffic and
other latter-day wonders,
scream at you
His-Lady-Love:

'Please shut up
questioning
my
money's
source, and
just do
me
the favour of
spending
it.'

Seeking Deep
Gina M. Streaty | *United States*

Stale liquor clabbers
in my mouth
sour, dry, sharp
like the breeze
shaving heat from my skin
My shoes scrape pavement
August sun licks the back of my neck,
yawns on my sweat-streaked face
Bitterness in my mouth;
regurgitated words
swell on my tongue
Once candy-coated phrases
I sucked to slivers, swallowed,
I consume
again
Exit the bus. I pass
broken Black forms on corners,
next Friday's cadavers
funneling whiskey
near gated storefronts, torn posters
Sing Be all that you can be?*girl*
I hear the missing lyric,
pray another tune
Up thirty-two steps
to the dark hall, the vacant room,
a broom or mop handle in my hands
gripped until nails pierce palm flesh
Dirt gray water floods cracked linoleum,
dilutes blood, chases dust from corners
Light escapes through open windows,
tugs webs trembling on high ceilings
and me. I hear
Lou Rawls in the distance,

age another year. $300 Later
Grandma's Bible *or* a needle in the alley?
Womb scraped clean of motherhood.
I choose the latter, blink away the pain
Slip?slip, again
fall slowly, sink,
seeking
some place
deep.

Eighteen Years Later for *Tia*
Gina M. Streaty | *United States*

I see your face
above a bowl
of cold cereal
Rush you to finish.

Baby brown orbs
pat me as I search
for a shoe, socks,
missing mitten.

Lost minutes
yell your name,
trip, fall across silence
as I spew.

Words taint you,
trail your small frame
out to the cold, wide,
gray gap of an orange bus.

Thoughts dodge incrimination
as I settle into space
left damp and warm
by five-year-old weight.

Glass of juice you didn't finish,
The vitamins you love, I forgot to give.
Twenty-seven pastel loops adrift in milk
A captious TV mumbles.

I wipe away the morning.
Tiny prints left by nervous hands
on a breakfast table mean nothing.
Traces of you resound.

Grandma Mariana
Alda Do Espirito Santo | *Sao Tome e Principe*

Grandma Mariana, washerwoman
for the whites in the Fazenda
One day she came from distant lands
with her piece of cloth round waist
and stayed.
Grandma Mariana stayed
washing, washing away, on the plantation
smoking her gourd pipe
outside the slave-quarters' door
remembering the journey from her sisal fields
on a sinister day
to the distant island
where the hard labour
erased the memory
of the bulls, the deaths,
away in the distant Cubal.

Grandma Mariana came
and sat outside the slave-quarters' door
and smoked her gourd pipe
washing, washing,
a wall of silence.

The years drained away
in the hot land.

'Grandma Mariana, Grandma Mariana
it is time to leave.
Go back to your vast lands
of endless plantations.'

'Where's the people's land?
Old woman comes, never returns...

Motherhood

I came from afar,
years and years spent in this yard...
Mad old woman does not have land anymore
I will stay here, silly boy.'

Grandma Mariana, smoking her gourd pipe
at the doorstep of your dark alley,
old little Grandma tell us
your inglorious story.
Live, vegetate
in the shade of the yard
you won't tell your story.

Grandma Mariana, my little Grandma,
smoking her gourd pipe
on the doorstep of the slave-quarters
you won't tell of your destiny...
Why did you cross the seas, old little grandma,
and remain here, all by yourself
smoking your gourd pipe?

I'm My Own Mother, Now

Stella P. Chipasula | *Malawi/United States*

Mother, I am mothering you now;
Alone, I bear the burden of continuity.
Inside me, you are coiled
like a hard question without an answer.
On the far bank of the river
you sit silently, your mouth shut,
watching me struggle with this bundle
that grows like a giant seed, in me.
In your closed fist you hide
the riddles of the fruit or clay child
you told before you turned your back
and walked, fading, into the mist.
But, mother, I am mothering you now;
new generations pass through my blood,
and I bear you proudly on my back
where you are no longer a question.

today, i smell like my mother
Carmen Gillespie | *United States*

Today, I smell like my mother,
mysterious alchemic combination
from grandma's perfume tray
sagging in its place beneath
my medicine chest with the weight
of my essences, some
older than my daughter,
who agrees,
"Mommy, you smell like Gammy."

Chance potion, inheritance
of fragrance and flesh, carpet-rides
through evenings
back over the rainbow—
her scent a censor's smoke,
nightly ritual of brush and braided
plaits, braced between her knees,
solid as cathedral arches angled
for me alone.
Or,
fighting flailing lids, awaiting
after-party kiss, feigning sleep
to still her presence, familiar as
sight, her smell, reassuring and lovely
as summer's cricket sounds.
"Mommy is home."

From behind the colored bottles,
the mirror crayons
the illustrations of my face,
linear legacies that will not soon lose
their form, permanent as the aroma of
memory, particular as my finger's print,
but also and always
like hers.
Today I smell like my mother.

Ode to Decima

Jane Alberdeston | *Puerto Rico/United States*

She is encincta,
pregnant, a kiln heavy with clay.

For what seems an eternity,
I make her belly round.

Her man creeps out, follows San Juan's neon,
her cravings callers, pregoneros, in the night.

She whistles. I recognize the tune,
tap along her rib, Carmen Delia's croon, a
cha-cha-cha.

When I come out, I will watch her like a new
husband, see she is beautiful with age.

Her years will count themselves in gray,
rest and

fold,
her landscape of skin washed burlap3
Just as coquis tick, her bones mark the
time
rattle with each movement: soft, hard, left,
right

butt, belly, back, side: I am a swimmer
greasing her channels.

She holds me, an uncoiling carpet python.
an unspoken dream for a son, baskets of bread,
fish

Soon I will press against blue Yemaja lips
split her salt waters: bacalao to asopao

Labour

Kristina Rungano | *Zimbabwe*

For nine months I had borne him in my womb.
Nine months of disillusionment and pain
Relieved only occasionally by the gentle kicking within me;
The gentle movement of the life I created within me
Nine months I waited for this day;
Nine months and the grotesque lump growing on me.
And Kit always making numerous sacrifices—of patience and
                                                    love—
Nine dreary months of waiting for this day.

And now I was beginning to feel sharp pains in me—
And mama saying they are labour pains—
The pains which will be the spring of new life . . .
Would it be a boy, I thought with intensified wonder,
How proud his father would be,
Or would it be a girl—
Someone I could teach to be just like me
And spoil with pretty frocks
And sweetly scented flowers to adorn her head?

I looked up into Kit's eyes
The eyes that had seen me through
The eyes that had known my sadness and joy for nine months
And saw in them all the love and care
The pain which he felt for me
And like the sun on a cold morning
Relieved me of all fright, all desolation.

I looked with warm contemplation
To the moment when his warm embrace would say
'Our very own baby—the very essence of our love'
And tiny little hands would cling to my breasts in hunger
Tiny mouth drawing warm milk from me

An innocent little face looking into my face.
With trust
Learning me, just as Kit did.

I felt him, Kit
Captured by a foresight of summer days to come
The days when we—no longer just two—
Would walk in the dusk
Caressed by the warm breeze
And our child would learn to sing the birds to sleep
And dance the kan-kan with the fireflies.

And thus I was borne to the labour ward
Whilst Kit waited
Waited again
Waited in warm anticipation
Waited for the awakening of my new beginning.

We Mothers
Ama Asantewa Ababio | *Zimbabwe*

we are the mothers
whose eyes water
with helpless tears
each time we watch
our sons bow brutalized
to the savagery
in the streets of
SOWETO, KINGSTON, HARLEM.
we are the mothers
living in tortured fear
of the ravaged ripping
of our daughters' flesh
by the inhumanity of your crazed desire

we are the mothers
whose sinews strained
in fields of sugar-cane
nurturing a sweetness
that only you could taste
and today
our bony fingers
shine the ornaments
that you display
in the show places
you call homes
reaped from the sowing
of our children

we are the mothers
who stretch a pound of flour
into a generation
of hungry bellies
and keep the fire of life burning

in the hearts of our children
robbed of hope
with stories of heroes
resplendent in cloaks of Afrikan greatness.
and the rumble of a song
whose spirit has ever lived
in the part of our souls
you have never touched
you can never touch

we are the black mothers
of Afrika, Jamaica, America

we are the mothers
wronged by history
we are the mothers
we will not forget
we are the mothers
whose seed
will extract justice
from your future generations

Early Motherhood
DeLana Dameron | *United States*

Early Motherhood

They looked at me funny
when they saw

                              When you gave it to me

Called me Mother Mary

                                        It was cold—
                                        December nights
                                        without protection
                                        from elements

Mama came to me
in sleep to explain
what was required.

                                        Our game
                                        resurrected itself
                              from my consciousness.
                              How reluctantly I played,
                                        because I liked you.

She explained
how I was come
to this predicament
          And wept
                    and you left
                          and he came
                                (I will call him David.)
and left.

What will prosper from this mound,
this earth where we planted him?
Who will believe in him after

he's gone?

I sprinkle olive-oil
for salvation,
childhood,
my first seed.

On Lies Mothers Tell

DeLana Dameron | *United States*

When I saw it burrowed
in the closet, I rummaged further beneath
mounds, unpaired socks, bills,
in dark, damp crevices.
I knew not how to decipher those announcements,
shuffling cards news clips,
I placed him in my lap; there,
as if I had given birth. I felt something escape
me when we locked eyes, presenting your
secret held for twenty-seven years. "Hello,
brother David" I said, half-expecting
a coo from new-born encased in plastic
and envisioned you, torn
apart at age eleven, in a sterile hospital room
hearing grandma yell "push", grandpa
holding your hand, praying
it'll be over soon enough.
I shuffle death certificates, sympathy
cards, tears. I bury him again.

Milk Children
Estella Conwill Majozo| *United States*

I nurse my infant son
at my breasts—
he does not know
that I am double-breasted—
that I lactate from sacred spaces
at cycles attuned to a spiritual spiral
that is the unwinding
of our freedom.

He does not know
that I am one of the seekers—
one of the milk children—
a disparate fold
made kindred
by the very food
that sustains us—
We have suckled freedom's breasts.

In our desert thirst
we drink the liquid manna
and it alone satisfies us
and then only for a while—
only long enough for us
to realize anew that this need
here—in this life—
is insatiable.

My son does not know
that at the sight of the oppressed
my inner breasts begin to change—
that my nipples grow rigid
and that the moans of the hungry
summon whole masses

Motherhood

of milk-swollen pain
from inside of me—
cries in the circling wind gone wild
force me to fill this wooden bowl
with words pumped out
for survival.

Afterspotting
Cherryl Floyd-Miller | *United States*

flat needle on E, the rancid sun-drench rotting the
dashboard
an almost greasy windshield conjuring pork rinds, old
cracklin'
skin. overexposed neckfat. i am empty with sweat. the
mouth
of a river has opened and screams out of me. at the
bend of
my fifth cramp, i begin to name the trees: Ezekiel (no
middle
name). or a girl: Ella Bijoux. i push harder. more
gas. more fat.
all blood.

push. name the blood Ezekiel at the middle of my fifth
cramp.
i am all windshield sun. almost girl greasy. more
rancid. i needle
the dashboard on E. no. gas. the flat rotting.
screams. i begin
to name a river of pork skin Ella Bijoux. or neckfat.
the fat, empty
mouth has opened. and overexposed the rinds of trees.
an out:
a harder drench, more cracklin' gut. the conjuring
bend. sweat.

Liberation
Amelia Blossom Pegram | *South Africa/England*

Birth
Blood
Afterbirth
Blood
Purification
Freedom
Celebration

Birthing
Amelia Blossom Pegram | *South Africa/England*

I thought I heard
the bleating lamb
But
It was the cry
of my new offering
to the world,
I thought I heard
the bleating lamb
But
At your birth
My daughter
It was your cry
For my pain
And for
your births
To come.

Snake Oil
Gina M. Streaty | *United States*

Clad
in pale blue

cotton gowns
exposed contours
pink flesh, brown flesh
no matter

they walk
gracelessly
leans against walls,
best friends, boyfriends
in nail-biting
waits

young, old
metaphors
with flushed eyes
rehearsed lines,
hand-carried foolish mistakes,
accidents, crimes

some pace cold floors
in blue paper shoes
as unasked questions
take a number,
pluck pills
from plastic trays
Dixie cups from gentle hands,
one by one

escorted
to the bright room

with glimmering steel,
a masked doctor,
and alabaster walls

where worries get sucked
from wombs, scarlet spills,
stains blue gowns,
relief arrives in spasms

Liberation
Abena Busia | *Ghana*

We are all mothers,
and we have that fire within us,
of powerful women
whose spirits are so angry
we can laugh beauty into life
and still make you taste
the salty tears of our knowledge—
For we are not tortured
anymore;
we have seen beyond your lies and disguises,
and *we* have mastered the language of words,
we have mastered speech.
And know
we have also seen ourselves raw
and naked piece by piece until our flesh lies flayed
with blood on our *own* hands.
What terrible thing can you do us
which we have not done to ourselves?
What can you tell us
which we didn't deceive ourselves with
a long time ago?
You cannot know how long we cried
until we laughed
over the broken pieces of our dreams.
Ignorance
shattered us into such fragments
we had to unearth ourselves piece by piece,
to recover with our own hands such unexpected relics
even we wondered
how we could hold such treasure.
Yes, we have conceived
to forge our mutilated hopes
into the substance of visions

beyond your imaginings
to declare the pain of our deliverance:
So do not even ask,
do not ask what it is we are labouring with *this* time;
Dreamers remember their dreams
when they are disturbed—
And you shall not escape
what we *will* make
of the broken pieces of our lives.

21 Years Grown

Gina M. Streaty | *United States*

You think

I didn't have dreams?
Spent days washing clothes,
Wiping floors, babies' behinds,
until my dreams seethed,
throbbed like an ache
at the base of my skull.
You think

I carried nothing to bed
except a worn out Bible, wet eyes
wrapped in red lines, and unpaid bills?

I emptied evenings
on my knees,
swallowed remnants of myself,
pieces left clinging to me
like dried food on a dirty dish,
or stink in piles of laundry¾
and you

Think!
Twenty-one years ago
pain walked the length of me,
scrawny legs trembled

On a blood-stained table
I forced out nine months
of dreams
trying to be grown

Guinea Woman
Lorna Goodison | *Jamaica/Canada*

Great grandmother
was a guinea woman
wide eyes turning
the corners of her face
could see behind her,
her cheeks dusted with
a fine rash of jet-bead warts
that itched when the rain set up.

Great grandmother's waistline
the span of a headman's hand,
slender and tall like a cane stalk
with a guinea woman's antelope-quick walk
and when she paused,
her gaze would look to sea
her profile fine like some obverse impression
on a guinea coin from royal memory.

It seems her fate was anchored
in the unfathomable sea
for great grandmother caught the eye of a sailor
whose ship sailed without him from Lucea Harbor.
Great grandmother's royal scent of
cinnamon and scallions
drew the sailor up the straits of Africa,
the evidence my blue-eyed grandmother
the first Mulatta,
taken into backra's household
and covered with his name.

They forbade great grandmother's
guinea woman presence.
They washed away her scent of

cinnamon and scallions,
controlled the child's antelope walk,
and called her uprisings rebellions.

But, great grandmother,
I see your features blood dark
appearing
in the children of each new
breeding.
The high yellow brown
is darkening down.
Listen, children,
it's great grandmother's turn.

Ludlow Street
Melanie Hope | *United States*

When I am no longer here

Children

You may not recall

My flat feet or

Dark brown eyes

But I hope you remember

I once sang you to sleep

In a small one bedroom

On the lower east side

Then scribbled into darkness

How I love you

Don't Call Me Mama
Carole Stewart | *England/Trinidad*

Don't call me Mama
Don't call me Mother
See me for what I am
A Woman.

Even though you crawled
I pushed you out from under me.
I teased you with my breast.
It gave me pain
It gave me pleasure
It gave you life.

Don't call me Mama
A stalwart of the nation.
Don't call me Mother
The backbone of the struggle.
See me here for what I am
A Woman.

Throughout our history
You call me Mother.
You ban your belly
And call me Mama.
How much longer?
Will you learn?
My Motherhood is not my Womanhood
Just another dimension
of me
A Woman.

I am here in the struggle
I am here—part of the nation
I am here in Afrika

I am here in Britain
I am here in the Caribbean
I am here in the Americas
I am here on the Frontline
A Woman.
Mama, Mother
A sign of respect.
When you call me Mama
Do you see my Woman?
When you struggle for sustenance
between my breasts,
Call me Mother, Tower of Strength,
Keeper of Tradition
Do you see my Woman?

Before my belly bloated with another life,
My teeth clenched
and the sweat of labour
burnt my eyes
I was Woman.
Before you called me
Before you whispered 'Mother'
Before you cried out 'Mama'
I was Woman.

When you mourn my passing
Mourn my Woman.
Don't call me Mama
Don't call me Mother
See me for what I am
A Woman.

Momma in Red
Nicole Shields | *United States*

They said
that the only reason
my momma wore a red
dress to her daddy's funeral
was because she hated him
and was just being sassy

I know she wore it
because it was
the only one she had!

Single Mom
Pam Ward | *United States*

somewhere between
a burnt marriage
a greasy kitchen
and a grey 22
sandwiched between
these smiling kids
and my painted teeth
somewhere way off
from coffee mugs
stained with
yesterday's paychecks
rent due
that last final kiss.
Choosing between
Disneyland or
Cybil Brand
murder or Mr.
Toads ride
driving all the way
from Anaheim to L.A.
Anxious as an inmate
passing your house
your new car
your girlfriends
red bike
smashing the snails
on my porch.
Somewhere between
what I didn't say
and my black
ajax mouth
scrounging for words
but spitting a shoe.

Motherhood

With two of you
in my back seat
sweet dreamy lugs
tasting of grape juice
and cherry
somewhere between
their breath at my neck
or them asking for water
or the fear
they'd call some
bimbo mommie
gnaws at me yanks
me straight back
from the brink
makes me face
one more sink
full of dishes.

Life Roots

Tureeda Mikell, Story Medicine Woman | *United States*

Life roots imitate
Mother Cells
Mammary wells
Water feeding trees
Fertile water weaves
Sun dipped in fire
Lips with tongues
Weave in tales
Encode in lungs and
Behave in behalf
Of memory sung
Flung in a wave
Weaves around the world
In all seed
Man Woman Boy Girl
Engraved in tones
Sown to bone
In each ones temple sternum
A Mother's poem
Where language sung
Survival's arrival in music
Chanted Vou Doun
Called it Hoo Doo to blues it
Have you been to the blue?
Certainly Lord
Versed a curse
On earth as it is on heaven
In meters that matter in 5, 6, & 7
In the DNA
The ground wire was laid
The law is in light
And Amen-Rah raided
Everyone's home
In everyone's Bone
Elementing life
In the Mother tongue tone
In the Mother tongue tone
In the Mother tongue tone

Double Exposure
Saundra Sharp | *United States*

in the mirror
she holds on
again

    if u can't leave
    u can't stay here
    get off my face!

if i leave this room
people will
see i am
not my own face

    if u can't leave
    u can't stay here
    get off my face!

she stays,
much too comfortable

    i left
    to flee your
    hand-me-down fears
    our answers
    no longer matched

she stays, as if i am
still on duty
in Her image

    i am not you anymore
    i am my own collection of
    gifts and errors
    so woman spirit

if u can't leave
u can't stay here

and finally, she moves off
(as in retiring to Her room
            after a trying day)

            don't you
            remember
            the sunshiny days?

i smooth in the camouflage
   smudge the brown red rouge
      assemble it all
       hoping
            if u can't leave
hoping to hold on
            if u can't leave
to my own face
            u can't stay here
for a few days
            get off my face!
please?

Crack Annie
Ntozake Shange | *United States*

i caint say how it come to me/ shit
somehow/ it just come over me/ & i
heard the lord sayin how beautiful/ &
pure waz this child of mine/ & when i
looked at her i knew the Lord waz
right/ & she waz innocent/ ya know/
free of sin/ & that's how come i
gave her up to cadillac lee/ well/ how
else can i explain it/

who do ya love i wanna know i wanna know
who do ya love i wanna know i wanna know

what mo could i say

who do ya love i wanna know i wanna know
who do ya love i wanna know i wanna know

it's not like she had hair round her
pussy or nothin/ she aint old enough
anyway for that/ & we sho know/ she
aint on the rag or nothin/ but a real
good friend of mine from round 28th
street/ he tol me point-blank
wazn't nothin in the whole world smell
like virgin pussy/ & wazn't nothin in the
universe/ taste like new pussy/ now this
is my friend talkin/ & ya know how
hard it is to keep a good man fo yo self
these days/ even though i know i got
somethin sweet & hot to offer/ even

then/ i wanted to give my man cadillac
lee/ somethin i jus don't have no mo/
new pussy/ i mean it aint dried up or

nothin/ & i still know what muscles i
cd get to work in my pussy/ this-a-way
& that but what i really wanted/ my
man/ cadillac to have for his self/ waz some
new pussy/ & berneatha waz so
pretty & sweet smellin/ even after
she be out there running wit the boys/
my berneatha *vida/* waz sweet & fine
remember that song "so fine"
so fine my baby's so doggone fine
sends them thrills up & down my spine
whoah-oh-oh-yeah-yeaeaeah-so-fine

well/ that's my child/*fine/* & well
cadillac always come thru for me/ ya
know wit my crack/ oh honey/ lemme tell
ya how close to jesus i get thanks
to my cadillac/ lemme say now/ witout
that man i'd been gone on to
worms & my grave/ but see i had me
some new pussy/ waz my daughter/ lemme
take that back/ i didn't have none/
any new pussy/ so i took me some/ & it
jus happened to be berneatha/ my
daughter/ & he swore he'd give me twenty-five
dollars & a whole fifty cent of crack/
whenever/ i wanted/ but you know/ i'm on the pipe/
& i don't have no new pussy/ & what difference/
could it
make/ i mean shit/ she caint get pregnant/
shit/ she only seven year old
& these scratches/ heah/ by my fingers
that's/ where my child held onto

me/ when the bastard /cadillac/ took
her like she wazn't even new pussy at
all/ she kept lookin at me &
screamin/ "mommy/ mommy help me/ help
me"/ & all i did waz hold her

tighter/ like if i could stop her
blood from circulation/ if i could stop
her from hurtin/ but no/ that aint how
it went down at all/ nothin like that/
trust me/ i got scars where my
daughter's fingernails broke my skin
& then/ when he waz finished wit my
child/ cadillac/ he jump up & tell me
to cover my child's pussy/ wit some
cocaine/ so she wdn't feel nothin no
mo/ i say/ why ya aint done
that befo/ why ya wait til ya done/
to protect her/ he say/ befo i lay
you down & give you some of the same/
dontcha know/ ya haveta hear
em scream befo ya give em any
candy/ & my lil girl heard all
this/ my child bled alla this/ & all i
could do waz to look for some more crack
wit the fifty cadillac done give
me/ but/ i wazn't lookin for it for
me/ jesus knows/ i wanted it for
berneatha/ so she wouldn't haveta
remember/ she wouldn't have to
remember/ nothin at all/ but i saw dark purple
colored marks
by her shoulder/ where i held her down for
cadillac/ i'm her mother & i held her
& if ya kill me/ i'll always know/
i'm gonna roam round hell talkin
bout new pussy/ & see my child's
blood caked bout her thighs/ my child's
shoulders purple wit her mother's
love/ jesus save me/ come get me
jesus/ now/ lord take my soul & do
wit it what ya will/ lord have
mercy/ i thought berneatha waz like
me/ that she could take anythin/ ya
know/ caint nothin kill the will of the

colored folks/ but lord i waz
wrong/ them marks on my child/ no/
not the marks/ from cadillac/ the scars
from my fingers/ purple & blue
blotches/ midnight all ruby on lenox
avenue at 7:30 on sundays/ that heavy
quiet/ that cruelty/ i caint take
no mo/ so lord throw me into hell befo
berneatha is so growed/ she do it
herself/ all by herself/ laughin
& shovin me/ & prowlin &
teasin/ sayin/ you a mother/ what
kinda mother are you/ bitch/ tell me/
now/ mommy what kinda mother/ are you/ mommy/
mommy/

i say i heard etta james in her eyes/ i
know/ i heard the blues in her eyes/ an
unknown/ virulent blues/ a stalkin
takin no answer but yes to me
blues/ a song of a etta james/ a
cantankerous blues/ a blues born of
wantin & longin/ wantin & longin for
you/ mama/ or etta mae/
song of a ol hand me down blues
hangin by its breath/ alone
a fragile new blues
hardly close to nowhere/ cept them eyes
& i say/ i heard a heap of etta james
in them eyes/ all over them eyes/
so come on Annie

so tell mama all about it

tell mama all about it
all about it
all about it

tell mama

Stepmother
Irma McClaurin | *United States*

She cannot see herself in me
I am not the daughter of her flesh
only the shadow of his last wife.
Inside the rolls of flesh,
a body no one wants
beats itself by eating more.
She does not understand this stringbean
of a stepdaughter is hungry too.
We both wait inside his house
for a man neither of us knows.

Motherhood
Rita Dove | *United States*

She dreams the baby's so small she keeps
misplacing it —it rolls from the hutch
and the mouse carries it home, it disappears
with his shirt in the wash.
Then she drops it and it explodes
like a watermelon, eyes spitting.

Finally they get to the countryside;
Thomas has it in a sling.
He's strewing rice along the road
while the trees chitter with tiny birds.
In the meadow to their right three men
are playing rough with a white wolf. She calls

warning but the wolf breaks free
and she runs, the rattle
rolls into the gully, then she's
there and tossing the baby behind her,
listening for its cry as she straddles
the wolf and circles its throat, counting
until her thumbs push through to the earth.
White fur seeps red. She is hardly breathing.
The small wild eyes
go opaque with confusion and shame, like a child's.

Mother Love
Rita Dove | *United States*

Who can forget the attitude of mothering?
    Toss me a baby and without bothering
to blink I'll catch her, sling him on a hip.
    Any woman knows the remedy for grief
is being needed: duty bugles and we'll
    climb out of exhaustion every time,
bare the nipple or tuck in the sheet,
    heat milk and hum at bedside until
they can dress themselves and rise, primed
    for Love or Glory —those one-way mirrors
girls peer into as their fledgling heroes slip
    through, storming the smoky battlefield.

So when this kind woman approached at the urging
    of her bouquet of daughters,
(one for each of the world's corners,
    one for each of the winds to scatter!)
and offered up her only male child for nursing
    (a smattering of flesh, noisy and ordinary),
I put aside the lavish trousseau of the mourner
    for the daintier comfort of pity:
I decided to save him. Each night
    I laid him on the smoldering embers,
sealing his juices in slowly so he might
    be cured to perfection. Oh, I know it
looked damning: at the hearth a muttering crone
    bent over a baby sizzling on a spit
as neat as a Virginia ham. Poor human—
    to scream like that, to make me remember.

Dear Mama (2)
Wanda Coleman | *United States*

she say that's what mama's for

you don't know or maybe you do
time you couldn't buy us shoes and asked grandpa
for money. he sent you one dollar
i remember your eyes scanning the letter. the tears
you got us shoes somehow by the good grace of a friend
maybe you are hip in your old-fashioned oklahoma cornspun way

or the time we sat in the dark with no electricity
eating peaches and cold toast
wondering where you'd gone to get the money
for light

grandma named you lewana. it sounds hawaiian
not that bastard mix of white black and red you are
not that bitter cast of negro staged to play to
rowdy crowds on the off broadway of american poor

and she added mae—to make it sound *country*
like jemima or butterfly mc queen or bobbi jo
it's you. and you named us and fed us and
i can't love you enuff for it

you don't know or maybe you do
it hurts being a grown working black woman
branded strong
hurts being unable to get over
in this filthy white world
hurts to ask your parents for help
hurts to swallow those old beaten borrowed green backs
whole
hurts to know
it'll hurt worse if you don't

Black Mother Woman
Audre Lorde | *United States*

I cannot recall you gentle.
Through your heavy love
I have become
an image of your once delicate flesh
split with deceitful longings.
When strangers come and compliment me
your aged spirit takes a bow
jingling with pride
but once you hid that secret
in the center of furies
hanging me
with deep breasts and wiry hair
with your own split flesh and long suffering eyes
buried in myths of no worth.

But I have peeled away your anger
down to its core of love
and look mother
I am
a dark temple where your true spirit rises
beautiful and tough as a chestnut
stanchion against your nightmares of weakness
and if my eyes conceal
a squadron of conflicting rebellions
I learned from you
to define myself
through your denials.

AGING

*(Women's) faces are maps of the hardships
they have gone through. The older women get,
the prouder they should be.*

—*Sothembiso Nyone (Zimbabwe) from*
The Black Woman's Gumbo Ya-Ya

The First Grey Hair

Mary Eliza (Perine) Tucker Lambert | *United States*

NO, let it stay. It speaks but truth:
    My Autumn's day is dawning.
The dream is past; sweet dream of youth.
    Hair, I accept thy warning.
With mournful thought, my spirit swells,
At the wild chime of memory bells.

Why will we in the present time,
    Of by-gone days be dreaming?
Say, why throughout the storm sublime,
    Is lightning ever gleaming?
Ah ! there is naught on earth that quells
The chiming of sad memory bells.

Hope, garlands fair of future bliss,
    With Fancy's pearls is weaving;
Alas ! we find in world like this,
    That Hope too is deceiving,
As on the past, our full heart dwells,
At your sad chiming, memory bells.

In youth all Earth was passing bright,
    And life with joy was teeming—
But hidden in each flower was blight,
    And happiness was seeming.
Yet charm me with your mystic spells—
With your sweet chiming, memory bells.

Why speak ye of the cruel wrong,
    That I am ever grieving?
I would forget, forgive, be strong,
    With faith in Christ, believing.
But oh ! the strain triumphant knells—

Aging

Cease, cease your clashing, memory bells.

Avaunt, dark image of despair!
    Why dost thou still go raving?
I would to Lethe's streams repair,
    And drown thy taunts in laving.
Alas! can nothing still thy yells?
Cease, cease your clashing, memory bells.

Now mournful is the solemn strain,
    And sadly I am weeping.
For those I love in battle slain,
    Who all unknown are sleeping,
Like murmuring of ocean shells,
Swells your sad requiem, memory bells.

Now much loved voices in their glee
    Their joyous shouts are sending;
And the sweet chorus, light and free,
    Of many a song is blending,
Yet bitter tear-drops, sad fare-wells,
Melt in your chiming, memory bells.

Yet I would fain recall the past,
    The bright celestial gleaming,
Which my first love around me cast,
    Too sweet to be but dreaming.
Like flowing water, in lone dells,
Is your sweet chiming, memory bells.

Yes, silver hair, rest thee in peace,
    I know that life is warning,
That soon will all my troubles cease,
    And I , the goal attaining,
Will list the joy your music tells,
And love your chiming, memory bells.

The Palm Wine Seller
Gladys May Casely Hayford | *Ghana*

Akosua selling palm wine
In the broiling heat;
Akosua selling palm wine
Down our street

Frothing calabashes
Filled unto the brim,
Boatmen quaffing palm wine
In toil's interim.

Tossing off their palm wine,
Boatmen deem her fair;
Through the haze of palm wine,
Note her jet-black hair.

Roundness of her bosom,
Brilliance of her eyes,
Lips that form a cupid's bow,
Whereon love's dew lies.

Velvet gleam of shoulder,
Arch of bare black feet,
Soft caressing hands,
These her charms complete.

Thus illusioned boatmen
Dwell on 'Kosua's charms,
Blind to fallen bosom,
Knotted thin black arms.

Lips creased in by wrinkles,
Eyes dimmed with the years,
Feet whose arch was altered,

Aging

Treading vales of tears.

Hair whose roots life's madness
Knotted and turned wild.
On her heart a load of care,
On her back, a child.

Akosua selling palm wine
In the broiling heat;
Akosua selling palm wine
Down our street.

Hands
Anita Scott Coleman | *United States*

Gnarled and knotty,
Iron-wrought hands,
Fashioned for the spade and plow,
Padded hard in calloused flesh
To rescind the spring of steel
Hands…his, yours…mine,
Old black working-man's hands!
They wielded an ax felling trees
In new country,
They have tilled the soil of an alien land
They have built a house in an unfriendly habitat.
Slender and lovely,
Muscical hands,
Dusky in hue, fluttering over ivory keys
Like a raven's wings;
Do raven wings make music,
Beating their way through inescapable air
Mounting higher?
Hands, brown as snuff,
Wash-tub hands,
Curled like claws from clutching and squeezing
Heavy wet garments.
Water-soaked, sudsy, rheumy, old hands-
Only when they are folded thus
In the quiescent pose of death
Are they stilled.

Beautiful Spirit
Barbara Thomas | *United States*

I watch them closely now
these seasoned daughters

Some moving slow silent
with daring distrustful eyes
others hitting the floor mad
spitting out pain masking taunts

I'm looking for those whose eyes still smile
whose grace and goodness come out to greet you
who say
> Yeah baby, I've lived
> but I ain't through yet

To tell me how to live in a world
that once clapped hands
and said *how beautiful*
and now turns its eyes away

Want to know how they live
in this special season of their lives

What did they say to the wicked witch mirror
when it began to give time reports

Did they accept it with grace and gratitude
seeing it as a time wrapped gift from Her
or
Did they cry out to hold back the tide

Tell me how to live within a tribe
that says aged grapes, brick boxes, barter paper
and even men are more valuable than they

I want to sit among the wondrous women
breathe in their funky fortitude
their wrap around wisdom

Want to taste that tartness
that tells an unseeing world

I'm here
I'm gonna sing dance make love
and continue to paint my life pictures
> *til my spirit leaves this holding place*
> *journeying to the next*
> *and even then*

> *I'll be beautiful*

Mama's Sugar
Carmen Gillespie | United States

Never could stand it. Later
when the girls came and
they was good, I'd make a
short bread and they'd like
it fine but there's not too
much in there. Mrs. Buchanan
up at the school liked it in
everything. Even
saw her sprinkle a little
on a doughnut once. Got
so that when it snowed I
would get a sick head
ache and have to take to
bed with a cloth and
Vicks and sometimes it would
be enough to forget all
that and remember the Lord
and how I said I'd be a good
girl and how, Mama, I
couldn't help Sister when
she started to drink,
and Mama, now I keep her
boy and Mama, I
don't know where Brother
is he wrote once after the war
sayin' he was getting out of the
service and that was two
years ago August and I haven't
heard since and Mama
do you think my Buddy
still loves that other girl?
I know his mama thinks he
married me only 'cause of the
baby, but Mama, I love
him and he is a good man
and Lord he works hard,

and Mama, I'm Mama
now and they look at me
with those eyes and I think
I understand Mama.

Why his Mama send him
home with only one piece
of cake on Sundays?
He brings it home
to the table and we
all watch and then
I put on a record loud

". . . I've got a sweet black angel, I likes the way she spread her wings
When she spread her wings over me, I gets joy and ev'rything"

'cause I know it makes
him mad 'specially on
Sunday, and Mama, my
head,   after you passed
we called the man and he
took the picture of you like you
said with the flowers in the
parlor and there was a little
sign that said, "Dearest
Mother" for fifteen cents extra
Mama and I show the
girls and I tell them
Mama I tell them how you were so
sweet

so sweet that summer before
my sixteenth birthday

so sweet
that your blood

your blood, Lord Jesus,
turned
    to sugar.

Letter from Mama Olewagi

Antoinette Ellis-Williams | *United States*

My dear daughter,

Today my arthritis is not so bad so I thought I would write you this letter. Imagine that I am still able to write some words on a paper and almost ninety years old. I keep following those spirits. When the spirit says move I move.

Remember growing up in Khamisi. I can still hear your great grand mother humming as she hung out the clothes to dry or my cousin Zambi playing with other children from our village. "ZZ jump, ZZ skip, ZZ play with a old chew stick…" Funny I can even remember my crying because ZZ kept teasing me because my feet were bigger than other nine year old girls and very ashy. "Ola, Ola big foot gal. Steps on the cat 'magine dat…" Those were good days. The air was fresh and I knew all my neighbors for miles. There were many days I left you with ZZ's mother or with Momma Ya's mother.. And I never worried about anything. I never had to carry food or clothes for you or your brother. We all ate out the same pot. Peanut stew was your favorite. Your little black eyes would smile at me each time you saw the peanuts and fish stew.

Remembering these things is easy. I can't even remember what happened yesterday or who came to see me. When did I see you last? I have 10 or is it 12 tablets I have to take every day. Blue, pink, green and black, red, and white. I keep telling them give me some cassava porridge and ginger tea with some hot pepper. Two lemons, green bush, some elyculptus rub and little castor oil. They think I am some crazy voodoo priestess. They don't respect scared things. Ancestors treatments, and prayers, songs and stories.

They just keep giving me these pills. Well darling daughter, I stopped taking them two weeks ago. I hide them under my tongue and just smile. Then I spit them in the trash. I have already begun to feel so much better. My stomach stopped hurting. Much better. At ninety I should know my own mind. Nothing wrong with my mind just my legs gone.

My dear Ife, Sitting in this wheelchair hurts my soul. My mind is still out in the village running after you and your brother. I am still flexible and nimble. But then I see a glimpse of myself in the closet mirror, I am afraid. Afraid I don't know who that old woman is steering back at me. She is a stranger to me. Her wrinkled fragile bruised body feels uncomfortable. My thick plaits are now gone. Even my teeth are gone. It's this American food and water polluting my body. But I know the good Lord still with me. He is a good God. Even if everybody left me.

Ife, I have lived a good life a full life. I have watched friends and family die, cars, trains and buses pass by, I have seen planes and computers all in my life. But I never thought that you and your brother would have put me in a place like this. A nursing home. A place with unloved and sick old strangers from a different land. No Africans my age here just some young rude selfish girls. Some of them from Nigeria, Uganda and Gambia. But they care for me like I am a stranger. But I am their Momma, there Auntie. They have no time to hear my stories. I kno w you are busy with your family and your travel plans. You have your own health problems I know. I know that your diabetes is affecting your eyes. But my own grand children hardly visit me. Never would know that I have 10 grandbabies. But they lives all busy too—Teachers, lawyers, doctors, administrators, construction workers, mothers, musicians, and artists. These my babies, my blood, my legacy.

Daughter dear, I don't want you feel no ways bad but I have always told you my mind. A white American nursing home is not home. I want to go home to my Africa soil and die. I need to see the Gold Coast one more time before I leave this place. I want to taste peanut stew and pepper pot soup. Not like the kind in America but the kind Momma Ya made.. The sun has to touch my gray skin. I am weary and all alone in this place. You have to let me go. I have to be free. I am caged up in this place. The smell of sickness and death is everywhere. I need to go home.

Ife, today I'm going home. I took the pills all 154 pills—pink, blue, white all the colors—like a rainbow to the ancestors. I will watch over you where ever I go. Just let me go to the land that I know. My mother and father are there. All of our people are there. Now its time for me to go.

You have been my joy, now it's time to say good bye. If you don't take me home I will set myself free.

Your Loving Mother

"Surely goodness and mercy shall follow me all the days, all the days of my life. And I shall dwell in the house of the Lord. And I shall dwell in the house of the Lord."

On Aging
Maya Angelou | *United States*

When you see me sitting quietly,
Like a sack left on the shelf,
Don't think I need your chattering,
I'm listening to myself.
Hold! Stop! Don't pity me!
Hold! Stop your sympathy!
Understanding if you got it,
Otherwise, I'll do without it!

When my bones are stiff and aching
And my feet won't climb the stairs,
I will only ask one favor:
Don't bring me no rocking chair.

When you see me walking, stumbling,
Don't study and get it wrong.
'Cause tired don't mean lazy
And every goodbye ain't gone.
I'm the same person I was back then,
A little less hair, a little less chin,
A lot less lungs and much less wind,
But ain't I lucky I can still breathe in.

miss rosie
lucille clifton | *United States*

when i watch you
wrapped up like garbage
sitting, surrounded by the smell
of too old potato peels
or
when i watch you
in your old man's shoes
with the little toe cut out
sitting, waiting for your mind
like next week's grocery
i say
when i watch you
you wet brown bag of a woman
who used to be the best looking gal in georgia
used to be called the Georgia Rose
i stand up
through your destruction
i stand up

Miss Willie
Sheree Renée Thomas | *United States*

She'll leave neckbones, laying on the altar
of her kitchen table, petrified stone gods
semi precious muse, won't hear the back door
slamming salutations, Miss B cussing kids
cutting through her yard. Won't see them
stomp her daffodils, reaching for dandelions
running across new buds in too little shoes.

Won't see her weekday stories or read
her Sunday funny blues. Won't scoop ice milk
in a glass dish or lick lemon pulp from sweaty
cups of melting ice. She'll leave the mailbox open
leave Miss Ida's snuff jar staining the last porch step.
She'll leave laughing, exhaling Indian blessing
pressing palm Sunday incense in our laps.

Love Loosely

Carmen Gillespie | *United States*

agilely she led me over the
loosened stones of ninety years,
her stained glass gently
coloring everything under
the vaulted ceiling—
original artwork and
        family pictures,
and books scattered on tables
like fallen leaves

"Education," said her father
is survival so she
mastered library shelves,
linen closets, and
lady's lunches, shadowed
by the laughing love
of a southern soldier

"Forget black and white.
Travel. Live your life.
Write, write, write.
Forgive your father. It'll
settle out all right. Remember
most of what you've read,"
and then she said,
        "love loosely."

dancer's lament
Shia Shabazz | United States

i wanted to dance
part my knees wide
into grande plie
chin up
return womb-round tummy
to washboard rippled and taut
lower steadily
straight
down

but these legs
once slender prima pliable
are now thick-thighed
tired in demi
knees arthritic with
the rigor of rowing
this stream more than
the merriment of dreaming
weak and wobbly
with the thought of separation
generally reserved for coitus and
rebirthing myself
by the time i am down
holding on to the illusion of balance
i can't imagine getting back up again

i wanted to dance
raise the sag of sere breasts
heart first into elegant arabesque
then plant ribs deep into earth
rest cheek at the summit of Mt. Bonnell
extend my arms
until my fingertips touch

Aging

somewhere near qamdo
on the yangtze river
lift my leg high
past this ass
that no longer tucks
nor tightens enough
anymore
waxes with age and the onus
of homeownership and college for my children

i wanted to dance
whip my head from side to side
in circles
do some flashdance move
that would make darren lie
bye, bye, bye
reclaim a hipness
that would mortify my six-year-old
but the pain of migraines
from sleepless nights and blank pages
heavy with the dolor of caterpillars
courses through my head like an amp for
music i cannot hear

i wanted to dance
eyes focused
flowering sojourns through
mwazindika
kishawi
kunjandi
wrapped in fibers reserved in america
as garniture for february and kwanzaa
dance for mkaba ngoma, the drummers
generations of my fathers
hands raining in rhythms that
fill my lungs with breath
songs of uja uvinagh, the dancers

generations of my mothers
call me beyond myself
into in the eyes of my children

in them
i learn to revere
this body
its service

the dawn of hips
the prize of thickness and thigh
the blossom of this belly
the eloquent wilt of these breasts
through them I realize

I have danced

I must dance

I will dance.

For Miriam

Marjorie Oludhe Macgoye | *UK/Kenya*

Children, why do you fear, why turn away?
Do you not know these knobbed, harsh hands are those
that turned and pulled your brothers from the womb?
These red eyes saw you first. These swollen feet
tramped to fetch water for your father's comfort.
This failing memory was quick to count
shillings to school him with, He'll tell you how.
It is still I.

Why do you doubt? Fingers are hard and stiff?
Hard, yes, to lift pots from the fire, to hoe
the heat-cracked furrow, husk the grain, split pods,
smack children hard, but shapely, straight, complete,
supple and loving. Laughter? When did they change?
I don't remember. True, the cup shakes, the needle
evades the thread. Joints creak. Yet I caress you.
It is still I.

Dress yourself child. See how I cover myself
carefully, unless now and then fever shakes me
and I forget the time and place. Yet truly
first cloth was a puzzle to me, we were ashamed
at new-fangled ways. We knew our modest duties,
walked blithely then, lithe, dutiful, expectant,
laughed at the stranger. You laugh and I laugh too.
It is still I.

We hid from vaccinators by the river—
laugh, you can see me doing that, typical me,
with a baby crying loudly among the reeds,
the medical people furious, road and market
growing till soon we could not hide. No fear now
so as long as you keep your blood to yourself and pray

separate bed and bedding. Now they cannot unmake me.
It is still I.

We cried for sorrow, stood rebuked, so turned
away to Jesus, changed and were made anew.
The pipe is broken and the beads dispersed,
the children schooled, the scriptures learned by heart.
I know new obligations, faces, buryings,
yet self of self in saviour still the same,
still hard, lithe, laughing. He returns myself.
It is still I.

This baby-face is pale, but see the features
line by line echo mine. This one will go to
school, that one also, one dig, one live in town.
You do not need to tell me. Have I not grown,
mounted steep stairs, seen whirling pictures speak,
eaten politely, begging whatever tools
they left out from my place. Old, no-one's fool,
It is still I.

Africa of your ancestry has not changed,
Is age unrecognized? The issues are the same,
the blood, guarded and grounded, feeds new life.
The artery-paths have hardened into highways,
tacit exchange crystallized into cash,
the morning sunward spit dries on our lips,
migration stilled, yet Mother Africa laughs,
It is still I.

Things that were open when we thought them good
are now discreetly covered, breasts by clothing,
blood-feud by boundary-mark, weapon by holster,
paternity by collusion. Things that were covered
those times we thought them bad now lie wide open,
unwanted babies, unpaid cattle, ways
of tying up the womb. Though witchcraft walks

Aging

It is still I.
Can you recall a time Misawa was
as strange as Jambo? Then we fed on pulse,
millet and milk, saw our dreams come alive.
Don't talk to me of change, even of freedom:
I have seen changes and I am content,
was saved, am free. If tongue and temper wander,
flesh stiffen and decay, why do you fear?
It is still I.

Death/Survival
Shooshilla Gopaul | *Mauritius*

Stealthily Cancer
crept in and settled down,
crow-like in silence.

First with anger I reacted,
but soon stepped in with care and cure.
Relentless it stood.

It grew and swallowed up all grace.
Quietly it gnawed away
a strong forty year knot.

II

With water they rubbed and washed away
The dear red dot on my forehead,
But my heart they couldn't reach.

In sorrow I got drowned.
His absence held me tight below
But duties pulled me up.

Schizophrenic I became
For dues a full citizen, for society only a half;
"Prepare and follow" I couldn't.

Then mixing past and present I built a whole;
Photographs brought proofs,
Memories they were, not madness.

III
A full bright moon rising
Behind the fragrant camphor trees;

Aging

Wafts of coffee intermingling with
Some tremulous notes from a sarod
or a touch.....

A touch, a gentle touch,
Yet a most abrasive one.
It's a silky soft pink petal,
But also a sharp electric blue sky
Torn by a sudden flash of lightening.

Memories swim up.
Disentangling dead dark kelp,
Gathering fresh sea weeds,
Awakening new desires.
Deprivation slides away like suds.

The body encapsulating the soul
Emerges, reaches out,
Gasps for breath, then
Gulps down draughts of fresh air.
The new blood merges slowly.

Two ways out:
Death by drowning
Or survival by the senses.

Old Women
Afua Cooper | *Canada*

When I am old
I would like to have my oldwomen friends around me
like Geraldine has now
they come and they greet her
kissing both cheeks
they sit on the porch and eat things forbidden by the doctors
and they laugh and chat in French
but they could be speaking in
English Swahili or Chinese

Old Women II
Afua Cooper| *United States*

They lament the passing of their husbands and with a deep
sigh say "it's better that way, he suffered much." They
still go to the hair stylist once a month and all except
for Josie who say she wants to see the a priest only at her
funeral, go to mass once a week. They feel sorry for me
because "young men today are not like the young men in our
days." And they brag and boast about their grandchildren.
I look at them and not feel afraid of growing old.

Resurrecting Great-Aunt Frances
Kamillah Aisha Moon | *United States*

They laid you out in pink,
rouged your cheeks,
painted you a saint between psalms.
Faced with whether to teach or marry,
you chose 40 ruler-straight years—
left here pristine at 74.

I saw you a handful of times,
said 'yes ma'am' and told you about my A's in class.
I remember how your veined hands cupped my cheeks,
the Hallmark cards filled with 5s and 10s.
One of 3 gray-haired ladies with oversized pocketbooks
who told me my father was a sneaky boy.
You were his stern spinster aunt he never tried
to know, the one who chose books over babies.

But looking at sepia photos of your solid 6' frame,
your face more handsome than pretty, I wonder
if labor laws and chalkboards saved you.
What stories could your blue house snug
between coal-mined bosoms tell?
What echoed after school bells?

Someone held you as your sisters married off—
you carried yourself like a loved woman.

Was she there when
they laid you out in pink,
rouged your cheeks,
painted you a saint between psalms?

Did she tremble before her sweetheart once more?
Sit in the back pew as family filed by?

Lodestone, or laying the trick
for Rushia Taylor Wade (1893-1998)
Sheree Renèe Thomas | United States

We only travel the blistering hill to follow the death march.
Three words,_Mount Zion Baptist_carved in faded
walls, proof our people gathered there. Under
billowing sky you wipe broad hands on stiff denim.
You bend from the waist and show me how to rise
with the cotton blossoms, nurse prickly stings. Our rhythms
quicken, my bend more shallow despite your years.
The sky whispers a warning, your story
judgment, what the old ones mean.

I sweat before the crooked house of praise,
timber cracked, pews swollen. Peebles Funeral
Home fans hide behind hymnals. Life lines on left
palm stamp memory into dirt. Nowhere to hide
from mosquitoes, under Somerville sun,
forty-two miles from the blues. I push roots back
to strength, gather a song for the fight. Deliverance,
when the full moon comes.

Silence lives here. So quiet where you stood. It ached
like temperance. He promised you dust, candles, crop loans
on bottom land. You brought your own seed. Copper tied
to stone with string, a bribe to feed stubborn earth. Worked
a fierce mojo, outlived your firstborn and three of seven
straightbacked children—Gus and Richard, Janie Mae,
Ezekiel. One hundred and five years. You made hot water
bread the centuries ate. Now the house in Klondike, North
Memphis holds your framed baptismal scroll. The recipe bound
in Isaac's book. We only travel the blistering hill
to follow the death march. Still, the lightning sky
whispers. The field holds your secret.

Protest Poem
Mendi Lewis Obadike | *United States*

Should the years continue
to press as they press now,
and in their pressing, press
the sugar from my skin, let
the stone that forms inside me
be amber.

Should there be aching,
then, for sweetness,
should they come looking
and find me, let them find
in me this rock, and not
my bitter carapace. This rock,
and think of honey, stored away
for safe-keeping.

Tomorrow, who knows?

Should the sun burn out,
as it plans to do, and as it burns,
burn down all the trees,
let my shadow be a cool thing,
reaching out to shade you.

When I Am Old
Nagueyalti Warren | *United States*

When I am old
I will sing unto the Goddess
a new song, walk naked in rain,
eat chocolates for breakfast
when I rise at noon.

When I am old
I will walk naked in rain,
celebrate my flab with ice cream—
Rocky Road—hand packed
by the pint—belch w/o an
excuse me.

When I am old
I'll walk naked in rain,
my sag giggling and maybe
give a toothless smile
to all surprised eyes.

Retrospect
Pearl Cleage | *United States*

Old woman—
I can see you
huddled in your
window
remembering now ancient
lovers
who are as withered
as you.
Wrapped tightly in
your shawl
your eyes no longer look
out
but only peer in.
The fragile gold frames
of your dusty glasses
are almost a shield
but not quite
and every once in a while
I can see you shiver
in a space between
memories.

Dust

Sheree Renée Thomas| *United States*

A woman sits on a porch of weathered board
her skin the texture of the dried apple dolls
grandmamas gave children years ago.
When asked about the past, she allows
only four words to peel back history
Them times was hard.

Her hands have worked iron
fashioned each bit into the tools
that make a home, axes and shovels
hinges and locks, gates and railings
skillets and chains, a harness
shaped by hands that gripped metal
as lungs grip air, grip breath
hands that could not protect
her or any of her children.

If she speaks, she might break apart
scatter like so many bits of iron
hot embers cooling in the wind
luminous as fireflies, the dust of her
flying across the backs of stooped men
two brothers, an uncle, a dead husband
chained by their debt to the fields.

Evening wears into night. The stars
gather like sisters, a shawl round her shoulder
she presses both lips together, then groans
the oldest language our land knows.

Mississippi Mammas
Phyllis J. Sloan | *United States*

for older ladies
    descended from southern places
with peach-cobbler smiles
and adoring praline eyes
    who say "how do?"
    and greet us others
as "baby" "honey" "dear" and "sweetheart"
you'll never know how many times
    your endearments warm me
while in your stores/cleaners/restaurants
        and homes
Missouri, Chicago, New Orleans, Alabama
    Mississippi Mammas

sometimes i'm yours
when being just mine
    is not enough

Grandma
Vergia Brock-Shedd | *United States*

Grandma said weakly
in her dying way
"where's the children?"
Her 91 years said that I heard
being 60 years younger
and knew
she wanted to see
how fruit from the
roots and soul of her tree
had multiplied.
She wanted to see
HER HERITAGE INHERITED.
She was no old folk
as kids sometimes would
laugh and say
"Look at that old woman!"
She was history
that we hated to see go.

Who Dunnit?
Melania Daniel | *St. Lucia/Canada*

This is a babe
Born on a beaming Sunday morning
Walked tall at midday
Grew grey with the evenings
Got smothered by a pile of falling darkness
Was interred in the heart of the night.
Who dunnit?

The assassin's a solitary prowler
Stalks his prey without a partner, no pattern
To his slaughter. Seers possess no prescience
On the game that's next to fill his platter.
Stake out his lair all day, he's never seen to leave.
Movements imperceptible, yet he covers so much ground.
Just a ticking announces his approach and
Cutaneous hairs jolt; a thousand hooves stampede in pulses,
Unsuspecting victims are rushing late—
They may miss their gravespace.

A phantom that's real; an entity
Ubiquitous with its menace, whose moving hand
Is death. Lethargy chipping numbers off one's life
While he remains immortal, passing glances at his serene face
And humans shriek in terror, lives drown in a flood of adrenaline.
He, languid in his deception, draws his hands together at twelve o'clock
As if in prayer for the departed. The faithful close their eyes
To join this newest convert; his hands transform to a dagger
That impales their eyelids, forever shut.

Sleuths, plodding through clues
To solve this gory mystery
May not know at death
That time
Is the killer.

You Dance

Jane Alberdeston | *Puerto Rico/United States*

You dance
Right into my dream in the haze of a purple robe
I her myself swear an old friend of your
daughter's gave you, those days your were alive
but not well, your face in the Antillean light,
hands curled beneath you like a palm frond
refusing morning sun. But back in my sleeping
dark rooms,

You salsa
(it seems like salsa, but I can't be sure—
There's no music and I don't look down for your
shoes). Your hipe shimmy, shoulders roll, there's
nothing grandmother about you, Dream-girl in
purple chenille, your left hand clutching my
right as if you were a gentleman leading me
onto the floor. We sashay right, then left,
skating the edges of my slepp. Your breath a bit
of butterscotch, you don't look me in the eye.

You just dance
Wild pulsing circles, your blooming grin,
Toothless and vast. The rest of you so new, I try
To tell you, but my voice is sugar, melting in a
boiling pot of water.

In a Breath
Dee September | *South Africa/Canada*

i drift between sorrow and joy
taste my loneliness
in sockets of darkness and fear
suckle my ecstasy
in smooth curves of the sea

given the circumstances
of cruelty or tenderness
i know i will plunge
deep into jagged pain
or soar on wings of laughter

in a matter of breath intakes
i pass through miraculous beauty
or fall victim to brutish terror
my emotional time-saver
is the smallest gift of life

death is life's mournful time-server
passing into the green of existence
from the fossil to the embryo
between the bomb and the heartbeat
i drift amongst passengers in history and blood

Sassafras Toned, My Grandma Sat

In memory of Elizabeth Storey (born circa 1859; died 1953)
Sarah Webster Fabio | *United States*

Stolidly silent, squaw-like,
thirty years past her promised
three score and ten;

despair, depressions, death
dismissed with a nod and a
whispered prayer, "The Lord
giveth and taketh."

Her silences broken usually
with proverbs and metaphor.

"Pretty is as pretty does,"
was her favorite yardstick
squelching easy praise.

Her words, so sparse, became
precious: quarrels were beyond
her; and having entered one,
she soon gave the final word.

"Gonna lay down my sword and
shield, down by the riverside,"
I'd play for her, time and time
again, on the pianos of my
childhood.

Often, I'd wonder how she'd
manage that in Tennessee
where rivers were scarce and
was sure she'd tripped herself
into a fatal lie.

But, then, when time came
snowing down to claim her
that winter, she gave up her
world in a quiet room overlooking
the red clay muddied waters
of the Cumberland.

House of White Carnations
Nagueyalti Warren | *United States*

She wore white to the funeral.
White was the color of death.
Strong black hair on her grandmother's head
was white, lifeless, and her once dark eyes
rimmed in white. White stole milky into irises
robbing her sight—
white etched the corners of her lips,
outlining and cracking once satin-brown skin.
White traveled up veins on her long sinewy hands,
white stole her grandmother's life.
She pulled a white veil over her own dark face
like some somber bride and rode the white limo
ordered especially for her, the child who knew
to refuse the black, blamed the white for smothering life.

Going Home
Jane Alberdeston | *Puerto Rico/United States*

If you had woken to call God's name, He
wouldn't
have heard it, the room struck deaf
by the blare of a television

and oxygen's dissonant hiss.
In the respirator, condensation buds
like drops of blood and iodine.

What's written on your body: all your
years and
ulcers, a tattoo of fallen veins,
cataracts,
diabetic blues and grays, needle pricks.

When nurses let your lips turn to salt in
that ocean of white, I pray to cups of water.
Today, a
forgetful nurse brings you lime jello

and mashed carrots,
your mouth a slit-gong,
deserted,

all of you tied to a coma's ribbon,
tubes and cords laced from under dress
 seams
to fingers.

The monitor's bleep suggests a ghost
of your campesina ways:
waist-bent over

dandelions, smacking them with your
machete. You
would never go the way of your mother,

roasting
coffee beans in a storm.

The hurricane days of loosed goats and
chickens.
Your mother, a Magdalena, fallen in the
dirt,
without a priest and his pocket of last
rites.

Where is the island woman's lunch: green
boiled banana, rice pearls drizzled in olive oil,
 a cup
of pineapple juice. A world in the ginepa
shell.

How could any one go hungry when
there are sweet fistfuls of malanga and
acerola
fruit, bread in your hands,

a grandchild's plaited hair.

Good night women (or, defying the carcinogenis pen)
Evie Schokley | *United States*

in memory of: audre lorde (1934-92), toni cade bambara (1939-95), sherley anne williams (1944-99), barbara christian (1943-2000), claudia tate (1947-2002), nellie mckay (cir.1933-2006)

they are rising like stars,
always brightly there behind our blindness,
pricking through the dark tent
with a fine, white rage
that burns trash to ashes,
that fires truth to ceramic strength.

they are shining like stars,
beaconing us to a north we bring along
in our pockets, constellating,
andromedas fighting their own monsters,
dipping into history and wisdom,
filling to overflowing the big and little gourds.

they are falling like stars,
ripping hot and fierce down the night sky
till they are out of our pining sight,
too quickly, more frequently than we can bear,
their incandescent metal, incinerating, is
the occasion and inverse of wish.

Ghaflah

June Jordan | *United States*

(In Islam Ghaflah Refers to the Sin of Forgetfullness)

Grief scrapes at my skin
she never
"Be a big girl!"
wanted to touch
much
except to disinfect
or bandage

I acknowledge nothing

I forget the mother of my hurt
her innocence of pride
her suicide

That first woman

lowered eyes
folded hands
withered limbs
among the plastic flowers
rhinestone bracelets
eau de toilette
trinkets from slow
compromise

Where did she go?

After swallowing fifteen/twenty/thirty-five pills
she tried to rise

and rising

froze
forever trying to arise
from compromise

And I do not remember finding her
like that
half seated half
almost standing up
just dead
by her own hand
just dead

I do not remember finding her
like that

I forget the burned toast/
spinach
cold eggs
taste-free tuna fish
and thin spread peanut butter
sandwiches
she left for me

I erase
the stew the soup
she cooked and carried
everywhere
to neighbors

I forget three or four other things
I cannot recall
how many pairs of pretty shoes

Aging

how many dressup overcoats
I saved my nickels
dimes and quarters

all year long
to buy
at Christmas time
to give to her
my mother
she
the one who would wear nothing
beautiful

Or how I strut
beside her walking anywhere
prepared for any lunatic
assault
upon her shuffling
journey
to a bus stop

I acknowledge nothing

I forget she taught me
how to pray
I forget her prayers
And mine

I do not remember
kneeling down
to ask for wisdom
high-top sneakers
or linoleum chips
to animate
my zip gun

I have never remembered
the blistering fury
the abyss

into which
I capsized
after her last
compromise

I wish I had found her
that first woman
my mother
trying to rise
up

I wish I had given her
my arm

both arms

I have never forgiven her
for going away

But I don't remember anything

Grief scrapes at my skin
she never
"Be a big girl!"
wanted to touch
much

RELATIONSHIPS

Spiritual

The True believer begins with herself.

—Berber proverb

I am one African who needs and wants my God Black,... preferably the female gender.

—Bessie Head, from *A Woman Alone*

You's a black queen Sheba
great black great grandmom
I love the you
that works in my flesh

—Jodi Braxton, from *The Black Woman's Gumbo Ya-Ya*

From the Thunder Perfect Mind
The Voice of a Feminine Divine Power | *Egypt*

Sent from the Power,
I have come
to those who reflect upon me,
and I have been found
among those who seek me.
Look upon me,
you who meditate,
and hearers, hear.
Whoever is waiting for me,
take me into yourselves.
Do not drive me
out of your eyes,
or out of your voice,
or out of your ears.
Observe. Do not forget who I am.

For I am the first, and the last.
I am the honored one, and the scorned.
I am the whore and the holy one.
I and the wife and the virgin.
I am the mother, the daughter,
and every part of both.
I am the barren one who has borne many sons.
I am she whose wedding is great
and I have not accepted a husband.
I am the midwife and the childless one,
the easing of my own labor.
I am the bride and the bridegroom
and my husband is my father.
I am the mother of my father,
the sister of my husband;
my husband is my child.
My offspring are my own birth,
The source of my power,
what happens to me is their wish. . . .

From Obelisk* Inscriptions

Queen Hatshepsut | *Ruled during the 18th Egyptian Dynasty*

I swear, as I am loved of Re,
As Amun, my father, favors me
As my nostrils are refreshed with life
    and dominion,
As I wear the white crown
As I appear with the red crown
As the Two Lords have joined
    their positions for me,
As I rule this land like the son of Isis,
As I am mighty like the son of Nut,
As Re rests in the evening bark,
As he prevails in the morning bark,
As he joins his two mothers in the god's ship,
As sky endures, as his high creation lasts,
As I shall be eternal like an undying star,
As I shall rest in life like Atum—

Good Lord in That Heaven
Penny Jessye | United States
A traditional African American Spiritual

Good Lord
In that Heaven,
Good Lord
In that Heaven,
Good Lord
In that Heaven,
I know I gotta home at last!

Go, Angel, and tell the news,
Go, Sister, and tell the news
Go, Elder, and tell the news,
I know I gotta home at last!

(transcribed by Eva A. Jessye)

The Prayer of Judith
From The Book of Judith in *The Missing Books of the Bible V. I*
(Poetic arrangement by Nagueyalti Warren)

O Lord, O my God, hear me a widow
My God take vengeance on the strangers
Who loosened the girdle of a maid
To defile her, to discover the thigh
To her shame—who polluted her
Virginity to her reproach; for Thou
Saidest, It shall not be so; and
Yet they did so.

The Shulammite *from* The Song of Songs
Song 1: 5-6

I am black, but lovely, O' daughters of Jerusalem,
As the tents of Kedar, as the curtains of Solomon.
Look not upon me, because I am black, because
The sun hath looked upon me: my mother's children
Were angry with me; they made me the keeper of the
Vineyards; but mine own vineyard have I not kept.

Makeda[1], Queen of Sheba
1000 B.C.

I fell
beause of wisdom,
but was not destroyed:
through her I dived
into the great sea,
and in those depths
I seized
a wealth-bestowing pearl.

I descended
like the great iron anchor
men use to steady their ships
in the night on rough seas,
and holding up the bright lamp
that I there received,
I climbed the rope
to the boat of understanding

While in the dark sea,
I slept,
and not overwhelmed there,
dreamt: a star
blazed in my womb.

I marveled
at that light,
and grasped it,
and brought it up to the sun.
I laid hold upon it,
and will not let it go.

1. Makeda, the renowned Queen of Sheba, beautiful Ethiopian woman who loved
wisdom and adventure, traveled to King Solomon's court to find out for herself if
he actually was as wise as his reputation claimed. Her relationship with Solomon
produced a son, Menyelek, who when mature returned to Israel to meet his father.
According to Ethiopian legend, he returned to Ethiopia with the Ark of the Cov-
enant where it remains to this day.

Religion, The Daughter of Heaven
Ann Plato | *United States*

Religion is the daughter of Heaven—
    parent of our virtues, and
    source of all true felicity.
    She alone giveth peace and
    contentment; divests the heart of anxious cares,
    bursts on the mind a flood of joy, and sheds
    unmingled and preternatural sunshine
    in the pious breast. By her the spirits
    of darkness are banished from the earth, and
    angelic ministers of grace thicken, unseen,
    the regions of mortality.

From "Religion," 1841

The Angel's Visit
Charlotte L. Forten Grimké | *United States*

"On such a night as this," methought,
    "Angelic forms are near;
In beauty unrevealed to us
    They hover in the air.
O mother, loved and lost," I cried,
    "Methinks thou'rt near me now;
Methinks I feel thy cooling touch
    Upon my burning brow."

Lady, Lady
Anne Spencer | *United States*

Lady, Lady, I saw your face,
Dark as night withholding a star . . .
The chisel fell, or it might have been
You had borne so long the yoke of men.

Lady, Lady, I saw your hands,
Twisted, awry, like crumpled roots,
Bleached poor white in a sudsy tub,
Wrinkled and drawn from your rub-a-dub.

Lady, Lady, I saw your heart,
And altared there in its darksome place
Were the tongues of flame the ancients knew,
Where the good God sits to spangle through.

Longings
Mae V. Cowdery | *United States*

To dance—
In the light of moon,
A platinum moon,
Poised like a slinder dagger
On the velvet darkness of night.

To dream—
'Neath the bamboo trees
On the sable breast
Of earth—
And listen to the wind.

To croon—
Weird sweet melodies
Round the cabin door
With banjos clinking softly—
And from out the shadow
Hear the beat of tom-toms
Resonant through the years.

To plunge—
My brown body
In a golden pool,
And lazily float on the swell,
Watching the rising sun.

To stand—
On a purple mountain
Hidden from earth
By mists of dreams
And teras—

To talk—
With God.

The Line of Clothes
Vibha Chauhan | India

The clothes on the line,
Washed, spread and clipped
To make them stay in place,
Will be worn and washed
And worn and washed,
Till becoming threadbare
They are thrown away
Making place for the new.

Much like all of us
Worn out and worked out
Stretched to the utmost
Till failing to stretch anymore
We give way, under the
Slightest touch of time's finger,
To new and newer lines
Of men and women.
New and bright, imagining
As they stretch out their strengths
In the glorious sun
That they nourish an eternal
Relationship with the sun.
Something that's special
And different from all others
From all else.

Till they suddenly notice
Their bright skins fading
And looking behind see
A long line of
New and bright clothes
Ready to be spread out
In the sun
To dry off.

416

Gettin' De Spirit
Una Marson | *Jamaica/England*

Lord gie you chile de spirit
Let her shout
Lord gie you chile de power
An' let her pray—
Hallelujah—Amen—
Shout sister—shout—
God is sen' you His spirit
Shout—sister—shout.

Shout sister—shout—
Hallelujah—amen.
Can't you feel de spirit
Shout sister—shout
Hallelujah—Amen.

Join de chorus,
We feel it flowing o'er us—
You is no chile of satan
So get de spirit
And shout—sister—shout—
Hallelujah—Amen—
Shout—Sister—Shout!

This Life

Claudia Rankine | *Jamaica/United States*

Each sensitive hour, every kicking day we sweep
the darkness mostly outside, wanting
the windows reflecting our lives to embrace a lit interior.
But then the blinds are closed, moths caught between
screen and window disappear, dust on the baseboard settling.

For what is hardest will persist in the world, an intrusion
that is forever; so it feels, of course,
we are open and vulnerable. Then the tears
start coming so fast nothing makes sense:
no blows, no blood, only hurt rearranging—

Who moves such pain?
its brokenness invisible, its breath at a loss.
And still the desire lives to shift its weight, to stand up
under it, to bring it forward out its awkwardness,
out of our breast. Each of us, disappointment

covered over by flesh. All this life we are unable to rest.

I Know She Will Pray for Me
Sharon Bourke | *United States*

Sometimes, when I become others of my people,
I become fervent in a different way,
Believing that if only we believe enough,
We can never be hurt,
That if only we are clean enough,
We can never be sullied,
That if only we love enough,
We shall be loved.

When I become these others of my people,
The bright, metallic discs of understanding, Yes, Lord,
Somehow shake and tremble on the tambourine,
And the rhythm, older than hymnals,
Is of a different Good.
Then the discs flash in the sun,
And my fervor becomes once more my fervor,
And I want to hurt and to sully,
Hating that vision of infinitely patient love.

I Know I Been Saved

Porchia Moore | *United States*

I was baptized in July.
It was a good month for reincarnation.
In July, barren Hindu mothers eat
the flesh of fish believing that fish
house the souls of the dead.
The souls of the dead,
thick and cumbersome
like whale sperm swim upward
into hollow wombs to be born again
I was saved in the seventh month
It is a good month to be
washed in Living Waters.

Lightness

Geni Guimarães | *Brazil*

Translated by Carolyn Richardson Durham

She closed her eyes;
Removed the flesh,
Separated the bones.
Seized control of the lung,
Put it on the table.

She returned:
brought the heart,
the stomach,
a piano,
a poem,

Some guts imprisoned on the bridge of a guitar.

And when
she was contemplating herself
viscerally,
intertwined with musical notes.
She felt hungry.
She fed herself with a verse.
She wavered.

Kali, The Mother Goddess
Usha Kishore | Isle of Man, UK

I am the drinker of blood, said Kali, the
Mother Goddess, I am pure energy that is
woman; I roam the dark, where no man
meets my eye!

I am the singer of songs, I am the slayer
of sorrow, said Kali, the Mother Goddess,
I am the queen of darkness, I am the
empress of light!

My garland of skulls shines like a thousand
moons; my skirt of hands, covers the earth,
said Kali, the Mother Goddess, my hair is
the sky; my teeth, the stars; my blood-shot
eyes, the fire that burns in all life!

I am she, who terrifies the dark hordes,
said Kali, the Mother Goddess, I am she,
who dances on Shiva; I am she, who is
the mother of the world!

I am born to destroy with my third eye,
said Kali, the Mother Goddess, I am
born to create order from chaos, I am
born to terrify fear, I am born to
bestow peace!?

My skull-bowl is full of demon blood,
said Kali, the Mother Goddess, my heart
is full of compassion; my hands, full of
blessing!

My trident draws blood, said Kali, the

Mother Goddess, *my red tongue lolls out*
for more; the sound of my anklets drives
away ghosts and ghouls, as each night, I
roam the earth!

My laughter is thunder; lightning, a flash
of my eye, said Kali, the Mother Goddess,
My hands are hot iron; my hands are soft
silk—they burn and they bless!

the coming of Kali
lucille clifton | *United States*

it is the black God, Kali,
a woman God and terrible
with her skulls and breasts.
i am one side of your skin,
she sings, softness is the other,
you know you know me well, she sings,
you know you know me well.

running Kali off is hard.
she is persistent with her
black terrible self. she
knows places in my bones
i never sing about but
she knows i know them well.
she knows.
she knows.

Cosmic Rhythms

Jacqueline Johnson | *United States*

Cylindrical view of the double
sighted vision. Mother, daughter
and the holy ghost—African ark
wings circumference centuries.

The path leads upward
through rumble of zigzag,
yin yang, DNA dance.
A double helix, splendid
thread life wraps around.

Ancient path the goddess travels.
Circle within the circle within.
Magnificent twirling that turns
women into mothers.

Look again could be a sombrero,
or Saturn's many rings.
See the dervish whirling
bringing with him a wisdom

that is always out of bounds.
In the center see the blink of
an iris open, blessed with vision.
Oh take me on the road that spirals round

and round. A galaxy of wombs teaming with life.
In a corner smooth, black aureole
of a nipple erect for sucking.
This great tit humanity feeds from.

The Blooming Thing
Donika Ross | *United States*

The blooming thing
pulled back into green
and you were talking of absence and people
walked away, laughing at nothing.
Your skirt gathered into disappointment
on the scuffed floors, and I wanted
to pull long pieces of you into pink
ribbons. I hated your paleness, the way you wore
my hands and pulled me into the soft,
bread smell of your belly only to fade.
I fought the stillness of your neck,
shook you like sheets,
like hands, but you
misunderstood the nature
of sleep and settled into the earth.

The Spirit at Rest
Sheree Renée Thomas | *United States*

Raw curbs
brittle as bone
amber floods of gravel
red eyes lock thunder
in a yard full of green
restless hand aches
guided by God
you sing
hymns inside stone

the wind sweeps in circles
showers the floor
with breath of dust
shards from earth's collarbone

in your house of broken light
the sun leans west
fire clings to trees, flickers
hard against bare stone

you rest, unafraid of storms
no music, just rain
and thunder growing

Pentecostals in the Attic

Phebus Etienne | *Haiti/United States*

Three sisters from the storefront church came
to pray for the patient propped up near the window.
Her eyes grew wide as shouts reverberated
against the chapel roof of her bedroom.

When she bent down to observe the wound,
the staples zipping south from navel to pubic line,
remembrance flooded the pilgrim
who was a cancer survivor.
"Oui, Bon Dieu!" her amputated
breast had leaked the same way. But she was
reborn in sacred blood and had the formula
guaranteed for promenades on streets of gold.

"Est-ce que ou kwè?" the zealots questioned.
I kneeled wanting the gift of two souls,
true communion with Christ to be the cure.

Psalm ninety-one did not usher salvation
as proclaimed. I brought bottles of milk thistle
until mom refused to swallow.
She asked for herbs, offerings
a priestess prescribed. Mixes from the altar
scented the room like sweat and musk
from lovers calm in the aftermath of sex. Her chants
summoned ancestors from Ginen, the Black gods.

Embolism weighed down her lung, halted pleas for mercy.
When the sisters returned to lay hands and crucifixes,
I turned them away like peddlers of sesame candy
at her childhood gate on Michel Oreste.
I had not been called to learn ceremonial songs
and could only beg the unseen universe
for her life to end.

"Oui, Bon Dieu!?" Yes, Lord!
"Est-ce que ou kwè?" Do you believe?
Ginen? Guinea.

Hoodoo Moma
Luisha Teish | *United States*

Wooden stairs scrubbed with red brick
Holy water sprinkled on the floor.
St. Michael slays that old demon
quiet-like behind the front door.
"Jesus, Mary and Joseph," she cries,
"C'mon in here and sit down."
Coffee is sipped from a demitasse cup
in my moma's part of town.
"Don't cross yo' legs at de table.
Beware the cook dat don't eat.
Mind ya home training for company.
Don't ya dare sweep dat 'oman's feet!"
A frizzy is running around outside
scratching up gri-gri. Rattlesnake skins
and mudbug fins 'round a blue plate of congris.
Back yonder in da burning barrel, there's
sulphur and rags aflame. Wrapped in red thread
up under it, nine times, she's writ somebody's name.
B'yond the fence things a growing: Cow greens, milkweed, and
Devil's Bread. Sunday mornin' she's stiff starched and
Catholic; altar night—white rag on her head.
Ask the woman where she going, or dare to ask her
where she been. You'll find bluing water on ya
doorstep, and ya breathin dis-eased by the wind.
Being as how I'm her daughter, I dared to ask her *one time*
"Moma you know about Hoodoo?" "Child ya must be outta ya
/mind.
Who don't hear the death rattle, or know howta talk wid a frog.
Common sense is what de lawd give ya. There's prophesy in
the bark of a dog."

Resolution
Lauren K. Alleyne | *Trinidad and Tobago*

If offered in all its sweetness, the world,
she would not turn. She would atone the body,
its complicated want; she would be *good*.
And it would begin here—she was ready.

The plan: to wake every morning at dawn,
reflect, read her bible, pray the rosary.
She would make a habit of devotion,
drape her flesh in new faith, wear it wholly.

Her morning meal would be humble, only
water would cross her lips until evening
– for these forty days she will be empty,
this daughter of Eve—hunger redeeming
her sins of inheritance, commission;
her wayward heart, its caution of Eden.

Love Up De Culture
Lelawattee Manoo-Rahming | *Bahamas*

It does hit yuh
Bam! Jus so
an sometimes dis culture
does wrap arong yuh
naked body
all slinky and sexy
slow and dreamy
like it want to make
love wit yuh

at other times
it does make yuh knees
get weak
yuh trimblin all over
moanin and gronin
like yuh is a Shango Baptist
ketchin de power

an den again
sometimes it does
get yuh excited
eyes open wide
an shining like black opal
heart ponging in yuh chest
like tassa drums in a
cooking night or hoosay

but always always
at de dead ah night
in ah silver riddum
ah crooning melody
wedda Baron or Polly Sookraj
steelpan or sitar
it does climax Bam!
an jus so it does go

Gospel

Patricia Spears Jones | *United States*

For my mother

She's been crying now
for hours
singing old songs
She is a blues song
8 bar   12 bar
blues song
long
long
past the last chorus
and it is midnight
or later
and there's a whiskey
or maybe just a beer
and it's quiet
so quiet
except for the music
of her tears

The sounds in her
throat
start waves of memories
suddenly
there is an echo
of a chorus
of a gospel pearl
about returning
to the temple
to be cleansed
to be cleansed

White uniformed sisters
stand guard 'round their

weeping comrade
and all the pain
goes away
in the shout
in the holding on of hands
in the sweat
sweet water
scent of cheap cologne
and talcum powder
returning to the temple
to be cleansed
to be cleansed

There are stars in her tears
Light-years have crossed her brow
She has traveled with this knowledge
of pain
of rape
of pain
for too long

and that gospel song
comes like a blessing
beautiful
black
loving
returning to the place
of mercy
of mercy on me/ she
stops her weeping
stops her dreaming
stops this silence
with the clenching
of her fist

with the opening
of her heart

much like a rose
under Arkansas sun

She has made her blues song
gospel
She has made her gospel
real
She claims all her powers
perhaps curses the darkness
and waits to generate new heavens
in her eyes.

(Wo)man

Javacia Harris | *United States*

God
Why would you make me a woman
Give me a womb
Then once a month call me
Unclean
When I shed the very blood used to create
Your precious man

                        Why would you make me a woman

Give me a name
Then smother it
With tradition and man's pride
As soon as my finger carries
The weight of wife

Why would you make me a woman
Give me a spirit
That burns with self-love and big dreams
Then stamp out the fire
With your heavy holy foot
A foot I love too much
Am too afraid of
To grab and push away

Revelation
Lita Hooper | *United States*

At the First Baptist Church of Christ the Living Redeemer
the holy ghost always comes on time
steals into the anxious room
just as the doors of the church are opened.
Pastor descends to the first row
his microphone a magic wand.

I know this ghost and its tricks
the ping-pong screams
the choir chanting up each swelling tide.
When the organ calls back
a fierce nudge brings someone else to her knees.

My son styles airplanes out of programs.
His legs are too short
to touch the planks of this old church.
Yet he absently rocks to the quickening drum.

Beneath the floor, a rumbling beast
but I will not be moved.
No list of this week's blessings
to set my back ablaze.
No knock-kneed clamp
to quit the dreaded quake.
Just a quick upstroke at the nape
for the strayed strands.

A woman near me is tagged.
She glides up the aisle
arms out like a fan approaching.
Pastor grips her willing head with his free hand.
Then she is a spineless thing collapsing.

My son sits up. Wide-eyed
he surveys the spectacle
a flurry of paper fans
wide-brim hats in orbit
a bevy of color erupting.

When I lead him out
his small hand tugs no
then minds the mother-grip.
In the parking lot
we are alone
under the wide, wide sky.

Delirium

Andrea Cristina Rio Branco | *Brazil*

Translated by Carolyn Richardson Durham

Here and now
In this mute silence
I'm a child, I'm a woman, I'm a lady...
Since dreams allow me everything.
I don't dream in vain, I know very well,
I have never nourished myself from illusions.
But without dreams, what would I be?
When life insists on saying "no."
Here and now,
In that solitude that vindicates
I am a queen, a princess, I'm a high born lady...
And a bountiful meal is on the table
And the silk sheets on the bed,
Will be a symbol of wealth,
Of all the nobility that sets me on fire.
Here and insistently now
In that thought that I'm thinking
I am his, so crazily his,
That I don't even know any more, how much of mine
belongs to me.
In that absurd delirium
Since dreams allow me everything.

Redemption in Our Time: A Promise, A Prayer
Hermine Pinson | *United States*

"cada poro tiene una luz"
    —victor hernandez cruz

i.

to those riding to the end
of the line
the train whistle warns
of preacher bird sermons
same same same same
screed that
builds word-bridges to
concession and guilt:

nobody's fall but mine

mary's daughter
in our time
ayida wedo's sister
queen of hearts rides an
appaloosa
and calls gaius, the folk,
to seal the lips of backdoor
oldtimey pumpkin-mouth haints

iii.

I know you will preach
on the last day
when trees make weeping motions
while their branches burn

ayida wedo, sister
pass your palm over a poisoned sky
find us in the bushes
hiding our naked need

iv.

ayida wedo tells us
one briar bush secret:
when you get there
the sun is setting and
the water's so blue
it makes you laugh
and cry at the same time
shanti shanti shanti

where are we, mary,
                estrella,

                      ayida wedo?

v.

almost here, sister
almost here

Fullness

Thylias Moss | *United States*

One day your place in line will mean the
Eucharist has run out. All because you waited
your turn. Christ's body can be cut into only
so many pieces. One day Jesus will be eaten up.
The Last Supper won't be misnamed. One day the
father will place shavings of his own blessed fingers
on your tongue and you will get back in line for
more. You will not find yourself out of line again.
The bread will rise inside you. A loaf of tongue.
Pumpernickel liver. You will be the miracle.
You will feed yourself five thousand times.

Small Congregations
Thylias Moss | United States

Look around at Sis. Elden's brim wider than the arms
of the crucifix but without promises; looking
into her eyes is impossible so what could be found
there must be sought elsewhere, Tahlma Ollet's
keyboard-wide bosom always in tune (can't tell
she most died bringing a no-count into the world) unlike
the old spinet whose keys look perfect but don't deliver
the notes, the pitches. Then they come; Tahlma Ollet
shouts, from kitchen below us, the sound coming up
through water pipes and plaster, threadbare rugs that
the patting feet beat to death, a demon-killing stomp;
through our own feet whose tapping is an African
distress call probably but we're out of range, out
of touch, although you can't tell from the way Tahlma's
shout comes on up through our root system then out
of our own mouths though we're out of range of the
pepper, out of touch with the onions she's peeling
in the basement, holding for a moment,
before the knife enters,
a globe, a honey-colored moon, a cook's bible that she chops
into scriptures and makes us eat, tossing them
into every course: soup, entree, dessert.
Our shouting, our jubilation scares the ominous into
crouching behind our ribs where it intercepts what
would best serve us if it reached our hearts.

It does sometimes in the hint towards boogie-woogie
courtesy the tic in Elder Simpson's fingers, the
improvised pauses, hops, physiological product of
arthritis, spiritual product of faith, a holy rolling
of the eighty-eights when he plays *Sweet Home, T''is the
Old Ship of Zion*. Church starts to drift there,
crucifix, hand carved, painted brown, life size becoming

mainstay, frame of the storefront ark serving Mt. Pleasant,
home of urban schools named for dead white presidents.

Ushers pass out bread slice—shaped weighty paper
stapled onto tongue depressors, fans from the House of Wills,
funeral parlor, black owned and operated—some might say
death always was.
Not just grief shouts, not just fury rages.
Go, Willa, go; dance that holy dance, shake
those sinful tail feathers off! *Go on, Girl, shake*
that thing; go on, Girl, shake that thing! Let God
have his way, let the spirit take control, get up, get moving,
get on board; that's what Elder Simpson's playing now; *there's*
a train a comin'; tilt the cross and it's a railway crossing
sign; a train's a comin' just like yesterday, simply
switching tracks, from underground to the sky; freedom
still the destination, hear the stationmaster call: Cleveland,
Ottawa, Heaven—that's right, *Heaven;* not New Haven
anymore!

RELATIONSHIPS
Family, Friends and Others

Ou okunda takushereka kigambo
One who loves you does not spare you the truth
                        —Kigezi proverb (southwest Uganda)

Ancestor on the Auction Block
Vera Bell | *Jamaica/England*

Ancestor on the auction block
Across the years your eyes seek mine
Compelling me to look.

I see your shackled feet
Your primitive black face
I see your humiliation
And turn away
Ashamed.

Across the years your eyes seek mine
Compelling me to look
Is this mean creature that I see
Myself?
Ashamed to look
Because of myself ashamed
Shackled by my own ignorance
I stand
A slave.

Humiliated
I cry to the eternal abyss
For understanding
Ancestor on the auction block
Across the years your eyes meet mine
Electric
I am transformed
My freedom is within myself.

I look you in the eyes and see
The spirit of God eternal
Of this only need I be ashamed
Of blindness to the God within me
The same God who dwelt within you

The same eternal God
Who shall dwell
In generations yet unborn.

Ancestor on the auction block
Across the years
I look

I see you sweating, toiling, suffering
Within your loins I see the seed
Of multitudes
From your labour
Grow roads, aqueducts, cultivation
A new country is born
Yours was the task to clear the ground
Mine be the task to build.

Old Maid's Soliloquy

Maggie Pogue Johnson | *United States*

I'se been upon de karpet,
    Fo' lo, dese many days;
De men folks seem to sneer me,
    In der kin' ob way.

But I don't min' der foolin',
    Case I sho' is jis as fine
As any Kershaw pumpkin
    A hanging on de vine.

I looks at dems sometimes,
    But hol's my head up high,
Case I is fer above dem
    As de moon is in de sky.

Dey sho' do t'ink dey's so much,
    But I sho' is jis as fine
As eny sweet potato
    Dat's growd up from de vine.

Dey needn't t'ink I's liken dem,
    Case my match am hard to fin',
En I don't want de watermillon
    Dat's lef' upon de vine.

Case I ain't no spring chicken,
    Dis am solid talk,
En I don't want anything
    Dat's foun' upon de walk.

Case ef I'd wanted anything,
    I'd hitched up years ago,
En had my sher ob trouble.

But my min' tol' me no.

I'd rader be a single maid,
　　A wanderin' bout de town,
Wid skercely way to earn my bread,
　　En face all made ob frowns,—

Den hitched up to some numbskull,
　　Wid skercely sense to die,
En I know I cud'n kill him,
　　Dar'd be no use to try.

So don't let ol' maids boder you,
　　I'll fin' a match some day,
Or else I'll sho''main single,
　　You hear me what I say!

I specs to hol' my head up high
　　En always feel as free
As any orange blossom
　　A hangin' on de tree.

Chant
Celinha | *Brazil*

Translated by Carolyn Richardson Durham

To braid your hair black woman is to
remember passionate songs of the sunny days
and the cold
nights of the seasons. To braid your hair
like ropes, like shackles and whips;
Is to feel the caress of the wind
Dancing in your hands.

It is to trace the lines
of the map of a nation.
It is to write on your head
a black song.

Between the twilight and the dawn, I invent a strong wind
and you come. I open the door to my verses, you come in and take
the whole room of my poem. I only understand and transcribe your
dreams. It's you who is the poet. My hands incriminate and leave
fingerprints within me. When desperate I look for an alibi in order
to run away from you, my verses betray me. I am changeable, a
black panther, and solitude goes down the steps of a poem with me.
Still, the only love that I possess, I dedicate to you.

Girlfriends for *Mungen, Rosen & Feldman*
Wanda Coleman | *United States*

we are faced with the irrefutable analyses
no one's gonna pay us for what's left of
our gal youth and our lady beauty

a connection in New York, London or the Vatican
is worth the expense of self-transmission as in
send bio demo-tape shoe size and lock of hair

there the need to be heard there the need there
are no proper men to fill there the nights so empty
we occupy ourselves with compulsive telephoning
and radio talk shows

forty smackers per diem and the secretarial pool
are alternatives to etching our names into toilet
stall walls with bobby pins (we shit, therefore)

we look after our mothers as we would have
our children look after us

we know the rhythms of loss and cancer intimately

we are constantly in the mirror of each other's
hope for "get over," networking against the next
wrinkle and unemployment check

we are the soft-armed stubborn avant grade
of the new cornucopia knowing we will be too
snaggle-toothed for the feast
once it arrives

we stroke each weary other to heal for this is
not about mutual masturbation but familial
respect and unmitigated pride. creativity is
the color of our skins

we write therefore we are

Change
Virginia K. Lee | *United States*

her arrogance grows obese
as a redwood
reckless as crabgrass
while she subtly
changes our friendship
from peers to

she as teacher
me as student

the condescending air
polluted with
verbal and written put-downs

fuels my anger
a most vicious creature
when full and let loose

what she doesn't know is
I'm a *sensitive*
I see her thoughts
when written in the clouds

the wind whispers
her motives and intentions
warns me to beware of
a she-devil deceiver

Friday Night: Two Kinds of Writing
Mendi Lewis Obadike | *United States*

I am alone in my dorm room,
writing at my little desk.
My friend comes to my room
to put on her makeup.

This is an act of generosity:
Her roommate is asleep. My
beautiful friend applies
her makeup in my mirror.

It is night. I am writing at my desk
with a lamp on. I am bending over
paper with a pen in my hand. The shape
of my head obscures my words.

My mirror has a florescent light.
My beautiful friend is standing in it.
My beautiful friend makes
a beautiful shadow on my floor.

My roommate is out dancing. My friend
puts on her makeup. I bend over paper
to write my sentence. My friend
leans in, very close to my mirror.

She is lining a silver eyelid. She is
painting her lips with a brush. I am
starting now to erase a word. My
friend begins to unbraid her hair.

What a Crazy Aunt Can Give
Tara Betts | United States

The one sign that I am the crazy aunt
is that I keep envisioning the gift I want
to give to nieces when they start to sigh,
write long letters or sneak off to horde
the phone and wear the tiniest clothes.

Before they repel the clutch of elders
entirely, I slide the pink box across
the kitchen table. It is light, thin
cardboard suitable for confections
or pastries. The creamiest pink
silk ribbon wraps itself in lush bow
that unknots with one gentle pull.

Before she loosens the blushing valentine
paper, I say, this is so you know
what you need, so you don't have to ask,
be ignored, be forced.

Pink paper reveals the battery-powered
device, not huge with length or girth
but dainty as a lip gloss or butterfly.
I expect the horrified look, nervous
bursts of laughter, a storm of footsteps
tromping out of the room, but the hope
lingers that she will take it
before someone tries to take her,
steal her first quivers & moans
or smash them
in a clatter of hips that sputters
without concern
for warmth.

This box
can open the crazy possibility
that she can please herself,
then let her pick the boys
as she pleases like a preference
for the most durable battery.

A Wife's Thought After 20 Years of Marriage
Kamilah Moon | *United States*

When we stood with moist, unlined
eyes and pledged

"until death do us part,"

did the loss   of who I was that day
or the killing   of who I might have become

count?

To a Dear Friend Mothering Misery

Kamillah Aisha Moon | *United States*

Every time your grief cries
you pick it up, cradle it
like a newborn. But your pain
isn't precious, not your life-long
responsibility. For each doting moment

your soul refuses to sing for days—and the world
needs your music too much.

Please leave it be; no more milk. Let it cry
for nights on end unattended. Let it
forget how your heartbeat sounds, the warmth
of your skin. Stop making it soup when it coughs,
setting a place for it at the table or buying it
new clothes. Convert its old room into
a sanctuary for things you adore.
Let your ache become self-sufficient
and grow apart from you.

Walk out the door
and forget to call home.

Same Difference?
Stella Abasa Dadzie | *England*

same taste in music
same taste in food
same sense of humour
same mellow mood

same love of cultural vibes
same black hair and skin
same taste for pepper sauce
same black kith and kin

same hot-chocolate kisses
same hot-buttered soul
same hot-chile lovin'
same cool-tempo stroll

same love of laughter
same love of life
onliest thing we didn't share?
his need for a blond wife!

Front Porch News
Stephanie Pruitt | *United States*

Big Millie done found her a new ole' man
She lay out a buffet for him every night
Nose so open he feed right out her hand
Everybody talkin' and say it ain't right

She lay out a buffet for him every night
Got him yawnin' all throughout the day
Everybody talkin' and say it ain't right
But Millie done put the swish back in her sway

Got him yawnin' all throughout the day
That big gal have him workin' overtime
But Millie done put the swish back in her sway
Gets more from him than a few good times

That big gal have him workin' overtime
They say the way she found him is the way he'll go
Gets more from him than a few good times
And she feed him in ways don't nobody know

They say the way she found him is the way he'll go
Nose so open he feed right out her hand
And she feed him in ways don't nobody know
Big Millie done found her a new ole' man

That's a Strange Question from a Stranger
Toni Asante Lightfoot | *United States* | *1974**

Zora was some kinda free.

Ain't gonna get me to say
No bad thing about a Black
woman prone to troubles.

I'll tell you this much
she smelled smoky but clean.
When she came to my place
kissed both my cheeks,
pinched my bottom hello.

I'd roll the reefer, pour the whiskey.
Wonder how long I'se supposed to be
somebody's closet for closeness?

Zora came in mad some days.
Complaining about how somebody
didn't flutter from her words.
Zora was soft when she cried;
Hard when you comforted her.

After the show ended we tired
of our futures conflicting.
She was a lit cigarette
To my 100 gallons of kerosene.

Did she send you?
Tell me how is she?

---

* Zora Neal Hurston and Jackie "Moms" Mabley co-wrote a Broadway production
 called "Fast and Furious: A Colored Review in 37 scenes". Zora died in 1961 and
 was buried in a potters field in Florida. No one knew what happened to her until
 Alice Walker looked her up in 1973.

Agnatha
Porchia Moore | *United States*

I.

In my dream I am spitting out
my tongue—chunks raw like
tuna until I am a hagfish
with no jaw and no bone.
I am a hagfish—
slick and firm
like a penis. I am only
a mouth; full of razor-sharp teeth.
I am a hagfish chewing up the
thin, red flesh of the piranha's eye.

II.

Fish scar too.
Our scars are hidden deep beneath silvery-green scales.
Our scars are hidden in our poetry
Our scars course in and out of our bodies
so that we will always move, forever restless.
Fish do not sleep.
Our scars rest within the
sweetmeat of our thin, slivery bones.
We scar and are scarred and are scared
of men with baited words
that dangle on silver hooks
words: *Bitch, I will kill you*—that pierce the skin
Have you ever seen a piranha grin?
The piranha with a cold, red eye.
Fish with just a little hope let their gills
gasp for air, making a scratching sound on
the front page of a damp newspaper:
Woman, 26, murdered by boyfriend.

Wife of the Husband
Micere Githae Mugo | *Kenya*

His snores
protect the sleeping hut
but the day's
load
and the morrow's
burden
weigh heavily over
the stooping mother as she

sweeps the hut
bolts the pen
tidies the hearth
buries the red charcoals
and finally seeks
her restless bed

His snores
welcome her to bed
four hours to sunrise
His snores rouse her from bed
six sharp
Arise
O, wife of the husband!

In Small Rooms
Donika Ross | *United States*

The nape of your neck smells of rain
again for the second time in four days.
You lie naked on the carpet,
holding your breath, and your edges
blur mildly against the floor. You are bodies,
and I must squint to see your horizons.
We dance near the windows and
you call that swimming.
We stop to catch our breath and
you call that dying.
You are mad for dry frosted flakes
and bread dunked in milk.
A knife waits,
serrated and crocodilian,
barely cresting the thick nap of a rag rug.
You cut me to ask what I will bleed.
Ink. Like anyone else.

I.

In my parking space
is the memory of a mother weeping.
There is a chalk outline no one has bothered to erase
or pay attention to except for you.
She should have asked me, you say from the window.
We both know that there are other,
less intrusive ways. Have both choked on pills
like salvation, let them melt like communion
on dry tongues. Believing
white to be the body of redemption.
Had she asked, you would have told her death
is best when the leaving is unobtrusive, less tidal,
doesn't inconvenience a soul.

II.

We should love each other, both being brown
in a small room. You are more but I don't breathe well
with scars. You let me shade the windows now when it doesn't matter—
our pasts walk through anyway, showing their teeth at the
range of our bodies. You are nothing like the last.
I close my eyes to apparitions, sleep to the rain smell of your nape.
But we don't. Love. It is anathema to opening an eye. Irises are
oceans with no edges. My skin has lined itself again. It lied
when it said ink. It meant something else entirely.

The Woman

Kristina Rungano | *Zimbabwe*

A minute ago I came from the well
Where young women like myself drew water
My body was weary and my heart tired.
For a moment I watched the stream rush before me
And thought how fresh the smell of flowers,
How young the grass around it.
And yet again I heard the sound of duty
Which ground on me—made me feel aged
As I bore the great big clay container on my head
Like a great big painful umbrella.
Then I got home and cooked your meal
For you had been out drinking the pleasures of the flesh
While I toiled in the fields
Under the angry vigilance of the sun
A labour shared only by the bearings of my womb.
I washed your dishes
And swept the room we shared
Before I set forth to prepare your bedding
In the finest corner of the hut
Which was bathed by the sweet smell of dung
I had this morning applied to the floors.
Then you came in,
In your drunken lust
And made your demands
When I explained how I was tired
And how I feared for your child in me
You beat me and had your way
At that moment
You left me unhappy and bitter
And I hated you;
Yet tomorrow I shall again wake up to you
Milk the cow, plough the land and cook your food,
You shall again be my Lord
For isn't it right that woman should obey,
Love, serve and honour her man?
For are you not fruit of the land?

No More Maypole Dances
Barbara Thomas | United States

I've decided. No more dances around the maypole
Remember those
Done sometime in May as a welcome to Spring

Several eager young girls dressed in soft pastel organdy dresses
holding ribbons tied to the maypole
as they danced and sang

Somehow the scenario reminds me of the womandance done around men
we primp, plan and pray to establish and maintain relationships with them

We dance around them hoping to move them one way or another
and like the maypole they never budge

Meanwhile our crisp dresses wilt and fall
the ribbon becomes moist in our hand from our own sweat
and finally the song we sing becomes ridiculous to even us

This day I solemnly vow to do no more maypole dances
I'll release the ribbon attached to some stationary object

No pleading

And any dance I do will be to celebrate myself
or to welcome someone who also wants to celebrate my existence

Do You Remember?

Stella Abasa Dadzie | *England*

Do you remember
my sister
those dark November nights
when we listened to the world
and sought to right its sorrows
with our clenched fists?

Do you remember
those languid summer days
when we raised our placards high
and sang sweet songs of freedom
certain that history
was on our side?

The world's cruel burdens
weigh heavy still
and though time may have tempered
our youthful dreams
we have come at last to know
a deeper truth

For it is people
not ideals
that are transient
and freedom's spirit lives
imprisoned in the shy smile
of a hungry child
and in a fierce, enduring love
that conquers fear

December 1992

Cash Cow Blues
Virginia K. Lee | *United States*

brother says good sister is a cash cow
brother says lonely sister is a cash cow
she don't even remember when or how

givin' all her money to that cheatin'man
sinkin' and slidin' with that slippery man
payin' for his time and everything she can

fallin' for his splenda smile and each new ruse
acceptin' fork-tounged promises and every ruse
trustin' his lyin' eyes and broke-man excuse

lulled by his allurin' flare and honeyed lash
afraid of his mad-eyed stare and stingin' lash
that's quelled only by her ready cool cash

keeps her hooked and deeply in debt
and all of her emotional needs unmet

Old Photo from a Family Album, 1915

Pinkie Gordon Lane | *United States*

for Inez Addie West Gordon and Ocydee Williams

I.

This lovely young woman,
with the elegant hat
and dress of flowing gauze,
sits in a chair (a rocker)
contemplating a feather
poised in two fingers
of her right hand

What photographer arranged
this photo in a studio
with the tapestried background
draped like a mural? See
how he catches
the pensive gaze,
face soft, unsmiling,
full of innocence and hope

She sends the picture
to her lover:

Dear William, again
I make another attempt
—Please send me
one of yours... or
else you can come
and make one
at our house

Her body curved, relaxed, slender,
the eyes returning into themselves

she is contained in her
assurance that leads
into the future

II.

Nothing in this photo
resembles the gross figure
the angry defiance
the abused spirit
of the woman I knew

The enlarged hand,
fingers swollen from years of work,
would no longer hold a bird's feather
but a torch to light
her way back to corridors
of love expected,
of fury diffused to a spiral
of smoke, and a gown
that (shroud of her life)
she might have placed
upon her unmarked
grave

Leaf-Of-Life Hands
Lelawattee Manoo-Rahming | *Bahamas*

When we were babies

You fed us hot lemon-grass tea
To ease our colds and flu

You bathed our heads with Limacol
When our skins burned like desert air

With sensitive fingers you squeezed
Warm Leaf-Of-Life juice into our aching ears

You satiated our hunger
With roti and dhal

Rubbed our wheezing chests
With heated soft-candle

You sang to us
On full-moon nights

And rocked us gently
In the crocus-sack hammock

But where were you Mama?

Where were your hands
Your herbs, your songs?

When your first daughter
My big sister needed them to protect her

She was twenty years old and being kicked
By your first brother

As your mother watched
Where were you Mama?

Where was the lemon-grass tea?
To warm us when we lay cold
Alone on wooden floors?

Where was the Limacol to cool
Our burning faces damp with tears?

Your fingers squeezing Leaf-of-Life juice
On the painful abscesses growing in our hearts?

Where were the roti and dhal
We needed to plug the holes in our bellies?

Our congested chests wheezed
Longing for soft-candle rubs

Songs about the full moon
And soothing hammock rocking

Because you had already left us
Nine years earlier

Where were you Mama?
Where were your Leaf-of-Life juice hands?

Your lemon-grass tea breath
Your dhal and roti smell?

Your bhajan chanting voice
To rock me steadily to my sleep?

Bitter Roots

Sheree Renèe Thomas | *United States*

today i chewed *calamus*
found it growing wildly
near a fallen pine in
the forest, tucked it
under my tongue
clearing my throat
of this nest you built
and abandoned
its eggs unhatched grown cold
and weeks later, the thin shells remain
too fragile to touch with hands
heavy with anger
like these empty words
i choke on

in the middle of the night
i woke, crying
over the memory
of the morning we walked
and found sassafras
growing in a stand
on the side of the road
laughing, we wove a mojo
together, then gathered our
hearts inside
and your tongue was
wild-cherry bark, sweet molasses
in my mouth

this morning i found a dream
tangled in the web
overhanging my bed
in it a river flowed

over
my split lips
chapped from the sea
of unspoken
words unsaid
words damned
with two black feathers
and a bone carefully carved
then sat in the nest lodged in my throat

and those waters filled my lungs
diverted to the dry cracks
of my barren heartland
overflowed the fields where a whole world
once grew

now when i speak
i spit up bits of broken shells
and dead stalks and leaves
rustle
in my mouth

while in the distance
the sound of rivers
echo their warning:

tomorrow I will
pull this love
by its roots

Denial
Melanie Hope | *United States*

I don't know
death

I don't know
a good friend
telling me she is going to die

I don't know
trying to get all of my
little hairs out of the tub
before its her turn to get in

I don't know
what to say

I don't know
what she
tells her son
he's only seven

I don't know
what death means
to a child

I don't know
how we will say
good-bye

I don't know
what else to ask

I don't know
what else to say
we are
running
out of time

I don't know
how to make it harder
for death
to carry
her away

I don't know
let's watch t.v.

I don't know
let's eat

I don't know
what should we do
tomorrow

I don't know
how much more
we can laugh

I don't know
heat

I don't know
what she says
to begin each day

I don't know
what to offer next

I don't know
thank you

I don't know
if
we
will
see
each
other
again

I don't know
if she's sleeping

I don't know
how
she
keeps
smiling

I don't know
why
I feel sick

I don't know
when she cries

I don't know
if she's warm
enough
in that spare bed

The Night Prayer
Javacia Harris | *United States*

Granny
Just before *Amen*
I ask for you

I blame you for my reluctance
To call out a fool when I see one
Or snap my fingers to gospel songs
But I'm glad you taught me
How to mend a hole in my shirt
And to wrap God around my shoulders
When the heat bill couldn't be paid

You never taught me
How to make your rice pudding
Or explained why you made Mama
Get rid of the baby
She just knew was a boy

Be sweet
You'd say before hanging up
When I was away at college
So I'd feel guilty
Every time I opened my legs

New friends see your photograph
And say I have your dimples
I don't interrupt with talk
Of my mother's adoption
Because I am certain I have your skin
I have a cheek you taught me to turn
Palms you taught me to press together

I still wake up at 3 a.m.
To check the balance in my bank account
Your obsession with money haunts me
But you refuse to
No matter how much I beg

Four Women (a cycle of poems because of nina simone, ray waller, & judith siegel pearson)
Esperanza Cintròn | *Puerto Rico/United States*

GRANDMOMMA 1928

Posed against a scarred backdrop
    of Lucky Lindy's plane
Brand new coat, coon collar
    pulled up high
Touching the snug felt head hugger
Dark fingers press gleaming bangs
    to a pair of sweaty brows

Car'mel man darting in and out
    of his camera box
Feeling rich, looking good
    hand on hip
Tightning knots on real silk stockings
Showing some knee and lean brown legs
    'cause he kind a cute

Thoughts of Greystone on Monday night
    of dance and The Duke
Big, fine, spending, yellow man
    on my arm
Blues swaying down in Paradise
Repenting in church on Sunday
    for temperance beer last Monday

Know I was born, just the right time
    of slavery gone
Smelling up-north promises
    kiss my free
Six dollar a day earning man
Sweat, dig, haul, colored jobs, for true
    but men bathe and money's good
Ice box, trolley, FORD, ain't no south
    of cotton Poplars

Don't have to clean they baseboards
     on my knees
There's two men to ev'ry woman
No need nursing no pale children
     'sides don't mind washing what's mine

Everybody come up this way know
     of the dark Valley
Folks squeezed in and piled atop
     pool tables
Looking toward ironing my man's clothes
North End moving and babies come
     'cause Dr. Sweet showed we got rights

Pat pasty powder on my face
     of Neisner's five and dime
Wish they made some for colored
     dull the shine
Lights blaring, glaring in my face
He say smile. Feeling good, collar high
hand on hip, smile sly, . . . there—POP!

MOMMA 1956

She talking on the phone
Hot comb heating on the stove
Sister gets out the Brownie
She laughed and cover her face

                            close-up, click

Lips painted a wild red
Part in an inviting smile
Fresh tinted jet black hair
Glistens as she tosses her head

Mouth wide, teary eyed laughing
At the lewd jokes of admiring men
Men dressed in loose cut suits

Small brimmed hats and shining shoes

Change jingling in their pockets
As they wait patiently, for her
Etta James's cool cuts through the heat
Nat grins out from the little round screen

Cain't be worried 'bout no bomb shelters
Air Raid Drills ain't gone save nobody
Folks sitting in where they not wanted
Boycotting, folks going to court, life's too short

She fans her hand at the TV
Crosses her leg, sucks on her cigarette
Switches to an interview with Dorothy Dandridge
Smiling, she sits back sipping her beer

click . . . click . . . click

DAUGHTER 1972

ungrown when 12th street went
smelled the fire, felt the flame
saw juice from Stein's
pickle barrel run down sidewalks

black boys wearing blue jeans
bent over with booty
scrambled amidst scattered glass
as shot-guns screeched from scout cars

clickclickclickfrontpage

young girls in short skirts
herded into wagons
saw wide-eyed wearied elders
point fingers screaming wait

Aunt Willie Mae
Audrey Tolliver | *United States*

You know they tell
She's that way
Never seen a man
Go in
or out
they say

And you were fully aware of their fence rituals
Where your idiosyncrasies were discussed daily

But you held your secrets closely to your bosom
No one knows about your turpentine cocktails
Entanglement with hangers in dim lit backrooms

Because that Tuskegee boy didn't mind pounding your pelvis
But couldn't take you home to his posh parents
you didn't beat the brown bag

Your people had paid prettily for your sheepskin
hoped that you would return home married well
You knew that they would never abide your bastards

You sat and waited for a suitable suitor and longed for labor

You offered sweets to the neighbor's children
Until they sheltered them from your strangeness
You only wanted to stroke their soft skin, touch their tenderness

Finally you mothered your brother's seeds

fed them fully
clothed them carefully
doted on them diligently

One day they were finished

Lured from you by the largeness and looseness of Bronzeville and Watts
Taken from you by The City of New Orleans and the Sunset

And you found yourself fifty-odd and fruitless

Your need to nurture, your capacity to comfort had not dried up

And one ordinary day faced with the magnitude of your barrenness
You burst onto the boulevard

Weeping, Weeping, Weeping

Where are my babies? Where are my babies? Where are my babies?

And you died your first death, all because you didn't deliver

Phyllis
Jacqueline Johnson | *United States*

It's strange
I know exactly what killed phyllis hyman
constant yearning for love deeply felt,
grounded with tenderness,
real is what she craved.

Bound and caught
like a slave
to a manic nightmare,
she learned to sing her way out of
and through blues.

Bearing a body too large to hold.
A body too large to hold up.
Big, diva lady,
a woman so beautiful
how could she live on
part time,
half time,
in-between,
co-wife,
liaison,
piece-meal
kinda' love?

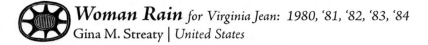

Woman Rain for *Virginia Jean: 1980, '81, '82, '83, '84*
Gina M. Streaty | *United States*

I suck air
through blood.
Mama's phone begs to ring.
Doorbell dozes
in frenzied space
vicious, violent
as flood waters.

He swells, surges.
Speaks thunder
while I crouch,
crawl to the rhythm
of fists on flesh.

Whimpers.
Moans.
Tears don't help.

I
can't
please him
      Don't!
sleep
      Won't!
eat.

Make believe
his mind fingers
visions of me
(soft / damp / black / scar-less)
as he
molests mine,
bruises it

to match my limbs.
I'm whole.

When he sleeps,
I wander, ghost my house,
choke down curdled chunks of time,
calm the part of him in my womb?
become my blues.

Crescent Moons of Christ

Porchia Moore | *United States*

...And Adam said, This is now bone of my bones, and fleshof my flesh: she shall be called ...

—Genesis 2:23

Fish-eyed and beautiful
like Kali, he whispers
with his warm, salty tongue
against my forehead,
he traces the cross
of two crescent moons.
He explores my vulva,
the overlapping space
between the cross,—
I am crucified over and over again.

Finished
Ai | United States

You force me to touch
the black, rubber flaps
of the garbage disposal
that is open like a mouth saying, ah.
You tell me it's the last thing I'll feel
before I go numb.
Is it my screaming that finally stops you,
or is it the fear
that even you are too near the edge
of this Niagara to come back from?
You jerk my hand out
and give me just enough room
to stagger around you.
I lean against the refrigerator,
not looking at you, or anything,
just staring at a space which you no longer inhabit,
that you've abandoned completely now
to footsteps receding
to the next feeding station,
where a woman will be eaten alive
after cocktails at five.
The flowers and chocolates, the kisses,
the swings and near misses of new love
will confuse her,
until you start to abuse her,
verbally at first.
As if trying to quench a thirst,
you'll drink her
in small outbursts of rage
then you'll whip out your semiautomatic,
make her undress, or to listen to hours
of radio static as torture
for being amazed that the man of her dreams
is a nightmare, who only seems happy
when he's making her suffer.

The first time you hit me,
I left you, remember?
It was December. An icy rain was falling
and it froze on the roads,
so that driving was unsafe, but not as unsafe
as staying with you.
I ran outside in my nightgown,
while you yelled at me to come back.
When you came after me,
I was locked in the car.
You smashed the window with a crowbar,
but I drove off anyway.
I was back the next day
and we were on the bare mattress
because you'd ripped up the sheets,
saying you'd teach me a lesson.
You wouldn't speak except
to tell me I needed discipline,
needed training in fine art
of remaining still
when your fist slammed into my jaw.
You taught me how ropes could be tied
so I'd strangle myself,
how pressure could be applied to old wounds
until I cried for mercy,
until tonight, when those years
of our double exposure end
with shot after shot.

How strange it is to be unafraid.
When the police come,
I'm sitting at the table,
the cup of coffee
that I am unable to drink
as cold as your body.
I shot him, I say, he beat me.
I do not tell them how the emancipation from pain
leaves nothing in its place.

Vacant Apartment, Austin, TX 1992
Amanda Johnston | *United States*

I stared over his shoulder,
counted ceiling tiles between humps,
prayed he'd find
what he was digging for.

I wanted him to leave
with more than rug burns.
I wanted him to take me with him.

After the blood dried
the doctor said he left
me with more than he brought.

I named it boy.
I never saw his face,
but I see him,
black as charcoal,
smoldering
in my dreams.

Octopus
Porchia Moore | *United States*

It was not until the tentacles
were around my neck and the
cups pressed my pipes and the
weight of his black evil

inked across my body in the bed
we had called Ours

that I heard myself such a long time
ago

say that I would never allow
a man to hit me

Never
without a fight

Hands
Riua Akinshegun | *United States*

Hands of all colors, yet no colors
Hands of all sizes, yet no sizes
It's in the tone, the reach
The smell, the texture
Tone of command
An octopus reach
Predator's smell
The texture of rough

Move in secrecy, behind closed doors
Crooked index finger points
Poking at scared spots
Digging, planting
"What goes on in this house
stays in this house"

Reducing all ten commandments into
Thou Shalt Not
Thou Shalt Not
Thou Shalt Not
Tell....

To a Jamaican Survivor with Love
Kamilah Moon | *United States*

You contain mettle
his gun-toting soul lacks—
his acid does not tarnish
your sheen.

His yellowed flesh plunged
into your bronze body,
raided your temple.
His sin is not your cross—
your heart beats sacred still.

You, a sturdy-petaled bloom
beneath howling sky,
weathering this hurricane.
Find the eye, begin to heal.
Fluff your hair back into place.
Stand on sinewy legs and walk, sister—
do not let this cripple you.

Seek the sun,
sweet daughter of Maroons—
until dragged into the depths
by God's blue, wet fingers,
the memory stops breathing.

Bless your reflection.
Float on currents
back to yourself,
back to peace,
back to the flavor of curried goat dancing
on your tongue.

Blackberry Wine
Nagueyalti Warren | *United States*

Dark, it is dark where fat Walley stands
starkly against artificial night.
Martha moves backward,
trips over the hay—
Jim, Tom, Herman,
Bill White's boys,
hold her motionless.

Down fat Walley comes
comes,
his alabaster fingers clutch
her blackberry breast,
comes
pork-smelling breath heaved in her
flaring nostrils,
comes
shooting his white-lightning into
unlit corners of her self.

Someone calls,
Bill White's boys let go.
Run.
Fat Walley is coming.
Martha doesn't weep;
she doesn't moan.
Her arms rise above her head,
hands finger a pitch fork,
lift it up
and bring it down

through fat Walley's red neck.
Fat Walley rolls away.
Martha gazes on a deep red sea
that seeps into the hay,
opens the barn door walks—
blackberry wine staining her dress—
into the Indian summer sun.

On the Turning Up of Unidentified Black Female Corpses

Toi Derricotte | *United States*

Mowing his three acres with a tractor,
a man notices something ahead—a mannequin—
he thinks someone threw it from a car. Closer
he sees it is the body of a black woman.

The medics come and turn her with pitchforks.
Her gaze shoots past him to nothing. Nothing
is explained. How many black women
have been turned up to stare at us blankly,

in weedy fields, off highways,
pushed out in plastic bags,
shot, knifed, unclothed partially, raped,
their wounds sealed with a powdery crust.

Last week on TV, a gruesome face, eyes bloated shut.
No one will say, "She looks like she's sleeping," ropes
of blue-black slashes at the mouth. Does anybody
know this woman? Will anyone come forth? Silence

like a backwave rushes into that field
where, just the week before, four other black girls
had been found. The gritty image hangs in the air
just a few seconds, but it strikes me,

a black woman, there is a question being asked
about my life. How can I
protect myself? Even if I lock my doors,
walk only in the light, someone wants me dead.

Childless, An Abridged Blues

Cherryl Floyd-Miller | *United States*

Man who took my children always said he never would.
Say the man who took my children always said he never
would.
But a man will say a thousand things when the
gimme-some is good.

A yippee-dog was howling when he laid me on my back
Oh a yippee-dog was howling when he spread me on my
back.
Felt the pillows wheeze and give, knocked the bed
right off its slats.

My spine stretched like a ladder from my tailbone to
my neck
My little spine rung like a ladder; he climbed my
tailbone to my neck
If I was a car that he could drive, we'd veer off the
road and wreck.

First time he was late for dinner, called me nicely on
the phone.
First time, late-for-supper sinner, called me nicely
on the phone.
When I called him back at midnight, I heard a hussy
voice just groan.

Packed my bags and quit that man, took my kids and
headed South.
Glad ragged, I went and quit that man, took my kids
and headed South.
By then I couldn't believe a word that came out his
no-good mouth.

He took the kids for early Christmas. Said he'd see me
when they got back.
Drove down to get them for Christmas. Grinned his
words, molasses black.
Two weeks late, my temper gone, police cars couldn't

hold me back.

Man sued me for custody, ran me low-down, dragged my
name.
That fool sued me for custody, low-down numnuts
dragged my name.
Brought that groaning girl to testify. Hussy didn't
have no shame.

People tried to feed me Jesus cause they thought I
wanted to die.
Came all holy and prestigious cause they thought that
I might die.
Told me saints were made to suffer, but they couldn't
tell me why.

When a man can take your children after saying that he
won't,
When his hands can snatch your children while his
mouth says he won't,
Scrawl his words in blood with a butcher knife. Might
be childless if you don't.

Don't get killed on your kitchen floor
Pam Ward | United States

He knocked me down so hard
I slid from my kitchen floor
to the living room rug
No man had ever done that.
I remember getting back up
and walking straight
to the butcher block
where I kept my knives.
I stared at them a long time
two steely rows
of neat metal points
to dice or to
dislocate textures.
Yes, I stared there
a long time
He saw me look too
and I saw the look on his face
ready to leap
if I got bold enough
to whip one out.
Well, the truth was I couldn't.
Couldn't bare the thought
of missing
and him slitting my throat
with one swift jab
like granddad did to chickens.
Couldn't bare the horror
of my children finding their mother
on the floor in a pool of red
like packaged meat
this vision their anguish
too awful to stand.
But I stood there

and watched each knife.
I wondered which one
would work best
could almost feel
the wood in hand
could picture fingers
skim the tip
how good it'd feel
to take him down
to take apart
like frozen skin
could almost taste
and almost did
but thought
what if...
I missed him?
What if I missed and he did me
and I end up
on floor again
my arm wrenched back
my throat exposed
a bone popped out
and I'd look up like chickens do
before the ax
like deer
before the highbeams.
Yes I'd stare up at his poised fist
that knife mid-thrust
I'd hear my mouth beg
"Please don't, wait
No, please not yet.
"Please let me raise my children."
Yes, this whole scene
played in my skull
I stood there still
before those blades
my rage thawed out

I changed my mind.
But just in case
I grabbed this pen.
I hid it
so if worst came worst
and he did try
he wouldn't suspect
that this inky blue tip
could be used as a weapon.
That this pen
that this ballpoint
was really my sword
my answer
my last word
my one final thrust
or maybe
to just write this down.

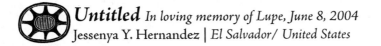

Untitled *In loving memory of Lupe, June 8, 2004*
Jessenya Y. Hernandez | *El Salvador/ United States*

Your husband
kisses your body
his tears
shower you
while you lay
in the hospital bed

I wonder
does he remember
you alive
instead of kisses
insults gushed from his mouth
his fists pounded your skin
furniture broke
when he threw you
and you landed
on it

I try to shove away those memories
bury them so they won't haunt me
instead
I think about Mexico
the times you and I shared

like when you bragged to your neighbors
that your cousin came from *el norte*
you let me sleep
in your bed
your sister Berta nagged you
to turn off the lights
but you stuck your foot out
wiggled your toe
pretending to say

dejanos jugar (let us play)

or later that week
you took me on the longest walk
I thought I'd ever been on

to play ball at La Unidad
a man on a
Motorcycle scared me
You told me not to pay attention
assured me I was safe

Later we walked under a tree
dripping with venomous insects
you pushed me aside
didn't want me to get hurt

but these memories fade
because I remember
the look of hurt
in you eyes
when you told me
at Bere's first communion
that he didn't let you eat
he called you a fat pig
so your sons waited till he was gone
to bring you food
assured you
you were no pig

Because I picture
the bumps on your head
the slaps on your face
from all the times
he came home too drunk
        he always came home too drunk
Because I remember the time

when I found his
brother
drunk
pointing a finger at you
screaming
fuck you
LUPE
fuck you

and I remember
my promise to you
when you told me
even the neighbors
heard him beat you
I promised I would help you
once I graduate from law school I'll help you
and now it's too late

the only thing I can do now
is thank God
you wont be
hit
punched
slapped
spit on
humiliated
dehumanized

in heaven

Sunday in the ER *for L.W.*
Gina M. Streaty | *United States*

With the butt of a handgun,
she said her brother beat her
one hundred times or more.
A twenty-dollar argument with their mama
lifted her left eye like jelly from its socket.
Subdural hematoma, one-hundred-sixty-four stitches
in her head, face; one hundred-fifty
in her hands
trying to protect myself.
CT of her abdomen, X-ray both arms,
fractured bones, too many to count.
Social worker photographs cuts, gashes.
Said he'd take more pictures after bruises emerge
because they'll darken in time.
She cries, bleeds on the edge of a stretcher
in front of two small children
who carry her blood on *Phat Farm* shirts and *Fubu* jackets.
Little black sneakers trail red footprints on white, waxed floors.
Her sister brings her Bojangles that she can't eat.
A nurses tells them, she must first drink dye.
Will it hurt me?
She screams as they stretch her swollen hand,
move her twisted fingers back and forth.
She moans, calls *Jesus* as needles puncture her skin,
penetrate pulpy raw flesh.
A sterile voice asks, "Why'd your brother do this to you?"
Twenty Dollars. Don't matter no how.
His ass is going to jail.
The answer makes no sense
to the doctor or me.
Time steps from wall clocks.
Blue lights stroke darkness.
Inside the ER fried chicken gets cold.

As mother-prayers parade
outside the door,
L.W. slips away.
Tears fall like rain tonight.
Blackened eyes seal in death-sleep.
Cops search the wet streets for Jr.

Ode to my bruises

Jessenya Y. Hernandez | *El Salvador/United States*

As a child I hated bruises
Thought they showed my clumsiness
But the bruises you leave
On my skin
Remind me of your clumsiness
The alleged explanation for every time
You allow your fist to slip
Again
And
Again
And
Again
On my arms
My thighs
My legs
My breasts

I find a new meaning for my bruises
I even take pictures of them and staple them
On my wall next to the phone
I like how they look

When you call me
My emotions betray me
I am tempted to stay on the phone
And listen to your excuses
But my bruises yell warnings
They forbid me from forgiving you
They make me hang up the phone

I still search for my self worth
I remain somewhat ashamed
Along with my blood vessels
You rupture my trust in men

But my bruises
They lift me off the floor
They push me to move on

I am fond of my bruises
They are my x-ray vision
They don't allow my eyelids to shut out your false claims to change
They remind me your empty promises are irrelevant

Ode to my bruises
Who will
Never
Ever
Permit you
To strike me
Again

Womanslaughter
Pat Parker | *United States*

It doesn't hurt as much now
the thought of you dead
doesn't rip at my innards,
leaves no holes to suck rage.
Thoughts of the four
daughters of Buster Cooks,
children, survivors
of Texas Hell, survivors
of soul-searing poverty,
survivors of small-town
mentality, survivors,
now three
doesn't hurt as much.

I. An Act

I used to be fearful
of phone calls in the night—
never in the day.
Death, like the vampire,
fears the sun
never in the day.

"Hello, Patty."
"Hey, big sister
what's happening?
How's the kids?"
"Patty, Jonesy shot Shirley.
She didn't make it."

Hello, Hello Death
Don't you know it's daytime?
The sun is much too bright today.

Hello, Hello Death
you made a mistake
came here too soon, again.
Five months, Death,
my sisters and I just met
in celebration of you.
We came, the four strong
daughters of Buster Cooks,
and buried him.
We came, the four strong
daughters of Buster Cooks,
and took care of his widow.
We came, the four strong
daughters of Buster Cooks,
and shook hands with his friends.
We came, the four strong
daughters of Buster Cooks,
and picked the right flowers.
We came, the four strong
daughters of Buster Cooks,
walked tall and celebrated you.
We came, his four strong daughters,
and notified insurance companies
arranged social security payments
gathered the sum of his life.

"We must be strong for mother."
She was the third daughter of Buster Cooks.
I am the fourth.
And in his death we met.
The four years that separated us—gone.
And we talked.
She would divorce the quiet man.
Go back to school—begin again.
Together we would be strong
and take care of Buster's widow.
The poet returned to the family.

The fourth daughter came home.

Hello, Hello Death
What's this you say to me?
Now there are three.
We came, the three sisters
of Shirley Jones,
and took care of her mother.
We picked the right flowers
contacted insurance companies
arranged social security payments
and cremated her.
We came, the three sisters
of Shirley Jones.
We were not strong.
"It is good," they said,
"that Buster is dead.
He would surely kill
the quiet man."

II. Justice

There was a quiet man
he married a quiet wife
together they lived
a quiet life.

Not so, not so
her sisters said,
the truth comes out
as she lies dead.
He beat her.
He accused her
of awful things
and he beat her.
One day she left.

"Hello, Hello Police
I am a woman
and I am afraid.
My husband means to kill me."

She went to her sister's house
she, too, was a woman alone.
The quiet man came and beat her.
Both women were afraid.

"Hello, Hello Police
I am a woman
and I am afraid.
My husband means to kill me."

The four strong daughters
of Buster Cooks
came to bury him
the third one carried a gun.
"Why do you have a gun?"
"For protection—just in case."
"Can you shoot it?"
"Yes, I have learned well."

"Hello, Hello Police
I am a woman alone
and I am afraid.
My husband means to kill me."

"Lady, there's nothing we can do
until he tries to hurt you.
Go to the judge and he will decree
That your husband leaves you be."
She found an apartment
with a friend.
She would begin
a new life again.

Interlocutory Divorce Decree in hand,
the end of the quiet man.
He came to her home
and he beat her.
Both women were afraid.

"Hello, Hello Police
I am a woman alone
and I am afraid.
My ex-husband means to kill me."

"Fear not, lady,
he will be sought."
It was too late
when he was caught.
One day a quiet man
shot his quiet wife
three times in the back.
He shot her friend as well.
His wife died.

The three sisters
of Shirley Jones
came to cremate her.
They were not strong.

III. Somebody's Trial

"It is good," they said,
"that Buster is dead.
He would surely kill
the quiet man."
I was not at the trial.
I was not needed to testify.
She slept with other men, he said.
No, said her friends.
No, said her sisters.

That is a lie.
She was Black.
You are white.
Why were you there?
We were friends, she said.
I was helping her move
the furniture the divorce court
had given to her.
Were you alone? they asked.
No, two men came with us.
They were gone with a load.
She slept with women, he said.
No, said her sisters.
No, said her friends.
We were only friends.
That is a lie.
You lived with this woman?
Yes, said her friend.
You slept in the same bed?
Yes, said her friend.
Were you lovers?
No, said her friend.
But you slept in the same bed?
Yes, said her friend.

What shall be done with this man?
Is it a murder of the first degree?
No, said the men,
it is a crime of passion.
He was angry.

Is it a murder of the second degree?
Yes, said the men,
but we will not call it that.
We must think of his record.
We will call it manslaughter.
The sentence is the same.

What will we do with this man?
His boss, a white man, came.
This is a quiet Black man, he said.
He works well for me.
The men sent the quiet
Black man to jail.
He went to work in the day.
He went to jail and slept at night.
In one year, he went home.

IV. Womanslaughter

"It is good," they said,
"that Buster is dead.
He would surely kill
the quiet man."

Sister, I do not understand.
I rage and do not understand.
In Texas, he would be freed.
One Black kills another
One less Black for Texas.
But this is not Texas.
This is California.
The City of Angels.
Was his crime so slight?
George Jackson served
years for robbery.
Eldridge Cleaver served
years for rape.
I know of a man in Texas
who is serving forty years
for possession of marijuana.
Was his crime so slight?
What was his crime?
He only killed his wife.
But a divorce I say.

Not final, they say.
Her things were his,
including her life.
Men cannot rape their wives.
Men cannot kill their wives.
They passion them to death.
The three sisters
of Shirley Jones
came and cremated her
and they were not strong.
Hear me now—
it is almost three years
and I am again strong.

I have gained many sisters.
And if one is beaten,
or raped, or killed,
I will not come in mourning black.
I will not pick the right flowers.
I will not celebrate her death
and it will matter not
if she's Black or white
if she loves women or men.
I will come with my many sisters
and decorate the streets
with the innards of those
brothers in womenslaughter.
No more can I dull my rage
in alcohol and deference
to men's courts.
I will come to my sisters,
not dutiful.
I will come strong.

Unknuckled
Cherryl Floyd-Miller | *United States*

I am not at the busted white plaster,
at his fist print in a broken wall.

I am not sitting vigil
for his amnesiac trigger finger,
not pressing fast tears
against a cold rifle barrel.

He is not gazing at his hands
as if they belong
to some other man.

He is not saying, "Someone's
gonna die tonight,"
and leaving.

He is not at an Elkhart hotel
with the second woman
on the night I discover
the first.

We are not debating
how she got our number.

On the days he makes it
for dinner, there is not a tidy table
where I host his chatter
with our children.

I am not the steam from skillet cabbage,
not the cast iron pan resting
on the stove's black eye.

We are not days deep in silence.

We are not entering
the months of absence,

abstinence.

We are not sleeping
back to back.

We have not parted our lives.

We are at an altar, promising
to be token and fire.

A man with a legal Bible
and an Indiana love edict
is asking us
if we will—until,

and we are saying yes,
for life.

One Thanksgiving Day
Pat Parker | United States

Priscilla Ford
got into her
Lincoln Continental
drove to Virginia Street
in downtown Reno
and ran over thirty people.
Six of them died.

. . .Priscilla Ford said yes
I drove my car
into the whiteness
of Nevada streets
she would say nothing more
and the state of Nevada
was frightened.
If Priscilla Ford could do it
who else?
How many Black faces
that emptied garbage
waited tables
bagged groceries
wrapped presents
were capable?

Rape

Jayne Cortez | *United States*

What was Inez supposed to do for
the man who declared war on her body
the man who carved a combat zone between her
breasts
Was she supposed to lick crabs from his hairy ass
kiss every pimple on his butt
blow hot breath on his big toe
draw back the corners of her vagina and
hee haw like a California burro

This being war time for Inez
she stood facing the knife
the insults and
her own smell drying on the penis of
the man who raped her

She stood with a rifle in her hand
doing what a defense department will do in times of
war
And when the man started grunting and panting and
wobbling forward like
a giant hog
She pumped lead into his three hundred pounds of
shaking flesh
Sent it flying to the Virgin of Guadalupe
then celebrated day of the dead rapist punk
and just what the fuck else was she supposed to do?

And what was Joanne supposed to do for
the man who declared war on her life
Was she supposed to tongue his encrusted
toilet stool lips
suck the numbers off of his tin badge

choke on his clap trap balls
squeeze on his nub of rotten maggots and
sing god bless america thank you for fucking my life
away

This being wartime for Joanne
she did what a defense department will do in times of
war
and when the piss drinking   shit sniffling guard said
I'm gonna make you wish you were dead black bitch
come here
Joanne came down with an ice pick in
the swat freak motherfucker's chest
yes in the fat neck of that racist policeman
Joanne did the dance of the ice picks and once again
from coast to coast
house to house
we celebrated day of the dead rapist punk
and just what the fuck else were we suppose to do

RELATIONSHIPS

Love and Sexual

Ruendo rutiri guoya
Love has no fear

—Gikuyu proverb

*By being sexually independent of men, lesbians, by their very existence,
call into question society's definition of woman at its deepest level.*
—Barbara Christian, from *Black Feminist Criticism*

Lines to an Old Dress
Mary Eliza Tucker Lambert | *United States*

ALAS! the time has come, old dress,
When you and I must part;
To say adieu, my valued friend,
Is tearing heart from heart.

Long years have passed since thou wert new,
Long years of war and crime;
But sight of thee to memory brings
The olden golden time.

I'd braid my silken tresses smooth;
Then cast thee o'er my form,
And press my hand upon my heart,
To quell tumultuous storm.

For well I know whose eye would beam
To see me thus arrayed;
'Twas one whose gentle tender glance,
His love for me betrayed.

Old dress, dost thou remember well
That beauteous moon-light night,
When the hoped-for truth o'erwhelmed my heart,
With a perfect blaze of light?

How he clasped us to his heart, old dress,
And he vowed beneath the stars,
That naught in heaven could us divide—
'Twas registered by Mars.

Ah, the Gods but mocked us then, old dress,
With a short, sweet dream of bliss,
That vanished, alas! from our mortal sight,

Like the dew at the sun's warm kiss.

In but a short year from then, old dress,
That sudden gleam of light
Had passed away, and left me naught,
But the darkness of midnight.

For Mars laughed at our arrogance,
And he hurled his mighty dart,
And my love lies in the battle-field,
And broken is my heart.

Ah, I cannot give thee up, old dress,
For thy threads are links of chain,
That bind my memory to the past—
To long gone joys and pain.

I Want To Die While You Love Me

Georgia Douglas Johnson | *United States*

I want to die while you love me,
While yet you hold me fair,
While laughter lies upon my lips
And lights are in my hair.

I want to die while you love me.
I could not bear to see,
The glory of this perfect day,
Grow dim—or cease to be.

I want to die while you love me.
Oh! who would care to live
Till love has nothing more to ask,
And nothing more to give.

I want to die while you love me,
And bear to that still bed
Your kisses, turbulent, unspent,
To warm me when I'm dead.

Touché
Jessie Fauset | *United States*

Dear, when we sit in that high, placid room,
"Loving" and "doving" as all lovers do,
Laughing and leaning so close in the gloom,—

What is the change that creeps sharp over you?
Just as you raise your fine hand to my hair,
Bringing that glance of mixed wonder and rue?

"Black hair," you murmur, "so lustrous and rare,
Beautiful too, like a raven's smooth wing;
Surely no gold locks were ever more fair."

Why do you say every night that same thing?
Turning your mind to some old constant theme,
Half meditating and half murmuring?

Tell me, that girl of your young manhood's dream,
Her you loved first in that dim long ago—
Had she blue eyes? Did her hair goldly gleam?

Does she come back to you softly and slow,
Stepping wraith-wise from the depths of the past?
Quickened and fired by the warmth of our glow?

There I've divined it! My wit holds you fast.
Nay, no excuses; 'tis little I care.
I knew a lad in my own girlhood's past,—
Blue eyes he had and such waving gold hair!

Rainy Season Love Song
Gladys May Casely Hayford | *Sierra Leone*

Out of the tense awed darkness, my Frangepani comes;
Whilst the blades of Heaven flash round her, and the
    roll of thunder drums
My young heart leaps and dances, with exquisite joy
    and pain,
As storms within and storms without I meet my love in
    the rain.

'The rain is in love with you darling; it's kissing you
    everywhere,
Rain pattering over your small brown feet, rain in your
    curly hair;
Rain in the vale that your twin breasts make, as in
    delicate mounds they rise,
I hope there is rain in your heart, Frangepani, as rain
    half fills your eyes.'

Into my hands she cometh, and the lightning of my
    desire
Flashes and leaps about her, more subtle than Heaven's
    fire;
'The lightning's in love with you darling; it is loving
    you so much
That its warm electricity in you pulses wherever I may
    touch.
When I kiss your lips and your eyes, and your hands
    like twin flowers apart,
I know there is lightning, Frangepani, deep in the
    depths of your heart.'

The thunder rumbles about us, and I feel its triumphant
    note
As your warm arms steal around me; and I kiss your

dusky throat;
'The thunder's in love with you darling. It hides its
    power in your breast.
And I feel it stealing o'er me as I lie in your arms at
    rest.
I sometimes wonder, beloved, when I drink from life's
    proffered bowl,
Whether there's thunder hidden in the innermost parts
    of your soul.'

Out of my arms she stealeth; and I am left alone with
    the night,
Void of all sounds save peace, the first faint glimmer
    of light.

Into the quiet, hushed stillness my Frangepani goes.
Is there peace within like the peace without? Only the
    darkness knows.

The Serving Girl
Gladys May Casely Hayford | *Sierra Leone*

The calabash wherein she served my food
Was smooth and polished as sandalwood;
Fish, as white as the foam of the sea,
Peppered, and golden fried for me.
She brought palm wine that carelessly slips
From the sleeping palm tree's honeyed lips.
But who can guess, or even surmise,
The countless things she served with her eyes?

To a Young Wife
Georgia Douglas Johnson | *United States*

I was a fool to dream that you
Might cross the bridge of years
From your soft springtime to my side.
Where autumn shade appears.

I am sedate while you are wild,
Elusive like a sprite;
You dance into the sunny morn
While I approach the night.

I was a fool—the dream is done;
I know it cannot be.
Return and live those burning years . . .
And then, come back to me!

Hunger
Kathleen Tankersley Young | *United States*

Your body is a dark wine
I lift to these trembling lips of mine.

Your body is a harsh dark bread
Broken that my hunger at last be fed.

At the end, this dreaming fantasy
Shall let my body and soul go free.

This Morning
Kristina Rungano | *Zimbabwe*

This morning I visited the place where we lay
like animals
O pride be forgotten
And how the moon bathed our savage nudity in purity
And your hands touched mine in a silken caress
And our beings were cleansed as though by wine.
Then you stroked my breast
And through love I shed the tears of my womb
O sweet fluid spilled in the name of love
O love
O sweet of mine existence
Your sigh of content as your lips touched my soul
O joy shared by the wilderness
O gentle breeze
O fireflies that hovered over our nest in protective harmony
How I yearn
I feel you here again with me.

To E.J.J.
Ethel M. Caution | *United States*

Sparkling eyes of diamond jet;
Wilful hair a-curling yet;
Rounded cheeks and lips well set—
Lips a-smiling, smiling yet;
Slender fingers quick to do
Gracious things for me and you;
Feet that never weary grow
Lightening of another's woe;
Heart a-bubbling o'er with love
From the Fountain-head above;
Life all laughter, words of cheer
Echoing down and down the year;
Loved her well when first we met,
And I love her, love her yet.

Acceptance
Donika Ross | *United States*

He is no surprise, a sweaty
palm muzzling me, a forearm embracing
my neck in anticipation. I am too resigned to scream,
have already been erased this way. We are a pathetic
fiction—I a mass of silence;
he a sharp toothed thing, a reoccurrence.
I unhemmed another once, became a hand
clamped against her nape, a bruising
at her back until she accepted the uselessness
of sound. She remained, blank and discarded, trickled deep
red from the corner of her smile.
We are the same, this thing with claws pulping my
memory, and I am beautiful now,
a rising in the dirt.

My Black Triangle
Grace Nichols | *Guyana/England*

My black triangle
sandwiched between the geography of my thighs

is a bermuda
of tiny atoms
forever seizing
and releasing
the world

My black triangle
is so rich
that it flows over
on to the dry crotch
of the world

My black triangle
is black light
sitting on the threshold
of the world

overlooking my deep-pink
probabilities

and though
it spares a thought
for history
my black triangle
has spread beyond his story
beyond the dry fears of parch-ri-archy

spreading and growing
trusting and flowing
my black triangle
carries the seal of approval
of my deepest self

Bougainvillea Ringplay
Marion Bethel | *Bahamas*

This me right here inside the ring
in March April May springing
from concrete tar and parading
passion purple ungoldly colors waving
cores of pink cream orange showing
my motion to you unsolicited
my months of dry rain sighing.

Ring center I come to you straight
shaping a vison beyond sugar in a plum
winding my waist tight in your face
clinging to a fence without shame
mounting it from rock and gravel
unhedged hips I raise
arching my back all over your wall.

This me now right here outside the ring
even in June July August fixing
to catch the color of your dream playing
biggety with your emotion working
up myself around edges of islands jumping
up even when poincianas sweat womanblood unconsoled
in full sea green I keep coming.

Back in the ring I aint shiftin for no one
under the shade of a dilly tree limboing
up the womantoungue and guinep climbing
wrapping my arms around a cerosee vine
rushing to the call of a lonely conch shell
fixed by a tongue-tied drum
we move ina circle shaking, flying, rising.

After the Storms
Delana Dameron | *United States*

We make music—
a higher frequency than those nights
we used to make love. Sharp soprano
aria of early morning, each discord is testimony
to our violations.

While the children lie
suspended in fitful sleep, forced to hear
our screams, products of this union
with eyes of yours;
hair curls at temple like mine—

Yes, while the children wonder
our secrets in their beds, conjure up
stories to our fighting,

We have the nights ahead, in bed we share,
where pillows barricade under blankets.

You have my hair in your hands,
caught in strangulation turbulence.

I have your drying skin
under my fingernails, flesh
sanguine and dying like faith.

We have this bedroom,
our thoughts of communion
as blurred as our marriage vows.

We have the scent of others
imbedded in our pores, mingled with the eternal
ambiguity of *I love you.*

Dead

Javacia Harris | *United States*

The two men I love most want me dead

He wants to behead my name
Set fire to my new favorite hobby
Of candle making
Melt down wax-coated pots
To mold chicken casseroles

And you

You make all things news
You are always green
Because when you envy it is not sin
You want me to die to self
Because you won't even share me with me

Sometimes I want to call you
Beg you to hide yourself in my bones
Beg you to come to my house
Because I hate what your roommates
Have done to yours

But sometimes I fantasize
About calling you by another name

But how can I be angry
I often cursed the clumsy syllables of my name
Tripping off Anglo and African tongues
And secretly I yearned to feed him until he was full
And love you until I was lost

Faded Roses
Afua Cooper | *Canada*

The roses you bought me on that Saturday evening
in summer, have now turned a dull brown in the vase
yet, I refuse to throw them out
these faded roses . . .
Because every time I see them I remember
with sharp precision every second we spent together
last summer
the seduction of a glance
the touching of fingertips
the tip of pink tongue on soft-hard brown nipples
the way you move under me
the way you move on top of me
and the way you nibble at me greedily
it seemed we spent the summer rediscovering
the wonders of love and the delight
Then one evening you had to leave
and you gave me red roses
"to honor our passion" you said
the passion that surges in me now
as I see the faded roses
and remember you

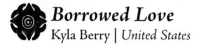

Borrowed Love
Kyla Berry | *United States*

because I look for him in the
crevices of rainbows, the shadows of stars

the underside of the sun &
the dirt in the fingernail moon

I look for him because I borrowed love from him
I asked and he gave

now I've got a funny feeling
in my bones telling me

I've looked for him through
a shard of pink glass &

if I move it thisaway
I'll surely get cut

I will always look for you
in the crannies of my pale heart

my heart that quickens like the
inverted echo of your voice

forever-whispering
forgiveness.

Uncivil
Venus Thrash | *United States*

I am wearing a white tux with tails,
or a baby blue one with a ruffly shirt,
or decked out in classic black, or coolly
clad in a pearl-white daishiki embroidered
in gold silk, or my favorite pair of holy blue
jeans & a white tee shirt that says *I? Pussy*,
or the green one with the velvet black fist
afro pick raised in the air, & you're not
wearing a white dress at all but a wispy
wraparound, strawberry-red that hugs
you warm & tight around the waist, cut
low at the small of your back, showing off
peek-a-boo cleavage & legs with no quit,
& our folks are there with tissue & hankies,
boo-hoo crying the way parents do at weddings,
& I won't be waiting for you at the end
of any aisle, but we will walk together,
side by side, arm in arm, our wrists tied
& bound with sheer purple scarves,
& we will be the only ones giving us away
under a moonlit sky spilling over in stars,
& there will be no wedding march
on the Steinway but Nina Simone
demanding *Be My Husband & I'll Be
Your Wife* or Aretha Franklin's luscious
You Make Me Feel Like a Natural Woman,
& we won't exchange vows or rings
but deep wet kisses & lingering hugs,
& there won't be a parchment certificate
stamped with any State's approval confirming
we're married or in love, but we will jump
over a brand new straw broom, we will
light candles & pour red wine into the soil

where our ancestors sleep, we will wash
& anoint each other's hair with frankincense
& myrrh, & the women will unwind butter-yellow
kangas from their hair & toss them upon
the ground before us to cushion our feet.

The Run Down

Linda Susan | *United States*

"How done is gone?"
                    —Rita Dove

1.

Her run down moccasins
with the backs bent flip-flop
from the bedroom to the bathroom
to the living room where two suitcases
hold her part of the three thousand six
hundred some odd days of their marriage.
Time is running down, and she thinks
about his three black suits, the line
of pin stripe, navy and charcoal gray
all weather-worsted wools, tropical
tan and seersucker summer suits,
double and single breasted blazers
with golden fleece buttons. Why
does a man need three black suits?

2.

And all those ties: regimental stripes,
muted somber solids, a few pale polka
dots, nothing whimsical dangling
from the carousel. That first year
she brought in a paisley was the first
time she tasted malice running
down and through the salty sting
of his words. She counts seventeen
pairs of shoes, lined up, toes forward,
facing her, colors running from coal
to kangaroo: wing tip, cap toe, tasseled
loafer, biscuit toe, cordovan, split toe,
even a pair of jodhpur boots, spit-shined
and creased where his foot bends.

3.

Running down the month's worth of white
and sky blue button down collared shirts
that line his wardrobe shelf, she memorizes
the crisp stiff smell of laundry starch. She
takes a moment to run her hand down
to the drawer in the high boy where his V-
neck cotton undershirts are folded in half,
then to the narrow drawer where all his over-
the-calf socks point in the same direction.
She never learned how to run her fingers
down the seam in his boxers, to fold
them in perfect thirds. Now, the last
ten years of her life running down, she
knows that leaving is not the same as left.

Every Goodbye Ain't Gone
Leleti Tamu | *Canada/Jamaica*

memories race pulse and heart to you
taking time with me through shivers
then laughter
you catching my tongue licking wetness
fingers rolling inside
your breath slips down my neck opening me
like morning.
you're gone
music and mangoes can't reach this heat
where your swiftness caught me and holds
me still hurry back love
i'm waiting.

Ain't Too Old To Be Out
Toni Asante Lightfoot | *United States*

loving an old man is like pushing a car uphill
with a rope. —Jackie "Moms" Mabley

My fingers wilt under your white cotton.
You giggles a tune of devious chords.

I'm gonna kiss every place you got
like joy is the right thing it is.

Virginia—v—Loving changed the rules
For white and black vows of forever.

What will the case be called that changes
it for woman on woman strolls down the isle?

Baby come set on this whiles I snuzzle.
Act like you ain't loving an old woman.

Please after all this time, don't feel like
being with me is like pushing a car

Uphill. Sugar, please don't make me
The laugh of a young woman's joke.

---

*   Moms Mabley revealed to the public that she was a lesbian in 1973. She then
began to produce lesbian party records.

Black Magic
Sonia Sanchez | *United States*

magic
     my man
is you

     turning
my body into
a thousand
smiles.
     black
magic is your
touch
     making
me breathe.

urban grind, first thursday *inspired by jon goode*
Tamara Madison | *United States*

this is not a "grown and sexy" poem.
at forty,
i lie somewhere between
a holler and a whisper,
pitch and throw,
grunt and groan,
breath and blow,
pant and purr,
blink and wink
with my eyes wide open.
i am more concerned
with cosmic cum and universal orgasm
than i am with changing sheets
and memorizing beats to archaic rhythms.
but
somewhere
in the cool beneath the fullest moon,
my monsoon begins to rise,
and i long to curl your bones,
make your muscles moan,
wet your loins with
ripe rush,
monk funk,
nun's lust,
a taste of church cheddar
and mo' betta' magenta
instead of blues.
we've both had enuf of those
in the octet of decades
between us,
so i conjure new magic,
at forty,
to make your "jones"
call my
name.

The Day You Became a Parent Without Me
Kamilah Moon | *United States*

Ache tugs at my bloated hips
like famished children.
This blood is old—a doomed,
mouthless river shedding
its banks.

Dusk sets fire to the porch
we should be sitting on together.
Beneath me, red floods into brown
trickle. Your baritone drowns
inside the roar of news.
A waiting room phone call
turns us into drops
swimming the Nile of yesterday.

My womb-jug empties, wasted
batch of lover's moonshine.
Afterbirth clings, Honey—
go bathe your son.

Ada and Fernando
Oktavi Allison | *United States*

Ada's flowered lap
Sways her bible
Psalm 130 blurs

In Sunday's pew
Saturday night
Undresses a moment
Shawl led, holy

Black eye
Snuck under
Fedora brim
Ada's kid pump
Taps a beat to
Throb of
Fernando's drunk fist

One eye
Roams stained glass
Ada's hand
Rests the verse
"My soul
Waits for the Lord
More than those who
Watch for the morning—"

Hocking a Wedding Ring
Ebony Golden | *United States*

dime store orbit
plastic sapphire
lodged against labyrinth
red metal cool on finger
           holds more weight
than your promise jewel

you are a vibeless trinket   flash
of some south african's salty flesh
lung pinched for this   insanity

apricot croissants
a film where acrobat tongues
sweet talk me butter thin
some sweet disco thigh
rub a french talking noir
you are deep gut laughs that
catch the ear of an old continent

i kept you longer
than i kept the man

pawn shop mistress
say 77 dollars
she got big bones
wide flat tipped fingers

sometimes
no black eyes
no fist to skull
imprints   only whispers
in the night that wring the melody
out of throats

how malleable is your protection amulet
insistent charm
shackle
binding contract
spherical prison
mythical reality
guardian talisman
for all this
keep yo damn rib

you tried to perm my pussy hairs
bucked against your chin
she knew you were not honest
hot comb eyes pressed against
pubic flesh like a last ditch mantra
for salvation

i imagine
some earthling
among silt and nile
declarations papyrus
reed sedge rush
smithing for the sista pharaoh
his hands articulate
obtuse as moonless sky

only the sweetest sternest
sprouts will do

i can see him
a mingling of bended
knee questioning eye taut
spine
        a whole body crafted
into her gateways potential key

she is aware

of his attempts to capture
her saliva portal

cast him out to the driest crust of the sahara
burn the metallurgy artifice
my destiny and my offspring are my own

like a wad of phlegm
lodged in waterless
mouth wedged between
gag and last nights dinner
you gotta come out
you are of better use
on somebody's curb
succumb to the elements male
be flaked off by the sun

when one sleeps
with fairy tale
she awakens with a nose high
on pixie dust

the kink in the fantasy
Teri Ellen Cross | *United States*

after the sex, it's drenched consummation
parched and panting lips, limbs buckled
then bent—now unfolding to the slowing
of exhausted breathing
she knows she can't sleep here.

not with kinked hair, sweated out, matted
and limp like overcooked pasta
if she were alone, fine she'd
take the time part it, grease it
let the fingers dance their nightly routine

sliding cross scalp, sectioning hair
pirouetting twists, the cursive braiding
the final bow—donning
the green and black silk scarf
the knot she ties unseeing

but *who* he would see if she unveiled this ritual
before his sleepy green eyes
would his tongue unlock rusted doors
and flood forth corrosive images
to infect their sweet sated silence?

so she mutters something about
an early meeting initiates a reluctant slide
from surprisingly warm arms, smiles as she
locates clothing tossed hours ago in passionate array
she gets dressed. she goes home.

Solitude Ain't Loneliness
Michelle T. Clinton | United States

Say for instance you're a girl/ but citified/ a hard sister
like to keep her eyes open when she fucks/ & carries weapons
for the urban night creatures on the prowl/ Say you ain't
got no freudian thing/ but you packing none the less:
your mucus is acid
your anger on a leash
& can't no wish from the mouth of a warm eyed boy
make you blink

Before the girl mist can enter you/ before you ever cop
a feminine buss/ & blow the urban rust out your uterus
you got to clear house
you got to clean out
all the greasy fuzz/ left behind by the rat pack lot
of ex-lovers

You got to celibate/ in silence
& wait & wait for a red blush to rise up
a sparkling rush as radical as your first blood
as muscular as your momma's hands in soapy water
cold as the shock of the first breath
the earth blew into your lungs

The black sky wants your ass purified
& clear enough to release this city's fear
free enough to close your eyes
go inside & hear her.

i need at least a half/moon to let the light in
Ebony Golden | *United States*

me: thin slit to wiggle through to get back
distorted vaginal breath

him: sit her on a glass shelf where she is disregarded i break
the excess away

me: and pain is right is normal and fair pleasure is sin the route of
evil

work the kinks out of the base chakra

mature untouched	peach
hardened layers	ripe swells
tissue paper softness	uneaten
form a burlap sac	and rottens

the aching is antique

me: i tend my garden

keep it good natural virtuous nature brazilian balmy citrus yes   long
wet kisses wet long kisses   a slice of honey dew sleeps against a nurtur-
ing tongue   open   bronze women well oiled hips
        call up the oceans   gyrate the yemeyah
yield magenta
velvet massages a stubble chin   natural
open

me: i am no hole to alter your mental disfunction
                    emotional disfunction
                    erectile dis/
      no figurine
      no statuesque melodrama

cupcake of a girl
no frame idol   for your
jagged finger staccato
or habanero tongue

i spit like billie holiday

Women of My Color
Wanda Coleman | *United States*

i follow the curve of his penis
and go down

there is a peculiar light in which women
of my color are regarded by men

being on the bottom where pressures
are greatest is least desirable
would be better to be dead i
sometimes think

there is peculiar light in which women
of my race are regarded by black men
     as saints
     as mothers
     as sisters
     as whores

but mostly as the enemy

it's not our fault   we are victims
who have chosen to struggle and stay alive

there is a peculiar light in which women
of my race are regarded by white men
     as exotic
     as enemy

but mostly as whores

it's enough to make me cry
but i don't
following the curve of his penis
i go down

will   i ever see
the sun?

A Piece of Tail
Teri Ellen Cross | *United States*

from their apartment's balcony
my girlfriends and I could see
their pale skins hear the clipped accents
the soldiers were British
and drunk with money flowing
the Kenyan women became
willing every stare every gesture
intoxicating they tore shirts, teased
skirts revealed panties gyrating
taunting those English boys
who'd never seen chocolate breasts
nipples tipped almost ebony
hips rounded to such a swelling
you needed two hands to grab
oh but they'd heard   how wild
black cats can be   scratching backs
lusty animals in vaguely human skins
it took me back to Ohio University's
frat row   drunk white faces leering eager
in mistaken belief embolden voices calling out
and I became   afraid
I was that exotic again   kin
to these Kenyan women
and all we were
dancing brown bodies
dancing on bar table tops
dancing for dollars or pounds
whatever brown bodies are
sold for these days

Where Our Hips First First Met
Kamilah Moon | *United States*

paradise resides. Exquisite
mountain women formed day
by fragile day, impressive
peaks merging at horizon's
blazing lips.

Luscious weave of limbs, sublime
slope of thigh. The sweet rock
of nipples rising, falling
into kisses without looking—
every landing plush, fathomless
as oceans. Sipping moonlight
pooled in the small of backs, grazing
deltas just beyond the rise
of round perfection.

This is how we beguile
demons, heal what ails.
Here, we are seraphim—
serene and satisfied, riding
each other until we are nothing
but stardust and musk.

From Running Come Touch
Gloria T. Hull | *United States*

For M.

You told me about
your fear of penetration—
men's maleness, people pushing
all thrusts you warded off
with weapons
your mother handed you
through pain

But, then, you touched me—
amazing move—
your shy sure fingers
unbalancing my reasons,
teeth biting off my breath

It was darkness come
daylight come morning
instinct and body love
coming through hands
and breakfast and questions leading nowhere
more clothes and passion
cocaine frost
the cat licking salmon
back darkness back rubbing
lessons hanging out pleasure
from running coming touching
deep
     into

Fall
Phebus Etienne | *Haiti/ United States*

We lay on our rented bed,
as rain taps a canopy of firs outside.
I stroke my love's forehead and
contemplate single motherhood.

I had watched a friend review a calendar
the October when I was seventeen,
listened as she recounted her conversation
with another man who could offer nothing.

We traveled by taxi from Lawrenceville
to Bordentown, the maple leaves on fire
against the sky. The driver paid, she shouldered
her bag heavy with loose change, remnants
of a financial aid check and savings account.

Across the waiting room, a woman had one arm
around a wailing younger version of herself.
"If my mother was alive," said the daughter
beside me as she gazed that the pair,
"I would be able to keep the baby."
My mother was still breathing then.

Dreadlocks brush my navel as the sleeper
raises his head for a kiss. He'll slip
his wedding band from his pocket
onto his finger as we hail separate cabs.
I take words from a motherless daughter,
use them as my compass.

Saint Chant
Gloria T. Hull | *United States*

Against your black shoulder
body quirky as a woman's

Muffled, still
picking responsibility from apple vines
heavy as stones
I take the weight

You can't bear it
can't bear me
opening like dark-thighed marble
pouring rivers oceans seas
sucking you in
and under—

primeval nightmares
men have always had:
the disappearance of the bone
annihilation of the self
in a swirl of blood
flooding

Look
I can't help this love
can't harness my passion

Flow with me—
or hold us drowning under—
chanting like the saint you are

My Lady Ain't No Lady
Pat Parker | *United States*

my lady ain't no lady

she doesn't flow into a room
   she enters & her presence is felt
she doesn't sit small
    she takes all her space
she doesn't partake of meals
      she eats—replenishes herself

my lady ain't no lady

she has been known to
    speak in a loud voice
    pick her nose
    stumble on a sidewalk
    swear at her cats
    swear at me
    scream obscenities at men
    paint rooms
    repair houses
    tote garbage
    play basketball
      & numerous other
      un-ladylike things.

my lady is definitely no lady
which is fine with me

cause i ain't no gentleman.

What About the Way You Love Me
Venus Thrash | *United States*

Al Green at four am,
pint of whiskey

stinking on my breath,
still hard, blood bursting

at the tip, a woman
in my head, asleep

beside me, drooling,
hair mussed, funk

of the day on us
& between us,

brine of her thighs,
musk of her breasts

on my lips,
dried trails of spit

on areolas, armpits,
crevices of toes,

four fingers drenched
in stale cum,

sheets funky
& twisted around

& beneath us,
Al Green at four am,

a woman in my head
asleep beside me,

simply beautiful
yeah, yeah, yeah.

mythology of the wide-open-pussy
Ebony Golden | *United States*

they say birds reincarnated her remains
clawed at sea's edge
into a pistol packing water woman
got magma and prayer beads tucked
under her left breast
hoists music in sugar uterus crinkles

some say she came back as mama
harriet and that's why she knew the swamps
and marshes so well   she gathered
steal aways in her tides and ripples
rushed them to safety

those birds costumed her regal plumage
some say   spit ruby
dust in her lungs   and she came back
as a mississippi delta blues empress
just a sanging

drink me plenty but don't suck me dry
i say
drink me plenty but don't suck me dry
i got lots of juice to give
but needs a little bit to quench the fire

she walked on water
part woman
part fish
all god
and she spit out the oceans
like a declaration
caught in mid air
congealed
then let go

 some name her whore
cause she be sexin loud
and juicy in the day light
and her babies ain't got no last names

the trees call her wide open pussy
jesus calls her indigenous womb
she walked seven days
spewing amniotic goodness seven
days birthing seven babies
seven days on seven continents seven days
and them babies be yo grandma

drink me plenty but don't suck me dry
drink me plenty but don't suck me dry
i got lots of juice to give
but needs a little bit to quench the fire

For Willyce
Pat Parker | *United States*

When i make love to you
i try
   with each stroke of my tongue
     to say
       i love you
to tease
       i love you
to hammer
        i love you
to melt
        i love you

and your sounds drift down
    oh god!
     oh jesus!
      and i think
        here it is, some dude's
         getting credit for what
a woman
has done
again.

Cum Tender: Blessing for the hard ex-
Cherryl Floyd-Miller | *United States*

The kind of tender —
disembodied —

that could turn
our salt to sugar,

could dimple
crisp fitted sheets,

and when re/coming,
could be the elegant onset

of used mattress sag,
make you arc your backbone

to catch each hot, dirty
secret I could gurgle

through sweat —ohhh
and oooh

that feverish tender
you owned

in the holy hours
of first woo,

while the ghosts
of our breath

loaned their first
two-faced promises

in the blind
but surefooted press

of involved skin,
yesss,

that kind of tender,
may it come in you again,

in every pore of your skin
a gingery clove scaling,

may it bloom
in the tally of hard regret

you nasty off to me now,
in this, the bitter scrap

of your ordinary life
without me.

Pink Poem
Jackie Warren-Moore | *United States*

This is a big girl's pink poem,
a poem about pinkness.
Deep dark shadowy rose I explore at the back of your mouth.
This is not a hot pink pinafore, lacy poem.
This is a poem about the long lean pinkness of your tongue
as it greets my lips.
This is about the sweet wet melt in my mouth motion of you.
This is not about the sashay,
turn around
curtsy pink cuteness.
This is about opening up and being gloriously pink.
This is a big girl's pink poem.

In Service
Linda Susan Jackson | *United States*

What do I dream when I remember
the first time you brushed your moist lips
against mine. I was young, you'd been places,
could please, each time an exploration
larger than yourself, on your way
to rapture in the sunken middle.

What do I dream after putting our last daughter
to sleep, and I crawl under the chenille
bedspread, flannel blanket and pale yellow
top sheet, my body rolls to that middle,
shivering.

What do I dream when in the mirror you're
sitting on the edge of the bed, watching me
slip off my panties, touch myself, my eyes
full of then. And now? Duty dulled,
sucked in a rut row of blues.

No heart stopping cerise, no crease
in my white blouse collar, no flip
of hair caught, no rapid jabber,
no wet skin, no polished rim,
no generous basin to catch the run off in,
no quick run to the store, no petals in pastel
palettes, no centerpiece, no Johnny
Hartman singing *You are too beautiful.*

I want a man, but no one dares
thrust his tongue in my mouth
since you, their shining prince, ambient.
Me, hermetic, in hand-blown glass
when twice a day a surprise of light
breaks through. Your reflection
swirls on the thick wall of one side,
slides smoothly down the other,
every hair on my body alert,
each hand in service.

On a Night of the Full Moon
Audre Lorde | *United States*

I
Out of my flesh that hungers
and my mouth that knows
comes the shape I am seeking
for reason.
The curve of your waiting body
fits my waiting hand
your breasts warm as sunlight
your lips quick as young birds
between your thighs the sweet
sharp taste of limes.

Thus I hold you
frank in my heart's eye
in my skin's knowing
as my fingers conceive your warmth
I feel your stomach
moving against mine.

Before the moon wanes again
we shall come together.

II
And I would be the moon
spoken over your beckoning flesh
breaking against reservations
beaching thought
my hands at your high tide
over and under inside you
and the passing of hungers
attended   forgotten.

Darkly risen
the moon speaks
my eyes
judging   your roundness
delightful.

is it true what they say about colored pussy?

hattie gossett | *United States*

hey
is it really true what they say about colored pussy?
come on now
dont be trying to act like you dont know what i am talking about
you have heard those stories about colored pussy so stop trying to
      pretend like you havent
you have heard how black and latina pussies are hot and uncon-
      trollable
i know you know the one about asian pussies and how they go from
      side to side instead of up and down
and everybody knows about squaw pussies and how once a white-
      man got him some that he wasnt never no more good

now at first i thought that the logical answer to these stories is that
      they are just ignorant racial myths
but then i thought: what about all the weird colored stories about
      colored pussy?
cuz you know colored pussies werent always treated with the high-
      est regard we deserve in the various colored worlds prior to our
      discovery by the european talentscouts/explorers

and we still aint
so now why is it that colored pussies have had to suffer so much
      oppression and bad press from so many divergent sources?
is it cuz we really are evil and nasty and queer looking and smelly
      and ugly like they say?

or
is it cuz we possess some secret strength which we take for grant-
      ed but which is a terrible threat to the various forces that are
      trying to suppress us?

i mean just look at what black pussies have been subjected to start-

ing with ancient feudal rape and polygamy and clitoridecto-
my and forced child marriages and continuing right on through
colonial industrial neocolonial rape and forced sterilization and
experimental surgery

and when i put all that stuff about black pussies together with the
stories i hear from the other colored pussies about what they
have had to go through i am even more convinced

we must have some secret powers!

this must be why so many people have spent so much time vilify-
ing abusing hating and fearing colored pussy

and you know that usually the ones who be doing all this vilifying
abusing hating and fearing of colored pussy are the main ones
who just cant seem to leave colored pussy alone dont you

they make all kinds of laws and restrictions to aparthedize colored
pussy and then as soon as the sun goes down guess who is seen
sneaking out back to the cabins?

and guess who cant do without colored pussy in their kitchens and
fields and factories and offices?

and then theres the people who use colored pussy as a badge of
certification to insure entry into certain circles

finally

when i think about what would happen if all the colored pussies
went on strike

(especially if the together white pussies staged a same day sympa
thy strike)

look out!

the pimps say colored pussy is an untapped
goldmine
well they got it wrong
colored pussies aint goldmines untapped
colored pussies are yet unnamed energies whose
power for lighting up the world is beyond all
known measure

Untitled
Renita Martin | *United States*

"it ain't nat'ral
just ain't nat'ral, jesus said"
say some sisters who
choose to talk still
after i tell them

some peers admire my
open/mind/deadness like
i *acquired* a taste for
my existence
was not born loving
but love women mechanically

while some brothers say i am
politically in—
correct that i one
woman must "build the nation
be fruitful and multiply. jesus said."

sometimes i feel like
the cigarette
butt i hold on to
walking down the street
        usefulness exhausted cannot
        be thrown on the ground to
        defy nature
        or in the garbage to
        start a fire
like my jesus had
nowhere to lay
lay his head.
sometimes i wonder why
they don't have ashtrays
on the street or why i
don't just start a fire.

You asked why I stayed married all those years
mistinguette | *United States*

Like water, love takes
the shape of what contains it:
cell, leaf
gourd, stream.
Runs wide or deep
to pass through barren places;
grows icy cold, and
sometimes disappears
underground.

Love, too
seeks its own level;
trace to lake,
like to like.
And a river will try
to flow uphill
in its sedulous race
to the sea

Womens
Sandra Royster | *United States*

I.

Mozetta Lee

Zetta used to call her man "Pig"
"Hey, Pig"
soft and succulent
round
brown
rollin flesh
against his tauntness
"How's my Pig?"
neon flash
of gold-white teeth
on
and gone
"What you bring me, baby?"
soft hand
movin
down his rigid back
ooo-whee
chittlin love
sho is good
if you don't mind
a little shit.

WOMENS

II.

Lou's Room

Lou's room in the afternoon

was crystal bottles
in multi-colored profusion
on purple lace doilies
catching dusty sun-shafts.
flower-shrouded bed
in soft lavender hues,
a chicken that laid plastic eggs
for the child
who had nothing else to do
but play in Lou's room.

Lou's room in the evening
was a heated darkness
alive
with sharply moving outlines,
stabbing acrid scent
of sweating thighs
and burning hidden juices,
and the deep and husky sounds
of love
for the men
who have nothing else to do
but play in Lou's room

WOMENS

III.

Miss Mary

Miss Marilyn
a cooly pale
moon maid
since her man's been gone
("She can have the nigger!")
delicate perfumes

surround each careful movement
and she whistled
sometime
in a trembling tremble
like the lonely call
of hidden birds.

she slept alone
in prudent
gown
opaque and full.
("Don't need no man—I've got myself.")
how cruel then
the accident of fate
that left her bedroom door
ajar
and made her restless limbs

kick back the covers
gown and all
and sent hungry eyes
of shufflin mr. Jackson
("he's a good, quiet roomer.")
to fasten on her fiercely risen
secret moons in sweating trembling awe
how cruel
that he only
shoved his hands into his pockets
deep
and walked away.

RELATIONSHIPS
Political

As a blackwoman
the personal is political
hold no empty rhetoric.
> —Maud Sulter, from "As a Black Woman"

From "To The Right Honorable William, Earl Of Dartmouth, His Majesty's Principal Secretary Of State For North America, ETC."

Phillis Wheatley | *United States*

Should you, my lord, while you pursue my song
Wonder from whence my love of *Freedom* sprung,
Whence flow these wishes for the common good,
By feeling hearts alone best understood,
I, young in life, by seeming cruel fate
Was snatch'd from *Afric's fancy'd happy seat*:
What pangs excruciating must molest,
What sorrows labour in my parent's breast?
Steel'd was the soul and by no misery mov'd
That from a father seiz'd his babe belov'd
Such, such my case. And can I then but pray
Others may never feel tyrannic sway?

White Things
Anne Spencer | *United States*

Most things are colorful things—the sky, earth, and sea.
Black men are most men; but the white are free!
White things are rare things; so rare, so rare
They stole from out a silvered world—somewhere.
Finding earth-plains fair plains, save greenly grassed,
They strewed white feathers of cowardice, as they passed;
The golden stars with lances fine,
The hills all red and darkened pine,
They blanched with their wand of power;
And turned the blood in a ruby rose
To a poor white poppy-flower.

They pyred a race of black, black men,
And burned them to ashes white; then,
Laughing, a young one claimed a skull,
For the skull of a black is white, not dull,
But a glistening awful thing
Made, it seems, for this ghoul to swing
In the face of God with all his might,
And swear by the hell that sired him:
"Man-maker, make white!"

From *The Crisis* (March 1923)

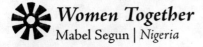

Women Together
Mabel Segun | *Nigeria*

Women's Lib
Women's fib;

Women together,
Women to get her!
Mocking solidarity.

Women strugglers,
Women stragglers,
More stragglers than strugglers;

Women leaders,
Women squealers,
Character stealers.

Women's Lib
Women's fib—
Liberation begins at home.

 *I Want a Space*
Marta André | *Brazil*
Translated by Carolyn Richardson Durham

that with the swindler's wad of money and the footsteps
of the past
became a sugar mill.

In the disorderliness of time
no one became a people
because of the negligence of the imperial stroke of the pen.

Two Strange Worlds
Francesca Yetunde Pereira | *Nigeria*

Women,
What fools we are,
Invading unprotected
The world of men so alien,
And ever manifesting
Weakness in tenderness.

In that world of reason,
Is it not reason to give?
Willing converst
Ardent learners
Giving, giving.

But, fools—
Our hearts have lost
The room for reason.
Can we unlearn
That which was taught?

Can we survive?
How can we live?
The flame is out,
The cinders
Painful memories.

Women's Lib in Black
Mary Carter Smith | *United States*

I want freedom
To stay home
And raise my children

I want freedom
From that
Long Blonde hair
Image of beauty

I want freedom
For my man
    To join the union

        So I can
                Come out of your kitchen

the myth of conception

for Metis and the early Greek belief that children were generated solely from man's sperm

Teri Ellen Cross | *United States*

take clay
round bones
anchor them to earth's spine
then breathe life
into ribbed hollow
swell the space
til it collapses
then rises again
on its own accord

call this conception
absent a canal for crowning
call it creation
call it myth
etch it in the looming
heavens above
and make woman
the floor
of this world

Hallelujah
Virginia Brindis de Salas | *Uruguay*
Translated by Ann Venture Young

Redeeming chorus shouting
from the Antilles
to the Plate River
and in the sea-like river
exclaims:
    Hallelujah!

People of America,
I am yours.
I was born in you;
because of you I exist
and so I say:
Hallelujah!

So many people
are there in the street
and there is no one
who maintains
silence:
    Hallelujah!

Many are those
who are going to work
and there are also many
who hardly eat
but yet would wish to sing:
    Hallelujah!

I have legs
with which to walk;
they will not falter.
I go everywhere

without hesitation.

Hallelujah!

I, a black woman,
you, a white American woman:
the same soup
we must both eat
for days and weeks;
even you, woman
of Europe,
have to eat, the same as I
the same soup
and you probably have the same faith
and the same clothes
and you have to drink your wine
from the same cup:

Hallelujah!

So many people
will be in the streets
whenever you go out:

Hallelujah!

✳ *Macho woman/Frail woman*
Brinda Runghsawmee | *Mauritius*

Macho woman comes from Macholand
With her freedom and equality philosophy
To save frail woman
From macho man

Frail woman comes from Frailland
With her orthodox and behind-the-scene philosophy
To bear with macho man
And macho woman

Both are brilliant
Top executives
Macho woman controls man
Frail woman works with man

Both are happy

Macho woman is a top model
In her tight sexy outfit
She runs the rat race
She keeps the image . . . panting!

Frail woman is her own top model
In her simple, smart outfit
She keeps up with the rat race . . . panting!
She has a good self-image

Macho woman drinks, smokes, dates
Equal is she to man
Frail woman does not drink, smoke, and date
Equal is she to herself.

Sister Outsider *for Audre Lorde*
Opal Palmer Adisa | *Jamaica/United States*

we
women black
are always
outside
even when
we believe
we're in
but being
out   side
ain't so bad
cause
we be
learning
to love
each other better
we be
learning
to listen
more closely
to one another
we be
learning
to allow
all of us
our humanity

sisters
are too often
out   side
fronting
trying
to get   over
but

we be coming
to   gether
coming
together
ending our silence
transforming
space and pace
searching
and finding
the most valuable
is often
that which is
overlooked   us

Shoes
Sylvia Hamilton | *Nova Scotia*

When I finally
got her attention
"Size seven and a half, please"
as I reached for the shoe.

Contempt, veiled
as laughter:
"You can't afford those!"

At that moment
I resolved to try on
every size seven and a half
in the store.

Not that I would ever buy—
only that I would try.

She needed to know
I had the right,
if I chose to
try and buy whatever
she had to show.

Very politely, "The grey pumps, please."
"The Almalfi in green."
(I hate green)
Canvas deck, why not.

When she was finally
surrounded by boxes,
her face truly red,
I left shoeless.
Only Ilmelda would not be pleased.

The Never Woman
S. Pearl Sharp | United States

She will never catch a May Co. white sale
on 200 thread percale

She will never exchange depression
for a new dress

She will never have an
overdue library book

She will never miss a mammogram or
forget to do her self exam

She will never chose from baby photos
snapped against blue velvet

She will never run out of tampons
or absent blessings

She does not get up from the TV
during commercials

She has insurance without assurance
a policy redeemed in food line broth.

Her taxes are on her back, due
every sunrise

The woman in the photo
one arm around her sucking infant

reaches through the
threads of fragile matte finish,

grabs my throat
chokes me on my plenty

My tears are no ablution for the
never hanging in her eyes.

✳ In Praise of a Woman I Know
Sylvia Jones | United States

A tall and beautiful woman
sat short
with a swollen stomach
by the window
and it rained from her eyes
she was either thinking about
all the coats she made on the line that morning
or
the man who had swollen her body
with her permission
and drove a truck
    who had not come home that Friday
    with the pay check yet!
    murder reflected in her face
    when she looked at the four of us
    some of us just sitting there looking
others standing there
old enough to understand
somebody had been wronged
    but more than that pain
love dominated her completely
    even knowingly oppressed
    even at that very moment of reality
    Capitalism had not taught her to hate
    the truck driver
    instead she passionately
had grown to hate that four room cold water flat
that small coat factory
that teacher who insisted on reminding us
we all had different fathers
    she had learned to hate gossip
and people with the authority
to tell you who you could love

when you could love them
and even if you could love them at all

when she finally did walk out of the door
to fight the truck driver
she did not hate him
but she did hate all the shit and
conditions
that had driven such a tall swollen and beautiful black woman
to trying to kill her husband
in the streets
an act that any of us can understand
if we ever worked
or tried to raise children with
no money
when we could barely read our income tax statements
and there was no one there to explain
why this shit was happening to us
I condemn my mother not
she and hundreds like her
did what they had to do, when they had to do it
cause she really never hurt, hurt him anyway
and out of raising six of us
she still managed to raise a communist

Black Woman Out Dere
Nefertiti Gayle | *England*

Black woman out dere have no fear
Fight back my sisters, Fight back.

An if you struggle is you fat
An you man pon you back,
An him say you too fat
Fight back my sisters, Fight back.

Black woman out dere, dem say
You gaan mad, dem wan put
You inna mad house, true you
depress an sad de pressure so
Hard . . .
When you man lef de yard,
You pickney in need an want
little feed
Fight back my sista, Fight back.

An you want little wuk and you
Can't get no wuk, all you can get . . .
Is de white man dut, so you resort
to crime to earn a dime an you en up on street a walk
frontline, an de man on dere jus a watch you behin.
Fight back Black sista, Fight back.

Black woman out dere wid troubles an fears,
Dem say you livin in sin
Cause you livin's thin an you givin away
A little sin ting.
You na beg no body no golden ring.
You only wan fe earn you own ting.
Fight back Black sistas, Fight back.

Black woman out dere you have to Fight back,
Jus come forward wid a double attack,
No boder weep
On no kitchen mat . . . Jus Attack.

Some Me of Beauty
Carolyn M. Rodgers | *United States*

the fact is
that i don't hate any body any more
i went through my mean period
if you remember i spit out nails
chewed tobacco on the paper
and dipped some bad snuff.
but in one year
just like i woke up one morning and
saw my mother's head gray
and i asked myself/could it have turned
overnight?
knowing full well the grayness had been
coming and had even been there
awhile
just like that i woke up one morning
and looked at my self
and what i saw was
carolyn
not imani ma jua or soul sister poetess of
the moment
i saw more than a "sister" . . .
i saw a Woman. human.
and black.
i felt a spiritual transformation
a root revival of love
and i knew that many things
were   over
and some me of—beauty—
was about to begin. . . .

✳ *shrapnel*
Shia Shabazz | *United States*

*"Although rape as a weapon of war has existed for as long as war, in today's
conflicts around the world it is taking a particularly heavy toll on women."*
   –from the article "Rape Now Taking the form of Genocide,"
                              The Japan Times, August 14, 2004

I.

this girl
eight the first time
she evaded her skin
retreated from her bed
to camouflage herself
in midnight corners
that harbor her fugitive
from her own innocence
this girl
unaware of what pieces of herself are lost
which limbs will grow back
what syndrome will thwart her growth
what it means anymore to not know
it is this girl
not the failing economy or the fallen new york skyline
not the fatigued and fatherless households
not the flailing red white and blue ribbons on car antennas
or affixed to beds of pick ups and minivans
but her
this girl
she reminds me
that we are at war.

II.

war looks different these days

some trenches resemble tract homes
tree-lined drives
cul-de-sacs
½ acre lots with 3 tree-lings on each
others
single/multi/extended families
sectioned eight ways
between liquor stores and Baptist churches
shrapnel lining streets
where shoeless vagrants pine for pennies
will work for anything edible
soldiers are
preschoolers
prepubescent
prementral
preteen
pre anything adult

latchkeys
casualties
who learn to live with a lack of
these soldiers
bury themselves nightly
craft foxholes of flannel and linens
prisoners of war
praying from morning to morning
submission silence amnesia
tactics for sub/urban warfare where
survival means more than memory
they plead for stays from sexual execution
for just one more day
to trust
before wounded and dying wolves
in sheep's clothing
feed on their need
    brothers uncles fathers steps and grands
    cousins once removed

sisters aunties mothers grand and steps
friends of the family
wolves, for whom real love is
as distant a memory
as a mother's womb
as distant as living

III.

living names plaster newspapers and war memorials
this girl
this Eve, this Elizabeth, this nine-year-old girl in El Cajon, this Jessica, this
fifteen-year-old boy in school closet, this Ida, this Kimberly, this Adam,
this eight-month-old baby in Africa; this Edward, this Ryan, this ten-year-
old boy in Tampa, this Jane Doe, this six-year-old girl on school bus in
New Mexico, this JonBenet, this ten-year-old girl in Arizona, this Polly,
this Samantha, this John Doe, this Jane Doe, this Jimmy, this Bonita, this
Shia

this girl and
this girl and
this boy and
this eight year old girl

IV.

my daughter is eight
she is consumed with bratz dolls
finally fashion
she covers her eyes when bodies go bare
still finds shock in four-letter words
giggles at what grown ups do
asks too many questions
she knows what private parts are
what boundaries mean
i pray her wits are about her
or a letter opener near
the day some dreamy eyed creeper

with a safe sounding biblical name
joseph, michael, john, david, abel, samuel or frank
tries to persuade her into submission silence amnesia
cajole her from being
"Salihah"; the pious, virtuous, upright one
she came into the world
eyes open, engaged

I knew
she had been here before
she would never walk alone
her roots are far stronger than the world
above this earth she belongs to
she will not wilt
this girl
my girl
i will teach her to fight

She Writes

Ayanna Black | *Jamaica/Canada*

these days
i'm cleanin' up
cleanin' up after these white women
scrubbin' floors
washin' dishes
cleanin' dem pickney behind
'nd dem husbands tek liberty
a bring chat to mi

mi da clean up
clean up
dem backra women
'tink dem better da mi
today mz. anne da bodda mi
wiz she crosses
eyes cold
cold and hard like diamonds
with fi she confusion:
har workaholic husband
and fi'im frozen cock
mi child
dem always wa fi mi advice
surprize da first time
mi cry buckets of wata
'nd mi da 'hink:
advice from dis a black woman?
dis a black nigger?
black mamma?
mi child
mi da sa' to all a dem
from mz. anne to mz. jane

mi nuh yu pyscharist

604

Fact

Esmeralda Riberio | *Brazil*

Translated by Carolyn Richardson Durham

They abolished slavery   as an institution

                                                                But

Not   as a condition

✳ Watching The Hours
Jadi Omowale | *United States*

Watching *The Hours*, I thought about the two servants in Virginia's house.
The women she was afraid of. The women who were paid to feed her, keep
her house clean and make a safe space for her to write. These women,
shadows in Virginia's house, who live within their own hour glass that
their mistress can't see into. Who never tries to see, beyond her own fear
of them, and their power as women who work and toil away from their
children, their lovers, their families, their own gifts. Women who live in
the shadows of your very clean house Virginia. Women who disappear in
the history, but make your bed and make your ginger tea, taking the train
to London to fetch it for the lady of the house who only wants the peace
of waters swirling over her, embracing her body and carrying her away in
its arms.

Watching *The Hours*, I thought about my mother and her mother, and
her mother and on down the list of brown women, cleaning and cooking
and picking and walking barefoot down dusty roads. I thought how they
would clean Atticus' house and watch Jem and Scout while he was crusad-
ing for the life of a black man raped by a white woman. I thought about
how Virginia would have been afraid of my mother who was so different
than her, so not a woman, because her browness kept her a world apart.
Because my mother, and hers and the line of brown women cling to life
with a fierce holding on. Where she and the other women sat an echo in a
corner kitchen which was miraculously clean every day and which Virginia
and her sisters never saw the spec of desperation in these women's eyes.

Watching *The Hours*, I wondered how a woman could love a man so and
never let him go. How another woman, his mother, could walk away so
she could live. I thought about my mama and those white servants who
worked for pennies for Virginia, or helped clean that NY apartment in
SoHo full of books and flowers, or the house in Florida in the 1950's
neighborhood where neither the servant girls or my mother would have
been allowed to live, accept as ghosts who sit quiet in the clean corners
until called to make tea, to watch the children, to worry about the woman
upstairs who wants only the comfort of water come to baptize her away
from the life these servant women, invisible, yet strong cling too.

✹ *Malini's Role Playing* a clichéd narrative poem
Sanjukta Dasgupta | *India*

I.

A speck of infant shame in the scared mother's arms
The newborn daughter curls and curls
Yearning voicelessly to re-enter the darkness
Of the uterine home that seems safer
As sighs and weak smiles of resignation
Infect the unhappy air around
Some placating murmurs buzz
As if to a failed examinee
 In a competitive national eligibility test
"Better luck next time"
Others smirk sadistically
While most openly lament
The unwanted birth of another girl child.

"we are not rich you know
(*then of course it would have been
 ultra sonography and foeticide*)
Let's save for the son to come"
Her lord and master's ring of authority
Counselling husbandry
For the nurturing of the unnecessary one!
The guilty mother weeps and rages
As the infant slowly but unmistakably
Becomes more and more girl
A tinkling voice, colt like grace
As she walks to the village school
For free afternoon meals and a few second hand textbooks
While neighbours greedily watch how Malini grows from girl to little woman
Salivating as the tongue tingling green raw mango mellows into ripe juicy fruit

"study further!"
Rages her industrial worker father
"Nonsense—I have found a suitable boy
Marriage next month—remember she is eighteen this year"
Without any records to prove dates or the flow of time
Malini, maybe now 14 or 13 or 16
Becomes eighteen on her marriage night
The members of the panchayat do not complain
Government officers of the district arrive as guests
As Malini garlands Dipak, the suitable boy
Who works in her father's factory
Follows him next day to the next village destined for her next home
Disappointed in-laws—her brand new mother, father and sisters complain
How they have been cheated by Malini's father Makhan Pal

II.

Malini now is re-born as wife
Good, obedient, submissive, sacrificing, self—effacing
Never asks for anything
Eternally grateful for all routine considerations
Working in the kitchen, washing clothes
 When permitted watching afternoon TV serials in black and white
Eating the meanest portion of each cooked meal
Malini still failed to make her new relations happy
Sighs rose as they exclaimed how Kanai's father-in-law
Had given his son-in-law's family a piece of land
Moti the jobless groom had not only got two sets of gold ornaments
But a motor cycle and Rs 20, 000
Malini's father Makhan Pal hadn't even been able to fulfill his promise
Of cash down Rs 30, 000 though he did gift a watch and a bicycle.

Then one day Dipak picked a quarrel
About a badly cooked meal and hit Malini
The bruises on her face and tears in her eyes
Made the in-laws smile
At last, Dipak is behaving like a man, they said

Makhan Pal and his wife Sandhya
Hear about the battering of their daughter
 From a neighbour's wife
"But that's so regular"
They know she'll get used to it
Which woman could say she had never been hit for her own good!
Malini knew slowly and surely
That this will have to be her life till death
Endless daily chores,
Relentless nights of callous lust

"That's an adult woman's life
You have to learn to live with it
Don't nag, don't ask
Accept, you are not to reason why
You are but to do and die"
Malini learnt the tricks
But the beatings became more severe
For a promise broken
By her liar father Makhan Pal
Maybe, they would have doused her in kerosene
Or pushed her into a well
But the arrival of her son Tapan one monsoon night
Saved her and thrust her into endless little deaths everyday.

III.

Yes, Malini was forgiven
She bore Dipak three sons—Tapan, Prabir and Mohan
The fourth son was still-born
Her in-laws praised this lucky plant that bore the right fruits
Makhan Pal was forgiven by proxy
For giving Dipak's family
A wife who bore only sons.
The neighbours were so green
Their gardens looked faded in contrast
Messengers and match makers

Rushed to Makhan Pal's house
"Do you have other daughters?"
They returned crestfallen, as Makhan's other two offsprings
Were sons not potential son-producing daughters

The three sons grew and grew
The mother smiled as she looked at them
"At last, Malini has done something right"
She told herself
As she heaped more steaming rice
On their waiting plates
Kitchen, washing and watching over others' needs
Malini rarely recognized her changing self
Her frail body, sure sign of malnutrition
Stared at her from the small mirror
Vermillion powder in her hair parting
Had cut a wide path
In what was once a head full of dark and thick wavy hair

IV.

Her sons had come within one or two years of each other
They went to school and graduated from college with Pass course degrees
Celebrating the subisidized education system of the State government
All three joined office, factory and small business respectively:
Thanks to globalization and open market economy
Small jobs for small people in small sectors cropped up
And then the world declared they were now ripe for marriage
Horoscopes were checked, dowry claims were settled
The sons participated eagerly
In this lottery programme
As chance and cash changed hands.

Soon enough three young women came in as wives
They were beaten, abused, bore children
Amidst nightly lusts and daily grind
But Malini could never use a harsh word

She declined the traditional role of the mafia mother-in-law
So these young wives and mothers
Ignored her and abused the soft target
Till she became a maid in her sons' home—
The young women she could not be unkind to
Became exploiters of the meek mother-in-law:
Then Dipak, Malini's husband, died in a bus accident

To cut a routine tale short
Five years later, Malini the widow, the unfortunate woman
Who did not have the sense to die before her husband did
 Was borne to the burning ghat by her three sons
And a few other male in-laws
The last glorious journey
Of the virtuous wife and mother
Loud invocations to God rent the air
As the sons chanted *Hari Bol* as they walked
With their incredibly light load—
Malini's dead body lay like a tired bird under a coverlet:
What glory to be cremated by her own sons
Not one, not two but three proud sons
Fulfilling the dreams of
Their mother, a penniless literate woman
 Who had secretly vowed
That she would never give birth to a daughter!
Sometimes, merciful God does grant prayers!

To be a Feminist is
Micer Githae Mugo | Kenya

Refrain: To be a Feminist is

For me
to be a feminist is
    to embrace my womanness
    the womanness of
    all my mothers
    all my sisters
    it is
    to hug the female principle
    and the metaphors of life
    that decorate my being

Refrain

For me
to be a feminist is
    to celebrate my birth
    as a girl
    to ululate that my gender
    is female
    it is
    to make contact
    with my being.

Refrain

For me
to be a feminist is
    to denounce patriarchy
    and the caging of women
    it is
    to wipe the fuzziness
    of colonial hangovers
    to uproot the weeds
    of neo-colonial pestilence

Refrain

For me
to be a feminist is
    to hurl
    through the cannon
    of my exploding
    righteous fury
    the cannibal
    named capitalism
    it is
    to pronounce
    a death sentence
    on the ogre
    named imperialism.

Refrain

For me
to be a feminist is
    to unhood racism
    to decry zionism
    to detonate apartheid
    to obliterate "tribalism"
    it is
    to necklace homophobia
    to drown fanaticism
    to strangulate classism
    to fumigate ethnic cleansing.

Refrain

For me
to be a feminist is
    to speak out loud
    to articulate my name
    to assert that I am
    to declare that woman is
    it is
    to water my fertility

to woman my womb
it is
to converse with my soul.

Refrain

For me
to be a feminist is
    to burst all the non-space
    between the bedroom
    and the kitchen
    of my life
    it is
    to grow wings
    and fly
    to unlimited heights
    it is
    to ride the sun
    of my visions

Refrain

For me
to be a feminist is
    to celebrate my mother
    to poetize my sisters
    to message their failures
    it is
    to savour their intellect
    to drink their feelings
    and to embrace
    their achievements.

Refrain

For me
to be a feminist is
    to curdle my children's hopes
    to infuse their veins
    with the spirit

of never-say-die
it is
to fan their wind
of resistance
to stroke them
with optimism
it is
to give them
to humanity.

Refrain

For me
to be a feminist is
 . to have dialogue
 with my father
 and my brother
 to invite their partnership
 as fellow guerillas
 it is
 to march with them
 to the war-torn zone
 of Afrikana survival
 it is
 to jointly raise with them
 the victory salute.

Refrain

For me
to be a feminist is
 to part ways
 with the bulging haves
 to merge paths
 with the stricken have-nots
 it is
 to know that
 deprivation consumes
 it is
 to see that

overeating constipates
it is
to level mountains
of obnoxious accumulation
it is
to rain upon deserts
of annihilating nothingness.

Refrain

For me
to be a feminist is
    to breathe the air
    of unpolluted peoplehood
    and to sing
    in harmony with nature
    it is
    to touch
    the soft earth
    it is
    to speak
    with the unknown
    it is
    to walk this life
    it is
    to hold up the sky.

Refrain

For me
to be a feminist is
    to unseat domination
    and forge a rock
    out of powerlessness
    it is
    to shake hands
    with people's struggles
    it is
    to disempower
    superpower arrogance
    it is

to conceive and deliver
a human world.

Refrain

For me
to be a feminist is
    to be me
    an Afrikan woman
    all Afrikana women
    and all who have walked
    their path of thorns
    it is
    to know herstory
    word for word
    it is
    to look history
    in the face
    and declare
    that I am
    because woman is.

Refrain

For me
to be a feminist is
    to be the mother
    of my daughters
    it is
    to be the daughter
    of my mother
    it is
    to be more than
    a survivor
    it is
    to be a creator
    it is
    to be a woman.

Refrain

You are Mad: and I mean It!
Phumzile Zulu | *South Africa*

What did you mean when you called me benighted
Savage pagan barbarian
You must have been mad
I know now
I say it and I mean it

When you found me here in Africa
You said I was hungry
You came carrying a big book called 'BIBLE'
And you called yourself 'missionary'

You were going to offer
Food for my life
But to my surprise
Never was I hungry like this before

Instead of bread you gave me crumbs
Maybe you just want me to salivate
Why do you act like this
Fat controlling experimenter
Who at the beginning called himself 'GOOD SAMARITAN'

I have realized that you did not mean all that good
You had come here to explore my wealth
Bloody spy in camouflage of a missionary
Did you think you would succeed forever and ever?

Look here . . .
Now that you are aware
That I am hard to get
You try and play monkey tricks
But you have failed with your BANTU EDUCATION
You thought I would bow down till when?

Relationships: Political

You stole my forefathers' land
You thought I would bow down till when? ... Huh!
I mean it
And I mean it
I am not going to stand your lie
You found me comfortable
You requested that I give you fresh water and vegetables
And at the end my blood has become your water
My body your vegetables
I have given a hand
But now you want the whole arm
You are not going to get me
And I mean it!

You tell me you are going to give me scattered portions
Of my own soil
And now you claim that this is a whiteman's country
You forget how you came here
You are a fool
You are mad
And I mean it!

Routine
Esmeralda Riberio | *Brazil*
Translated by Carolyn Richardson Durham

There's always a man
telling me

what to do.

✳ *Political Union*
Iyamide Hazeley | *Sierra Leone/England*

You call me 'Sister' Brother,
yet it seems you speak with the empty kernel of the word,
and sometimes
when you talk to me
there lingers after
a void
far more empty than existed before.
When you hear my anguished silence and are reassured by it
     then I know that your strength depends on my
     becoming weak
     that you have not questioned
     the bars, deeply entrenched,
     of the barbed cage, externally defined
     that is the oppressor's role you so emulate.
When you look above the waist
     see my face
     touch my skin,
     nestle on my breast as though
     to reclaim the ease of infancy
     then I know
     that you have concretised my body
     in your mind, into a temple
     for your fantasies.
When you fraternise with my sisters while demanding my
fidelity
then I know that you yourself are unfulfilled.

Many times you have seen my nakedness
     but not noticed my eyes
     as you surround me in your taunting caress.
Can you, physically a part of this body
Try to see, inside this body
     the joy and the pain at once housed side by side?

Can you stop wearing me, playing me
      stop strumming my emotions?

You call me 'Sister' Brother,
      yet I know
      that it is simply a psychological lever to prise apart
      my legs.
'Sister, make coffee for the movement,
Sister, make babies for the struggle'
You raped my consciousness with your body
      my body with reason,
and assuage your unconscious guilt by oral politicking
                        make believing
'Sister, Sister'.

When you yourself acknowledge the Occidental fetters
that truss you,
When you yourself see the hidden fenders that seal the
seal
over your mind's eye
against me
When you can see that my political significance is
          a vertical one
      that my contribution is
          a vanguard one
          and you can see my total
Then you can call me Sister
Then you will be my Comrade.

Equality
Gwendoline C. Konie | *Zambia*

I shall not stand
on mountain tops.
Indeed, I shall not shout
at the top of my voice,
nor stamp my foot in rage.
I shall not take
unusual steps for recognition.
But, I shall stretch myself.
I shall spread my wings
and in so doing, lift myself up!
I shall use my intellect.
Brother, father, husband!
I shall not challenge you
as my brother,
nor as my father.
No, not even as my husband!
But I shall challenge you
as a worker.
I shall challenge you
as a scholar.
Indeed, I shall challenge you
as a whole human being.
I shall use my intellect
to prove my point
that you and I are mortal.
That you need me
as I need you—
until we stand shoulder to shoulder,
eye-ball to eye-ball—
and I see the miraculous
softening in your eyes
a prelude to respect
an acknowledgement of each other.
Then, and only then
shall you deserve
my undivided loyalty and love.

Candidacy in the Making
Gwendoline C. Konie* | *Zambia*

Mine is a candidacy
for every ordinary man and woman
who ever believed in the God given ability
for a human being to rise above the ordinary.
It is a candidacy
for every man born of a woman
who has revered that woman for having given him life.
Mine is a candidacy:
for every man who ever wanted his woman to excel.
It is a candidacy
for every man who ever fathered a daughter
who was a potential president.
Mine is indeed a candidacy
for every mother who ever spent countless hours
grooming her daughter for a fuller life.
It is a candidacy
for every brother whose sister's leadership potential
drove him up the wall and generated sibling jealousy!
Mine is indeed a candidacy
for every sister who ever had to stamp her foot in rage
at her erstwhile brother, demanding recognition
of her leadership qualities!
Above all,
Mine is a candidacy
for every girl whose dreams on countless occasions
transported her to a world of unlimited freedoms,
where she was unafraid to be who she wanted to be.
To crown it all,
mine is a candidacy
for that special woman with sufficient courage and arrogance,
coupled with the right amount of humility
to stand her in good-stead, when she had to cross
her political threshold, as a liberated soul,
capable of becoming whomsoever she was destined to be.

---

*   Candidate for First Woman President of Zambia 2001 and 2006.

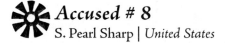

Accused # 8
S. Pearl Sharp | *United States*

"I stand accused
    Of loving

you too much ..."

Accused # 8
they call her.
Accused # 8
Name by number.

Accused # 8
accused of
kidnapping the spirit of those
in need of vision/sight

Accused # 8
accused of assaulting the senses of the world
with beauty

Accused # 8
accused of turning a "banning"
into a world movement

and who stands accused?
of burning down the woman's home
who stands accused?
of removing the woman's love mate
who stands accused?
of keeping the pregnant woman
on a prison floor
who stands accused?
of creating a nation of Winnie's

unnamed
but not unfelt?
who among us is not accused?
of being wrong
of being Black
of freeing ourselves in
our own recognizance

8 cannot be banned
dance on it:
8 cannot be banned!

8: circular power
8: love locking arms
  8: bonds unbroken
    8: lotus regenerating
      8: circle of protection
    8: the unmoved mover
  8: omega chained at the waist
8: infinity on end

Accused # 8
accused of kidnapping and assault
and, " I stand of accused
Of loving you too much
And I hope it's not a crime. . ."

Canto I
Dionne Brand | *Trinidad/Canada*

ashes head to toes
juju belt
guinea eyes unfolded impossible
squint a sun since drenched
breasts beaded of raised skin
naked woman speaks
syllables come in dust's pace
dried, caked rim of desert mouth
naked woman speaks
run mouth, tell.
when the whites come they were dead men
we did not want to touch them
we did not want to interfere in their business
after the disappearances
many times there were dead men among us
and we cursed them
and we gave them food
when the whites came they were dead men
five men died in our great battles before
guns gave us more heads of our enemies
and those who disappeared were dead men
and the dead take care of their own
for things come and they leave
enemies were dead men and whites were
    dead men
and our city and our people flourished
and died also,
naked woman speak
syllables come in water's pace
long river mouth, tell.

Canto III
Dionne Brand | *Trinidad/Canada*

one thing for sure
dismembered woman,
when you decide
you are alone
understand,
ugly faced woman
when you decide
you are alone
when you dance
it's on your own
broken face
when you eat
your own plate of stones
for blasted sure
you are alone
where do you think you're going
dismembered woman
limbs chopped off
at the ankles.
when you decide,
believe me
you are alone
sleep,
sleep,
tangential face
sleep
sleeping or waking
understand
you are alone.
diamonds
pour from your vagina
and your breasts
drip healing copper

but listen woman
dismembered continent
you are alone
see
crying fool
you want to talk in gold
you will cry in iron
you want to dig up stones
you will bury flesh
you think you don't need
oils and amulets, compelling
powder
and reliance smoke
you want to throw people
in cesspits.
understand
dismembered one
ululant
you are alone
when water falls back
land surfaces

    they're like bottle-flies
    around my anus
    look at their blue mouth on my excrement
    when my face is bandaged up
    like war,
    white and cracked
    like war
    I know
    I am alone.
    You think I don't know
    I am alone
    when my foot
    is cracked and white
    like hungry people
    I have a stick for alone

tell them to come for me
and bring their father too
fly will light on him before day finish
my face will set up
like the sky for rain
for them
tell them to come for me
and bring their brother too
all that can happen to me
has happened
I have a big stick for alone.

I was sent
to this cave
I went out one day like a fool
to this cave
to find clay
to dig up metals
to decorate my bare and painful breasts
water and clay
for poultice
for this gash
to find a map, an imprint
anywhere
would have kept me calm,
anywhere
with description.
instead
I found
a piece of this,
a tooth,
a bit of food
hung on,
a metatarsal
which resembled mine,
something else
like a note, musical

ting ting!
but of so little pitch
so little lasting
perhaps it was my voice
and this too
a suggestion
an insinuation
so slight
it may be untrue
something moving
over the brow
as with eyes closed to black
the sensate pole
phantom!
knocks
the forehead back
the middle of a dance
no, I cannot say dance
it exaggerates;
phantom
a bit of image
a motion close to sound
a sound imaged on my retina
resembling sound.
a sound seen out of the corner of my eye
a motion heard on my inner ear
I pored over these
like a paleontologist
I dusted them
like an
archaeologist
a swatch of cloth, skin
artless
coarse utility
but not enough.
yes enough
still only a bit

of paint, of dye
on a stone
I cannot say crude
but a crude thing
nevertheless
a hair
a marking
that of fingernail to rock
an ancient wounded scratch
I handled these like
a papyrologist
contours
a desert sprung here
migrations
suggestions, lies,
phantom!
a table land
jutting up,
artful
covert, mud
I noted these
like a geopolitical
scientist
I will
take
any evidence of me
even that carved
in the sky
by the fingerprints of clouds
everyday
even those
that do not hold
a wind's impression.

✳ Women's War: Nigerian Delta
Jacqueline Johnson | *United States*

Praise to the grandmothers in lappas and T-shirts
protesting against low wages and poverty
who commandeered southwest delta ferries
pushing back the gates of Chevron-Texaco oil.

Praise to all those secret society women
who took over five hundred and eighty three acres
of Delta oil land, now Chevron Texaco property,
staring down the ghosts of their future.

What if we here in America had joined them,
made stronger their protest.
It's so hard to think of global freedom
when you don't have local freedom.

What if we here had joined them
shut down Texaco and Shell oil USA?
Demanded, no oil sales,
until you do right by my sisters in Escravos.

These ordinary women shouting for jobs,
blocked the airline terminal stopping
Chevron=92s presidents from escaping,
back to Europe and the safety of empires.

Great grandmothers in geles and braids
demand more housing, new towns,
twenty-four hour electricity. Call for
their wealth to come back to them.

Praise to the grandmothers from fifty to ninety
Who strapped grandchildren to their backs,
camped out on the concrete grounds of Chevron

as husbands and children brought food each night.

For ten days they stopped production,
took seven hundred workers hostage.
Grandmothers who were not making mash
but war, like their foremothers 1929 Women's War.

Praise to Nigerian Delta grandmothers
threatening to go naked in front of
male workers and foreign power brokers
shaming Chevron oil thieves into negotiation.
Praise to the grandmothers for the new women's war.

(based on incidents that occurred in the Nigerian Delta during the
summer of 2004)

✸ Just Becuz U Believe in Abortion Doesnt Mean U're Not Pro-Life

laini mataka | *United States*

recently i read a medical report that claimed
women who had abortions were not traumatized.
the person who said that, shld have been aborted.

it was probably some right-to-lifer
who believes that all pregnant women shld be made
to have babies even if they've been raped, even if
it was incest, even if it means their sanity, even
if they can't take care of a baby.

that same right-to-lifer
wants children to have the right to be born in dire
poverty, to have the right to live with rats and roaches
to have the right to have a number instead of a name,
to have the right to be born into a situation they
can't possibly live thru.

just let the babies come; it doesn't matter what they're
coming into; it doesnt matter whether they're wanted
or not; it doesn't matter whether they'll be welcomed
by crack-heads, alcoholics, pimps or molesters.
lifers believe in quantity not quality, and they almost
never volunteer to take care of some of these babies
they want to force to be born. yet, when it comes to
killin babies in somalia, uganda or yugoslavia:
no problem. no demonstrations. no blocking the entrance
of invading armies. no protest against dropped bombs.
they only understand the concept of life within the
context of amerika, which everybody knows is the center
of dead meat.

to hear the lifers tell it, it's a pleasure for a woman

to lay up on a table and have her insides sucked out by
a human-eater—vacuum-cleaner. they think all u have to
do is blink yr eyes and u're thru and ready to go
to the club later, and meet mr. destiny. yet some
lifers are women who wear make-up which they're too
stupid to kno was made from the dead fetuses.

lifers wanna tell u it's murder to abort a fetus.
and i say, if it must be done, its better to abort at
3 weeks than at 13 yrs of age. look at our city streets
and there are unwanted children walkin, beggin, sellin
rippin, killin: becuz nobody wanted them, and they know it.

lifers claim they've got the church on their side
(hell, the church started chattel slavery) but
we wont talk about the baby bones that have so often
been found when convents are torn down.
they say the wrath of God will visit anyone who has
an abortion/but i got news for them—most women
punish themselves more severely than God ever cld
or wld. and any God that cant forgive, needs to
be replaced.

nobody really wants to get up on that table!
nobody really wants to kill a part of themselves.
nobody wants to meet their ancestors with blood on
their hands/but when a woman knows she CANT
handle bringing a new life into fullness/she *more than*
has the right, to beg that life's forgiveness
and send it back to the spirit world.

there are women who say they dont believe in abortion
and they have baby after baby by man after man
and their children suckle themselves on empty tits
and later kill somebody over a pair on tennis shoes.

there are men who say they dont believe in abortion
and finesse their way into the front door to knock
somebody up before they slide out the back door.
and like bees they go from flower to flower
flying forever away from tiny faces that look
just like them.

i hate this society for creating an atmosphere so terrible
that good, clean women feel compelled to stop life
from coming fully into being/and yet
i thank the Mother-God for the technology
that allows a woman to free herself from the possibility
of becoming a horrible mother.

Feminist Poem Number One
Elizabeth Alexander | *United States*

Yes I have dreams where I am rescued by men:
my father, brother, husband, no one else.
Last night I dreamed my brother and husband
morphed into each other and rescued me
from a rat-infested apartment. "Run!"
he said, feral scampering at our heels.
And then we went to lunch at the Four Seasons.

What does it mean to be a princess?
"I am what is known as an American Negro,"
my grandmother would say, when "international friends"
would ask her what she was. She'd roller-skate
to Embassy Row and sit on the steps of the embassies
to be certain the rest of the world was there.

What does it mean to be a princess?
My husband drives me at six A.M.
to the airport an hour away, drives home,
drives back when I have forgotten my passport.
What does it mean to be a prince? I cook
savory, fragrant meals for my husband
and serve him, if he likes, in front of the TV.
He cooks for me, too. I have a husband.
In the dream we run into Aunt Lucy,
who is waiting for a plane from "Abyssinia"
to bring her lover home. I am the one
married to an Abyssinian, who is already here. I am the one
with the grandmother who wanted to know the world.
I am what is known as an American Negro princess,
married to an African prince,
living in a rat-free apartment in New Haven,
all of it, all of it, under one roof.

For Those Who Are Trying to Understand Black Women

Gloria Wade Gayles | *United States*

You are searching for
trying to find
wanting to understand
Black women?

You want to look inside
our dreams and journey through
the dense forest of our desires?

You want to see us walk in bare feet
through alleyways of pain, stepping
on neglect and loneliness and your
prediction that we will bleed to death?

You want to hear us hum just hum because
we are sometimes too weary from singing
the blues to remember the words?

You want to see us in midnight lace
stroking our men whom
you have not found whom
you refuse to understand?

You want to touch our field-heavy
dishwater hands and trace the lines
that tell a story whose beginning
was the beginning?

You want to know how we do it
love
smile
dance

plan
achieve
dream
stay sane
and walk affirmed
in your world?

You want to know us,
Black women,
who do it all
in spite of it all?

First:

Do you believe in miracles?

✳ Traditional Post-Modern Neo-HooDoo Afra-Centric Sister in a Purple Head Rag Mourning Death and Cooking

Michelle Clinton | *United States*

1.

Traditional:
>that mean has a voice & a person
>you can relate to
>& probably a plot w/ a beginning, middle & end
>& if you don't understand it, the poem don't work

Post-Modern:
>is because of 1945 when the americans dropped
>the first nuclear bomb
>on nagasaki asia
>& got everybody thinking about death of the species
>more problems, more paranoia

Neo-HooDoo:
>1972, *Conjure*, by Ishmael Reed
>deals out of a black bohemian mentality
>also post-nationalist BoHo Nats of new york city

Neo-HooDoo:
>sound a lot like voodoo
>also new, which is not real

Afra-Centric:
>afra-centric
>like first colored was the compliment
>then negro was the compliment
>& nigguh was always the insult
>then change happened
>& black was everything beautiful
>& africa was new
>then nigguh was the precious secret
>then afro-mantic

now everything
now afra-centric
now of course news of the first mother of the first womb
in the first cave of afra-centric
africa
Afra-Centric:
coined by Asungi, womanist artist
Sister:
this means of a woman
of the uterus root
In A Purple Head Rag:
Purple:
a color
a color like colored like
nigguh was so black he was blue
girl was so blue she was purple
the color purple
which is Alice Walker which is our time
A Head Rag:
this is a head rag
as relaxed
as home
as natural
Mourning Death:
Morning:
as the sound of the first day
Mourning:
as the sound of hurting for the loss of a dead person
Death:
as barrier to the spirits
And Cooking:
as sexual energy
as communal response
as human feeling

2.

Morning was the softest hum
an anti-music buzz that ached
in my face when he died
a white boy suicide
in love w/ the evil in elvis
& conjured a heart attack
w/ cigarettes & despair

All the hard & good people
who loved him at a funeral
party freak out

I was about to call
I was ready to wail
        ready to grieve & receive
the basic wisdom to deal w/ the situation
I was trying to be connected
to the black at the bottom of my genes
bad enough to box w/ grief
that plus some impulse to take
care of business & feed people
to taste & stir & season
& pass out plates solid w/ material radiance

It's me thinking
cooking is sometimes a contradiction
folks w/ european privilege
people w/ penis privilege
get happy on the service
& greedy w/ my love
I won't be nobody's mammy
but at a wake when folks mourning
when common & good sense both take a whipping
when understanding sits down, trembles & falls into fits
it's a sin not to cook

it's a sin to hold back any kinda magic you got going

It's me thinking
I gotta come across
so I put an honest drain on my mystery
I cooked
I tried to look good
I ate & danced w/ strangers
I listened for the echo that the dead heart leaves
& wore the color purple

It's me remembering
trying to sing
that plus holding myself
I had to soothe & quiet somebody
& ended up witness
to this pain washing through
a body of people
who came together
because he left us
because he had to
do what all bodies have to do
sometime

which is pass on
let go
& finally say good bye.

✳ Ten Essential Rules to Live By to be the Best Good Girl on the Planet *for Kate Hymes*

Jadi Omowale | *United States*

1. Wish only for the happiness of your loved ones. Say no only to yourself.

2. Wait your turn. Though angry, say nothing though the vein in your right temple pulses.

3. Make sure you hold your tongue when you want to scream. You break a promise instead or lie, but smile nicely while doing it.

4. Say you are sorry. Frequently. Convincingly.

5. Smile so much your cheeks feel like pulled taffy. You sometimes practice frowning.

6. Always give things away. When you run out of objects, time and money, give blood or bone.

7. Never complain. Slam doors, drawers, dishes. Create arguments when you are alone in the house.

8. Feel guilty when something gives you pleasure.

9. Lie to keep the peace though you have none.

10. Never leave. Wait for him to die instead.

✳ *Nok Lady in Terracotta*
Ifi Amadiume | *Nigeria/England*

If I were to write with my blood,
dip deep in the stream of my tears
to tell what sorrow my heart bears,
still I would not have made history,
as I seem not the first to tell my story;

Sad-eyed Nok lady
captured here in this terracotta,
I see reflections in your valley;
that fine deep curve
moulded by the course of sweat-drops
which have run down your brows,
mingled with your tears,
trailing down to leave
the telling marks of time
at the corners of your eyes,
running to the very base of your cheekbones;
delicate, mysterious to the stranger
but special truly to you
Nok lady.

And sad-eyed sisters I see daily,
I know by your looks,
though recorded in no books,
we too have travelled the same road,
carried the same load,
and sipped of the same sorrow;
knowing we are the beginning of
that distant road of long ago-
the very basis; the grass roots-
the mystery and the secret of which
locks behind those sad lines
running along the curves

of the eyes of the Nok lady in terracotta.

Sister-tears of denial I share today;
same sap which ran through the mother stem
now runs in her off-shoots and grows on;
once ploughed, she will crop,
though she reaps not what she sows,
for the planters pick her harvest;
pitcher of water, not your water;
river-bed carrying not your water;
so mother do you carry their sons
who in turn will marry off your daughters!

Weak-kneed sisters sitting trembling
with nostrils flaring
and that rhythmic shake of the feet,
telling tales of anger and defeat!
Weep not sister, you are not alone,
for you are just one branch of the tree-
The Tree of Life; The Tree of Africa;
stretched out across the black land
is that dark mysterious valley
between the legs of Great Mother Nile,
the cradles of our birth
we dare not deny.

Still Mother!
you should not have flirted,
mating with the current
to give birth to civilization,
deserting your children
in your careless amorous trips
between the current and the sun.
Your sons in vengeance,
did they not desert you?
appropriate your daughters?
take control of the lands?

ces exchanging sisters?

er!
were thus left neglected,
ose sons left you unprotected,
then the rape began:
persecuting Persians!
merciless Macedonians!
ruling Romans!
ruthless Arabs!
torturing Turks!
treacherous French!
leech-like English!
You see sister,
the beginning of your anguish.

They too cunningly control lands,
mindlessly exchange sisters,
purposely pass on knowledge
controlling your minds
as you deny yourselves
and refuse to look into her eyes-
the eyes of the Nok lady in terracotta.

✳ *Your Only Mission* *for Elizabeth*
Mendi Lewis Obadike | *United States*

bleeding, she said. *I'm a bleeding,* she said,
I'm a bleeding heart, she said, reaching in the air
for what she'd never grasp.

I'll never forget the back of her head, her ugly hair
shaking over her neighbor's plate as she started to tell it,
the dream the poet's dream had made her remember.

over the stove, she said, *I was standing over the stove,*
she said, *I was standing over the stove cooking a black woman's body*
that kept coming up, that I kept pushing down.

Adding, *And I'm a,* adding, with a straight face, *And I'm a bleeding,*
Adding, with her hand, reaching towards the poet, *And I'm a*
bleeding heart, her hand, her reach for redemption, *a bleeding heart liberal.*

And so free now, I note, absolved from her guilt, no longer a secret,
left blossoming on an altar. It's my stomach turning over
with her spoon, blood at a rapid boil.

These are things that keep coming up as my student tells my class that
when he first saw me he thought to himself, "ghetto porch bum" and I
think, *I should write a poem about this,* but when I get to the stanza where
I'll say it, I don't want to write the poem anymore. I don't want it beautiful
or ugly or clean. I don't want it to have line breaks or structure, to make
sense or feel chaotic. I just want to tell it so I don't forget that happened.
I don't like how writing can mean that I don't scream or don't need to
scream because I know I can use it. I don't thinking, *Now this will make*
an interesting poem before I think, *This is making my veins hurt.* Later I'll
go have coconut soup on Chapel Street and tell my husband how my day
went while we eat. He'll be wearing the blue sweater I bought him and
I'll be thinking about how black his eyes are when I let it slip that I keep
wondering what I could have done to fix this child's head. And he'll say,
trained, he'll say, *not trained,* he'll say,

trained to exorcise white people's demons. And he'll tell me,
  n those black eyes, *cross the water,* with those black eyes
  a me, *You'll have to cross the water if you want to do that.*

 we'll go home and sit in the bean bag chairs and I'll twist his locks.
And when I lie down on one side he'll whisper, *mission,* he'll whisper, *only mission,*
he'll whisper, into my gaping ear, *Your only mission is to not be stopped.*

✺ Need: A Chorale for Black Woman Voices
Audre Lorde | United States

For Patricia Cowan* and Bobbie Jean Graham** and the hundreds of other mangled Black Women whose nighmares inform these words.

tattle tale tit.
> *your tongue will be slit*
> *and every little boy in town*
> *shall have a little bit.*
>> —Nursery rhyme

I.

(Poet)
This woman is Black
so her blood is shed into silence
this woman is Black
so her blood falls to earth
like the droppings of birds
to be washed away with silence and rain.

(Pat)
For a long time after the baby came
I didn't go out at all
and it got to be pretty lonely.
Then Bubba started asking about his father
made me feel
like connecting to the blood again
maybe I'd meet someone
we could move on together
help make the dream real.
An ad in the paper said
    "Black actress needed
        to audition in a play by Black Playwright."
I was anxious to get back to work
and this was a good place to start

so Monday afternoon
on the way home from school with Bubba
I answered the ad.

In the middle of the second act
he put a hammer through my head.

(*Bobbie*)
If you're hit in the middle of Broadway
by a ten-ton truck
your caved-in chest bears the mark of a tire
and your liver pops like a rubber ball.
If you're knocked down by a boulder
from a poorly graded hill
your dying is stamped with the print of rock.

But when your boyfriend methodically
beats you to death
in the alley behind your apartment
while your neighbors pull down their window shades
because they don't want to get involved
the police call it a crime of "passion"
not a crime of hatred.

Yet I still died
of a lacerated liver
and a man's heelprint
upon my chest.

II.

(*Poet*)
Dead Black women haunt the black maled streets
paying our cities' secret and familiar tithe of blood
burn blood   beat blood   cut blood
seven-year-old-child rape-victim   blood
of a sodomized grandmother   blood

on the hands of my brother
as women we were meant to bleed
but not this useless blood
each month a memorial
to my unspoken sisters   fallen
red drops upon asphalt.

(*All*)
We were not meant to bleed
a symbol for no one's redemption
Is it our blood
that keeps these cities fertile?

(*Poet*)
I do not even know all their names.
Black women's deaths are not noteworthy
not threatening or glamorous enough
to decorate the evening news
not important enough to be fossilized
between right-to-life pickets
and a march against gun-control
we are refuse in this city's war
with no medals   no exchange of prisoners
no packages from home   no time off
for good behavior
no victories. No victors.

(*Bobbie*)
How can I build a nation
afraid to walk out into moonlight
lest I lose my power
afraid to speak out
lest my tongue be slit
my ribs kicked in
by a brawny acquaintance
my liver bleeding life onto the stone.

(*All*)
How many other deaths
do we live through daily
pretending
we are alive?

III.

(*Pat*)
What terror embroidered my face
onto your hatred
what unchallenged enemy
took on my sweet brown flesh
within your eyes
came armed against you
with only my laughter   my hopeful art
my hair catching the late sunlight
my small son eager to see his mama work?
On this front page
My blood stiffens in the cracks of your fingers
raised to wipe a half-smile from your lips.
Beside you a white policeman
bends over my bleeding son
decaying into my brother
who stalked me with a singing hammer.

I need you. For what?
Was there no better place
to dig for your manhood
except in my woman's bone?

(*Bobbie*)
And what do you need me for, brother,
to move for you   feel for you   die for you?
We have a grave need for each other
but your eyes are thirsty
for vengeance

dressed in the easiest blood
and I am closest.

(Pat)
When you opened my head with your hammer
did the boogie stop in your brain
the beat go on
did terror run out of you like curdled fury
a half-smile upon your lips?
And did your manhood lay in my skull
like a netted fish
or did it spill out like milk or blood
or impotent fury off the tips of your fingers
as your sledgehammer clove my bone
to let the light out
did you touch it as it flew away?

(Bobbie)
Borrowed hymns veil a misplaced hatred
saying you need me   you need me   you need me
a broken drum
calling me   Black goddess   Black hope   Black
strength   Black mother
yet you touch me
and I die in the alleys of Boston
my stomach stomped through the small of my back
my hammered-in skull in Detroit
a ceremonial knife
through my grandmother's used vagina
the burned body hacked to convenience
in a vacant lot
I lie in midnight blood like a rebel city
bombed into submission
while our enemies still sit in power
and judgement
over us all.

(*Bobbie & Pat*)
Do you *need* me submitting to terror   at nightfall
to chop into bits and stuff warm into plastic bags
near the neck of the Harlem River
they found me   eight months swollen
with your need
do you need me to rape in my seventh year
bloody semen in the corners of my childish mouth
as you accuse me of being seductive.

(*All*)
Do you need me imprinting upon our children
the destruction our enemies print upon you
like a Mack truck or an avalanche
destroying us both
carrying their hatred back home
you relearn my value
in an enemy coin.

IV.

(*Poet*)
I am wary of need that tastes like destruction.

(*All*)
I am wary of need
that tastes like destruction.

(*Poet*)
Who learns to love me
from the mouth of my enemies
walks the edge of my world
a phantom in a crimson cloak
and the dreambooks speak of money
but my eyes say death.

The simplest part of this poem

is the truth in each one of us
to which it is speaking.

How much of this truth can I bear
to see
and still live
unblinded?
How much of this pain can I use?

"We cannot live without our lives."

---

* Patricia Cowan, 21, bludgeoned to death in Detroit, 1978.

** Bobbie Jean Graham, 34, beaten to death in Boston, 1979. One of twelve black
women murdered within a three-month period in that city.

TRIBUTES

For Women Famous and Ordinary

A Poem for Ella Fitzgerald
Sonia Sanchez | *United States*

when she came on the stage, this Ella
there were rumors of hurricanes and
over the rooftops of concert stages
the moon turned red in the sky,
it was Ella, Ella.
queen Ella had come
and words spilled out
leaving a trail of witnesses smiling
amen—amen—a woman—a woman.

she began
this three aged woman
nightingales in her throat
and squads of horns came out
to greet her.

streams of violins and pianos
splashed their welcome
and our stained glass silences
our braided spaces
unraveled
opened up
said who's that coming?

who's that knocking at the door?
whose voice lingers on
that stage gone mad with
        perdido perdido perdido.
        i lost my heart in toledooooooo.

whose voice is climbing
up this morning chimney
smoking with life
carrying her basket of words

Tributes

a tisket a tasket
my little yellow
basket—I wrote a
letter to my mom and
on the way I dropped it—
was it red . . .no no no no
it was green . . . no no no no
was it blue . . . no no no no
just a little yellow

voice rescuing razor thin lyrics
from hopscotching dreams.

we first watched her navigating
an apollo stage amid high-stepping
yellow legs

we watched her watching us
shiny and pure woman
sugar and spice woman
her voice a nun's whisper
her voice pouring out
guitar thickened blues
her voice a faraway horn
questioning the wind,
and she became Ella,
first lady of tongues
Ella cruising our veins
voice walking on water
crossed in prayer,
she became holy
a thousand sermons
concealed in her bones
as she raised them in a
symphonic shudder
carrying our sighs into
her bloodstream.

this voice chasing the
morning waves,
this Ella-tonian voice soft
like four layers of lace.

> *when I die Ella*
> *tell the whole joint*
> *please, please, don't talk*
> *about me when I'm gone . . . .*

i remember waiting nite for her appearance
audience impatient at the latness
of musicians,
i remember it was april
and the flowers ran yellow
the sun downpoured yellow butterflies
and the day was yellow and silent
all of spring held us
in a single drop of blood.

when she appeared on stage
she became Nut arching over us
feet and hands palced on the stage
music flowing from her breast
she swallowed the sun
sang confessions from the evening stars
made earth divulge her secrets
gave birth to the skies in her song
remade the insistent air
and we became anointed found
inside her bop
> *bop bop dowa*
> *bop bop doowaaa*
> *bop bop dooooowaaaa*
Lady, Lady, Lady.
be good. be good

to me.

     to you.   to us all

cuz we just some lonesome babes

in the woods

hey lady. sweetellalady

Lady. Lady. Lady. be gooooood

ELLA ELLA ELLALADY

    be good

        gooooood

           goooooood. . .

Song for Alice Coltrane
Ellease Southerland | *United States*

Alice.
At the river where
water is changed to wind
clay changed to fire.
The sun translates to a mute thought
caught in the bitter grace of her hands.

     Leroian rivers run
through a psychological country.
Sun translates to a mute thought
caught in the bitter-grace of her hands.
Music is changed to wind
clay changed to songs.
The hollow rush grows in
the wet places of her music.
The river.
The river.
It is a sign of deeper love.
It is a sign needed in these times.
Alice.
The river.
Water is changed to wind
clay changed to fire.

Portrait

Virginia Brindis de Salas | *Uruguay*

Translated by Ann Venture Young

Where do you come from,
passionate and exalted one?
Your blood saw the ardors
of expectant Nigeria.
Curved
and arrogant like the ebony
contour of your face.
Your fragrant armpits
like the flora of the jungle.
Like the undulation of the snake
your hips,
black girl.

Diva *for Abby Lincoln (Amenata Moseka)*
Jadi Omowale | *United States*

The Diva
>   Shimmering eyes wrapped in kohl
>   Black silk, head to foot
>   Smile, wavering in the bright glare of stage lights

Looked lonely, lovely on the bare stage
Was said to be difficult, acting Diva-ish when the mike went dead...

The audience wanted to pull close
She kept them at arms length
but made them at home when she sang "Joe"

Later, she signed autographs, tried to forget tonight's performance,
wanting the next one

The Diva
Ripped herself apart after each performance,
searching for her inadequacies
Cried at them
Then stitched her skin tightly around the faults she found

She wanted the world to be blinded by her perfection
and was careful, to not let slip her perceptions of herself

The Diva is—
The first lady
The one who makes her world her art
She is the Goddess delivering herself to us on a platter decorated with her
soul

The Diva
We call her that
(it is a caress)

Amazed at the gifts she shares with us
The gifts she remakes nightly, behind locked doors
Alone with materials, God given, that she knows to live
She must give back

Queen-Mothers
Oktavi Allison | *United States*

We walked
With Pharaohs
Maiden head
Low in
Egyptian dust
Bearing princes

Gazed our sons
Groveled in clay
Crack-tear of whip
Slumped them like
Drought magnolias
Over southern terrace

From fields of
Crack pipe concrete
Men-Son folk are
Lifted shoulder high
Suited in
Blue, midnight
Body bags

Over funeral song
Pine, mahogany
Cranked below a
A mothers' weep

Queen-mothers
Sanctify squalor of
Desecrated gardens
Plant prayers for
Cherished, best
Tend seeds of
Princes
Yet to rise

Letters to Our Ancestors

Gloria Wade Gayles | *United States*

To Sojourner Truth

you wear your name well
sisterwoman of truth

riding your chariot
hard and fast
through mud puddles
leaving brown tracks
on the faces of men
ashamed to show their arms

hard and fast
with your skirt raised
by your own hands
and your Bible raised
and your anger raised

hard and fast
through the births
and the thefts
and your mother's pain
which none but your Jesus knew,
and understood

you wear your name well
sisterwoman of truth
whose dressed-down words
rode hard and fast
through the centuries
arriving in time
and on time
to dressusup

for change.

To Phillis Wheatley

a million regrets we owe you
singer of songs
dancer with words denying
truth in every couplet
pain rhymed

they decorated you for royalty
we hanged you for treason

they stole your life
we threw away your art
which was the only life
you ever owned

a million regrets we owe you
sister poet
genius woman
mother of the free ones
writing freely

NOW

To Harriet Tubman

Time means nothing to those
whose suffering continues time
and time again to be ignored
by Time which takes no time
to end the seconds, minutes
hours and centuries of
our pain

Tributes

It is time, I say,
to close the books
which lock you in a time
called yesterday
so removed from now that
only somebody else's words
can tell me who you were
and what you did
then

today
this moment
this second
(not a century ago)
but today
this moment
this second
I see your anger silencing a chorus of fears
your skirt brushing the earth clear of tracks
your courage calming the waters
your teeth
   biceps
legs
    arms
pulling the train to freedom.

To Ida Wells Barnett

from your womb
the children
you held with love
and released
for others to hold
while you held
the race

from your mind
the words pressed
into action
and history
from your rage
the knife
that cut the rope
and the gun
your woman's hands
would have cannoned
even at moving targets

To Mary McLeod Bethune

your dark skin and body
too large for dainties
meant by their definition
beauty was not yours

but it was not beauty you sought
or needed in their conference rooms

wearing the aroma of pies
passion
and the people's dreams,
you walked in
thunderously
sat down
proudly
took off your white gloves

ceremoniously
and moved your dark hands
fast
like scythes cutting through
thickets of lies

your lips
pursed with Africa
preached the plans
and sang the alma mater
yet to be

when you finished
talking and singing
(you never danced for them)
you
left sane
with your bodacious hat
cocked arrogant
and
victorious

it was their world
their game
even their words

but your school

Fire the Canons (and let me stain the picketed tightly fenced borders of our history)

Stephanie Pruitt | *United States*

for the every day Women
who labor
continuously
wanting
no more than
earned wages
and everything beyond touch
intimately familiar with held breath
and love on lay-a-way
skin stretched
marked with bulging memories
canons
heavy
loaded
waiting for ignition

Maria Pina & the B & G Grill

Mari Evans | *United States*

Maria Pina
brown coffeevoice pinched
thin jamaican edges
sings to the red vinyl
nowhere do she smiling

Sullied sagging fakefurred
nowhere do she smiling
singing to the vinyl
to the bougainvillea
graceful in the hot cup
of her sightless seeing
she singing purple agony
waydown deep in black necks
singing crystal laughter
frothingfresh in white eyes
sings she man/ driven
whiskey mad
by d'white fo'ks

Maria Pina
sullied sagging fakefurred
nowhere do she smiling
singing to the vinyl
she see bougainvillea
Only bougainvillea

Special Dedication To Jamaican Women
Afua Cooper | *Canada*

To all those women
who rise at 5 in the morning
to prepare food for their children and
send them off to school
while their men lay in bed

To those women who have no food to give
their children
and cannot afford to send them to school
and whose men have disappeared

To those women who struggle to raise their children
while at the same time fighting to earn a living
from inside stinky factories
or from lying on cold sidewalks
or from hacking an existence from rocky hillsides
or taking abuse from men who are their only
source of survival

To those women who spend their nights and days
in the marketplace
through good weather and through bad
not because it's something they love to do
but because they cannot bear to see
the haunting eyes of their children

And to the new breed
Those women conductors
who operate buses between Papine and Half-Way-Tree
who have masculinised themselves
so they can better withstand
the abuse men hurl at them
To you I dedicate this poem

Authentication

Geni Guimaraes | *Brazil*

Translated by Carolyn Richardson Durham

When she saw herself
she wanted to turn away
to hide herself
to disappear
to deny.

She did so much to undo,
she bled so much not to bleed,
she aspired,
she spat,
she drank,
she dedicated herself, she struggled,
so upon conquering herself, she loved herself.

Today she exhibits her beautiful black face
To the fierce sun that dresses the road.
She is satisfied.
Life is a head
The mind is hers.

Pregón Number Two
Virginia Brindis de Salas | *Uruguay*
Translated by Ann Venture Young

At six in the morning
through the streets of the city
a voice rings in the air;
the cry of the vendor, Marimorena.

What news, what news
of the world does the newspaper bring?

At five in the afternoon;
the call of Marimorena
like a loud bell
in the popular neighborhoods;
the call of Marimorena!

Old colored woman, who gave you
that strident melody
that comes from your lungs,
proclaiming night and day
the dramas of the world?

Peddler of hopes
with newspapers under your arm;
four cents and small talk
which you forget down the block.

Nights in the suburbs
come back to your mind;
troubled hearts spin
so that others may live.

What do the editors know about
how to sell a newspaper,

or politicians or professors
beyond their primer?

You, black illiterate woman,
Marimorena,
day to day, face to face
you fill the streets
with provocative sounds:
first in the morning
then in the afternoon
for thirty or thirty-one
days of each month.

No amount of sun keeps you away,
nor does the rain drive you back;
and if you get sopping wet
or your boots get soaked,
you keep right on peddling
like a herald at a rally
and you even make the names of your
papers flow like music from your lips.

When a man of the press
passes by you, and hearing your voice,
from which no one escapes,
yet he pretends not to hear:
so that when you can no longer
peddle the paper which he writes
you will be without a crumb,
and no one will subscribe to you.

Tell him that in the columns
of the newspaper that they produce
they can certainly announce
the retirement of the street vendor.
Let there be bread for the one who works
and has worked in her lifetime

and who struggles to make quick money
for the papers;
and tell him to remember always
that the pioneers of the industry
—the newspaper industry—
are all hawkers
who do the same things you do.

Listen politicians,
journalists
who pretend not to see;
look you selfish gentlemen
how Marimorena, who has never
asked for anything,
has lived.

Sound your pitch, saleswoman
of the daily press,
brown-skinned Marimorena
with your strange look.
You do more than the printing presses
and more than the linotypes
which hum in the workrooms.

What would become of their news
without your sound support,
those administrators and clerks
and other sedentary workers?

For four cents a paper,
Marimorena,
the cloth of her shroud.

Ambrosia: A Poem for Black Women

Joyce Carol Thomas | *United States*

You are the girl in an exquisite painting
You wear your pride on your head

You are the woman standing naked without
     Her judgement
You, asked to pay dues because your voice
     Is silver

You sing sparrows out of trees
With your voice you would change night
     To morning; hear it

You are the mother whose children are
     Golden
Whose love is immediate and deep
The lover who smells of gardenias

Your will is a fine thread of steel. You are the watcher
Fashioning grace out of men's laughter
A molasses child straying into light,
Dressed in a soul bright like the sun

You are the traveler warming the world
     With peace
Carrying culture in your belly and
Caravans of bones carved on the

                Bottom of your feet

You are the impatient one impatiently

                Being patient
You cry. You are laughter.
You are the guitar twang.

You are the mother of the church
Rocking the foundations on Sunday,
Draping goodness on the back of your pew
Placing happiness in your feet

You are the sway of the rocking chair
You are the painter intruding upon eyes
And staining them even when your palette
      Is not before you

You are the hoodoo queen and Marie Laveau
At three in the morning you get back
At the world as you mix your portions
Of love and wrath

You are the Calafia, Sojourner Truth,
And the Black Madonna
You are the Egyptian cat of the species
You want what you want when you want it

You turn mountains to valleys
Turn houses into trees

You are free
You cease to cry
And wonder if you ever
Liked the sound of that weeping

You smile in spite of this strange place
You are all that you are
And some of what you hope to be

21st century black warrior wimmins chant for strengthening the nerves & getting yourself together *for edwina, donna, joan, debbie, roberta*
hattie gossett | *United States*

sisters   mothers   cousins   girlfriends
aunties   lovers   grandmothers   daughters

we honor yo bad wimmins selves

we pour libation   to   you

sisters   mothers   cousins   girlfriends
aunties   lovers   grandmothers   daughters

you who sing the original break(out) songs: steal away/steal away/
steal away/cuz we aint got long to stay here

you who wont bow down to no father or husband or lover or boss
or government

you who are the womanlover or the manlover

you who waylay rapists and child abusers and absentee landlords
in alleyways and on rooftops

you who resist the dopedealer and outslick the pimp

you who keep mr executives hands in their place

you who plan and carry out the work slowdown and the strike

you who outmaneuver the overseer in the fields under the hot sun
or in the factory on the airconditioned assemblyline

you who break up all madames fine china and sprinkle rust on her imported linens

you who mixed dried blood and powdered glass into mastas quiche& salad

you who raise children to love themselves and create solutions

you who dream and plan and work with us for the future

     with

     yo

     bad

     wimmins

     selves

       we honor you
  with yo bad wimmins selves

     we pour libation to you
  with you bad wimmins selves

     we wear your colors
  with yo bad wimmins selves

     we eat your foods
  with yo bad wimmins selves

     we dance your dances
  with yo bad wimmins selves

     cuz you give us something
  with yo bad wimmins selves

that is carrying us through this world

    with yo bad wimmins selves

      we honor you

    with yo bad wimmins selves

we call on you

    with yo bad wimmins selves

      witness us in our battles

    with yo bad wimmins selves

      witness us in our battles

      with yo bad wimmins selves

        witness us in our battles

      with yo bad wimmins selves

with

yo

bad

wimmins

        selves

Litany
Lourdes Teodoro | *Brazil*
Translated by Carolyn Richardson Durham

we neither are alive
nor do we keep on being,
we hold on.

neither do we have hope
nor do we kill ourselves in despair,
we hold on.

obsessed in fear
without running away from the powers that be,
we hold on.

living images
of our death anew,
we hold on.

neither do we strike the blow
to scarify banners
nor do we clamor the scratches
torn on others,
we hold on.

made of lack,
we hold on.

where we hide the pain
we don't even know,
we hold on.

Woman Talk
a-dZiko Simba | *Jamaica*

Sisterwoman sisterwoman
Talk about the pleasure
Talk about the pain

Don't save up your emotion
for a stormy day
Don't let pent-up anger reign
rain, reign, rain, reign, rain
down
on the ones you love

Take that feeling
don't fake that feeling
　　make that feeling your own

Sisterwoman sisterwoman
Talk about the pleasure
Talk about the pain

Don't hide your feelings behind blank eyes
(a thin disguise for your hurt)
Don't cry
behind closed doors
Don't try
to smoother the sobbin
the sobbin, the sobbin, the sobbin, the sobbin,
the sobbin and the heavin
of a million tear-filled moments
strangled into silence.

Take that feeling
don't fake that feeling
　　make that feeling your own

Sisterwoman sisterwoman
Talk about the pleasure
Talk about the pain
and when joy and laughter
overwhelm you
and threaten to split you
from head to toe
let them know
Throw back your head
open your mouth
and laugh
    laugh
     LAUGH
     OUT
     LOUD
let the highest leaf on the tallest tree
let the smallest ant in the deepest valley
    dance
     to the rhythms of your fun
Take that feeling
Don't fake that feeling
     make that feeling your own

Sisterwoman sisterwoman
Talk about the pleasure
Talk about the pain

and sisterwoman know yourself
and sisterwoman feel yourself
and sisterwoman be yourself

and

Sisterwoman

find peace

Movement in Black
Pat Parker | *United States*

Movement in Black
Movement in Black
Can't keep em back
Movement in Black

I.

They came in ships
from a distant land
brought in chains
to serve the man.

I am the slave
that chose to die
I jumped overboard
& no one cried.

I am the slave
sold as stock
walked to & fro
on the auction block.

They can be taught
if you show them how
they're strong as bulls
& smarter than cows.

I worked in the kitchen
cooked ham and grits
seasoned all dishes
with a teaspoon of spit.

I worked in the fields
picked plenty of cotton
prayed every night
for the crop to be rotten.

All slaves weren't treacherous
that's a fact that's true
but those who were
were more than a few.

Movement in Black
Movement in Black
Can't keep em back
Movement in Black

II.

I am the Black woman
& I have been all over
when the colonists
fought the British
I was there
I aided the colonist
I aided the British
I carried the notes
stole secrets
guided the men
& nobody thought
to bother me
I was just a
Black woman
the Britishers lost
& I lost
but I was there
& I kept on moving.

I am the Black woman

& I have been all over
I went out west, yeah
the Black soldiers
had women too,
& I settled the land
& raised crops & children
but that wasn't all.

I hauled freight
& carried mail
drank plenty whiskey
shot a few men too
books don't say much
about what I did
but I was there
& I kept on moving.

I am the Black woman
& I have been all over
up on platforms & stages
talking about freedom
freedom for Black folks
freedom for women
in the Civil War too
carrying messages
bandaging bodies
spying & lying
the south lost
& I still lost
but I was there
& I kept on moving

I am the Black woman
& I have been all over
I was on the bus
with Rosa Parks
& in the streets

with Martin King
I was marching
and singing
and crying
and praying
I was with SNCC
& I was with CORE
I was in Watts
when the streets
were burning
I was a Panther
in Oakland
in New York
with NOW
in San Francisco
with gay liberation
in D.C. with
the radical dykes
yes, I was there
& I'm still moving

Movement in Black
Movement in Black
Can't keep em back
Movement in Black

III.

I am the Black woman

I am Bessie Smith
Singing the blues
& all the Bessies
that never sang a note.

I'm the southerner
who went north

I'm the northerner
who went down home.

I'm the teacher
in the all-Black school
I'm the graduate
Who cannot read.

I'm the social worker
In the city ghetto
I'm the carhop
in a delta town.

I'm the junkie with a jones
I'm the dyke in the bar
I'm the matron at county jail
I'm the defendant with nothing to say.

I'm the woman with 8 kids
I'm the woman who didn't have any
I'm the woman who's poor as sin
I'm the woman who's got plenty.

I'm the woman who
raised white babies &
taught my kids to
raise themselves.

Movement in Black
Movement in Black
Can't keep em back
Movement in Black

IV.

Roll call, shout em out:

Phillis Wheatley
Sojourner Truth
Harriet Tubman
Frances Ellen Watkins Harper
Stagecoach Mary
Lucy Prince
Mary Pleasant
Mary McLeod Bethune
Rosa Parks
Coretta King
Fannie Lou Hamer
Marian Anderson
& Billies
& Bessie
sweet Dinah
A-re-tha
Natalie
Shirley Chisholm
Barbara Jordan
Patricia Harris
Angela Davis
Flo Kennedy
Zora Neale Hurston
Nikki Giovanni
June Jordan
Audre Lorde
Edmonia Lewis
and me
and me
and me
and me
and me
& all the names we forgot to say
& all the names we didn't know
& all the names we don't know, yet.

Movement in Black

Movement in Black
Can't keep em back
Movement in Black

V.

I am the Black woman
I am the child of the sun
the daughter of dark
I carry fire to burn the world
I am water to quench its throat
I am the product of slaves
I am the offspring of queens
I am still as silence
I flow as the stream
I am the Black woman
I am a survivor
I am a survivor
I am a survivor
I am a survivor
I am a survivor

Movement in Black.

Performed at the Oakland Auditorium on December 2 & 3, 1977

Remembering Fannie Lou Hamer
Thadious M. Davis | *United States*

Precious night-blooming cereus
You flowered once in Mississippi
Red clay blistered your bare feet
Kept you burnt-out sharecropping
But you blossomed out of Ruleville
A new field worker
Losing job, house, family, health
A new field worker committed in strength
Organizing, registering, mobilizing
Teaching us how to flower in battle
How to free our lives ourselves
How to move powerful in love
How to make "joyful noises" for ourselves

In the barren morning after you
Silences inside match the flowerless clay
We won't blossom the same any more
And we won't sing the old hymns
Because your passing into Mississippi dust
Teaches us
It's not for our song
We will be remembered
But for strong new growth
Under midnight moons

To a Woman Poet That I Know

Pinkie Gordon Lane | *United States*

I.

When you lie again
In the street of forgetfulness
Smashed beyond recognition
Courting the dark avenue,
When you wake to the alien
Walls that do not touch
Your battered flesh,

Your other self
Will fall into the locket
Of your mind and wait
For truth

A creature without roots
Standing on the brink
Of private ruin
Your voice will not save you
For you have found the power
Of destruction

I weep for your lost
Self that stands on the edge
Of the terrible wood
Whose darkness draws

II.

If I could I would make
A gift: the magic of souls
Spinning in the great center
That place where love meets

Merged in the light

I would dispel your personal
And private hell
You, woman: black, lovely,
And lost
You, poet
Whose voice cries out
To the silent air
That dissolves you

This elegy, this inscription
Becomes the dichotomy,
The oxymoron, the paradox,
The beauty, the strength
Of your existence
The destiny of this earth

Testimony *for a poet i admire*
Nagueyalti Warren | *United States*

She spun a soft black song
gave birth to true love
and her motherhood

created a new poetic dimension
that turned girl into woman
manchild into warrior.

She smiled on her childhood
and we remembered the joys
of our childhood too.

She dreamed
and we awoke to dig
the natural dream.

She was the revolution—
her RE: Creation was
the ripple on the pond.

She taught us the colored concept
of hue man beings
put the "S" back in his-story
to show us why
we ain't part of it.

She put the "N" back in
demoncracy—to help us
understand the present system.

She told us we could fly
high like a bird in the sky.

for our lady
Sonia Sanchez | *United States*

yeh.
      billie.   if someone
had loved u like u
shud have been loved
ain't no tellin what
kinds of songs
         u wud have swung
gainst this country's wite mind.
or what kinds of lyrics
         wud have pushed us from
our blue / nites.
       yeh.   billie.
if some blk / man
       had reallee
made u feel
      permanentlee warm.
ain't no tellen
      where the jazz of yo / songs.
      wud have led us.

Our Gardener *for Gwendolyn Brooks*
Naomi Long Madgett | *United States*

You are our gardener in a land of blight.
You enrich arid soil, purify
polluted air, shower on us benedictions
of sun and rain.

Because of your hands' gentleness,
fragile stalks grow strong,
healthy roots burrow deep
expanding their power.

Strengthened by your spirit,
nurtured by your caring,
we blossom for you, dear sister.
We give you our sunflower faces
as a token of our love.

Something Like a Sonnet for Phillis Miracle Wheatley

June Jordan | *United States*

Girl from the realm of birds florid and fleet
flying full feather in far or near weather
Who fell to a dollar lust coffled like meat
Captured by avarice and hate spit together
Trembling asthmatic alone on the slave block
built by a savagery travelling by carriage
viewed like a species of flaw in the livestock
A child without safety of mother or marriage

Chosen by whimsy but born to surprise
They taught you to read but you learned how to write
Begging the universe into your eyes:
They dressed you in light but you dreamed with the night.
From Africa singing of justice and grace,
Your early verse sweetens the fame of our Race.

So Many Feathers
Jayne Cortez | *United States*

You danced a magnetic dance
in your rhinestones and satin banana G-strings
it was you who cut the river
with your pink diamond tongue
did the limbo on your back
straight from the history of southern flames
onto the stage where your body
covered in metallic flint
under black and green feathers strutted
with wings of a vulture paradise on your head
strutted among the birds
until you became terror woman of all feathers
of such terrible beauty
of such fire
such flames
all feathers Josephine
This Josephine
exploding red marble eyes in new york
this Josephine
breaking color bars in miami
this Josephine
mother of orphans
legion of honor
rosette of resistance
this Josephine before
splitting the solidarity of her beautiful feathers

Feather-woman of terror
such feathers so beautiful
Josephine
with your frosted mouth half-open
why split your flamingos
with the death white boers in durban south africa

Woman with magnificent face of Ife mask
why all the teeth for the death white boers in durban
Josephine you had every eyelash in the forest
every feather flying
why give your beaded snake-hips
to the death white boers in durban
Josephine didn't you know about the torture
chambers
made of black flesh and feathers
made by the death white boers in durban
Josephine terror-woman of terrible beauty of such
feathers
I want to understand why dance
the dance of the honorary white
for the death white boers in durban

After all Josephine
I saw you in your turquoise headdress
with royal blue sequins pasted on your lips
your fantastic legs studded with emeralds
as you kicked   as you bumped   as you leaped in the
air
then froze
your body breaking lightning in fish net
and Josephine   Josephine
what a night in harlem
what electricity
such trembling
such goose pimples
so many feathers
Josephine
dancer of the magnetic dancers
of the orange flint pelvis of the ruby navel
of the purple throat
of the feet pointing both ways
of feathers now gone
Josephine   Josephine

Tributes

I remember you rosette of resistance
southern flames
Josephine of the birdheads, ostrich plumes
bananas and sparkling G-strings
Josephine of the double-jointed knees
double-jointed shoulders   double-jointed thighs
double-jointed breasts   double-jointed fingers
double-jointed toes   double-jointed eyeballs
double-jointed hips doubling
into a double squat like a double star into a giant
double snake
with the double heartbeats of a young girl
doubling into woman-hood
and grinding into an emulsified double spirit
Josephine terror-woman of feathers i remember
Josephine of such conflicts i remember
Josephine of such floating   i remember
Josephine of such heights   i remember
Josephine
of so many transformations   i remember
Josephine
of such beauty   i remember
Josephine of such fire   i remember
Josephine of such sheen   i remember
Josephine
so many feathers   i remember
Josephine Josephine

What Has Yet to Be Sung In Tribute to Audre Lorde
Malkia Cyril | *United States* | *January 18, 1992*

Backing to breaking down
I always come to why, to
the unfair, painful
part of life
which runs through everything
like children's crayons
or mud streaked
into the secret rooms of my house.

It gets easier and easier to sit
and watch the sun set
forgetting how it rose
how the glow lifts
black children's faces toward
tomorrow and another chance
waiting with everything that I am
to know the world
and fill it up with one mighty word
one poem to rage catastrophic
on my enemies
one powerful poem to fly past silence
and bleed will into children trapped
by public schools and private traumas.

Forgetting in between spaces
that deny opposition I invite chaos;
the only direction for me is out.
Audre, I am learning not to sacrifice
belief, not to murder hope.
Still sometimes I wake in the middle
of the night screaming dark alleys
and an ex-lover's body desecrated
and buried in time for papers

to catch the story.

That is not
the whole of life,
whole—I can't explain is where
she took me, is where you bring me
to become the poetry of our mothers,
the survival of our fathers
to love beginnings
taking trips back to loving hands
into the sit back, yes on track
stand up way Audre had of obliterating
silence so that even while midtown maniacs
with billy clubs are smearing
our future with blood
we know we are still the plenty of our love
the height of promise.

I have known a woman who was a movement
in my life,
like welcome back to love;
we become the women
whose tongues have been stabbed
and sing anyway,
the women who learn from
teargas and tears how to make
a bomb cry, the soul rise
to meet the earth
crushed under buses
splintered onto sidewalks
we learn death is not the end of life
that language and change
are the beginning
I want to be a beginning
for me
for you.

Mother Afrika's Matriots
Micere Githae Mugo | *Kenya*

A contribution towards the urgent task of engendering our language and concepts such as "patriots"

Refrain: Mother Afrika's Matriots

When we surmount
                      an attack
on the unfinished
                      business
of historical stock-taking
we shall begin
with dynamizing
              freezing silences
              now paralyzing
our womanful lives.

We shall recount
              our herstory
dramatizing it
and illustrating it
with rainbow colours.

We will pour lavish
              libation
              honouring
named
un-namable
yet to be named
Mother Afrika's matriots.

Refrain

We will sing
              without counting time
We will dance

Tributes

        hearts touching earth
We will map
        the A and the Z
of our unfolding
epic journey
        of womanful living
We will compose
        immortal verse
in living praise of
Mother Afrika's matriots.

Refrain

Nefertiti, the ever poised gazelle
legendary beauty, granary of culture
whose stunning reign rained sparkling stars.

Refrain

Hatshepsut, grand political architect
who artfully engraved plateaus
of human development while Europe still slept.

Refrain

Cleopatra, commanderess of matriotic forces
strategist of unfathomable battlecraft
whose stature not even William can shake or spear.

Refrain

Anne Nzinga, proud, stately daughter of the Matamba
unconquered queen of Ndongo, abolitionist supreme
who etched liberation anthems across Angola's valleys and
hills.

Refrain

Harriet Tubman, orature artist from Afrika's health
uncaptured guerilla of the underground railroad
whose untiring feet carved corridors of freedom south to
north.

Refrain

Jane Lewis, detonator of America's dungeons of slavery
who engineered highways across Ohio's angry waters
navigating slave rescue boats under the enslaver's jaundiced
eye.

Refrain

Mary Prince, fearless daughter of sustaining Afrikan soil
who spat on the virulent crumb-eating housenigger cult
burning with each stroke of her pen Caribbean's slave-ridden
fields.

Refrain

Mary Seacole, Afrikan of undying Jamaican maroon seed
whose womanful vision uncovered all male chilvarly myths
urging sisters to pilot their herstory to newly aimed heights.

Refrain

Gertrude Gomez de Avellanda of defiant, revolutionary Cuba
who composed a resounding feminist choral poem ages gone
since highjacked by plagiarizers and forgers of the feminist
text.

Refrain

Sojourner Truth, earthquake that shook pillars of racism and
   sexism—
Mary C. Terrell, educator, life-long campaigner for women's
   rights—

Tributes

Ida B. Wells, journalist-activist, source of liberating
    consciousness—

Refrain

Frances Harper, poetess and orator of melodious anti-slavery
    tunes—
Lucy Parson, unsetting sun on black working class life of
    struggle—
Ella Baker, weaver of grassroots networks for civil rights
    activism—

Refrain

Fannie Lou Hamer, resister before whose vision Mississippi
    trembled—
Audrey Jeffers, clarion for Afrikana sisters to combat racial
    assault—
Amy Ashwood Garvey, Pan-Africanist feminist who
    unchained wifehood—

Refrain

Mary McLeod Bethune, heartbeat of Afrikan war drums for
    freedom—
Clara McBride, "Mother Hale", utmost symbol of Afrikana
    motherhood—
Queen Mother Moore, Audley of Louisiana, spine of Afrikana
    struggles—

Refrain

Women valiants, whose fighting spirit was a mighty wall of
    defence—
surrounding Afrika, stretching defiantly east to west, north to
    south—
Yaa Asantewa, Mihayra Bint Aboud, Queen Aminata,
    Mamfengu, Ma Rarabe—

Refrain

Sisters who took over guard, fortifying the wall with gallant
    resistance—
Nyakasikana Mbuya Nehanda of the undying Munhumutapa
    fighting stock—
Me Katilili wa Menza, daughter of Kenya, orator, mobilizer
    unsurpassed—

Refrain

Rosa Parks, whose enthroned dignity no racist bigot could
    unseat—
Mary Muthoni Nyanjiru who reignited a retreating volcano of
    workers—
Muthoni wa Kirima, last fieldmarshall of the Mau Mau
    landfreedom army—

Refrain

Mother Afrika's matriots will raise the earthshaking power of:
the Aba women
the Abeokuta women
the Maji Maji women
and the *jua kali* women

They will rise with the roaring fury of:
the Dakar railway strike women
the Defiance Campaign women
and the Black Panther women

They will rise with the sweeping force
of Mother Afrika's struggling women
Our matriots will surely rise
with the gun salute
          of the final *chimurenga*
picking up the molotovs

Tributes

                    that missed the target
last *chimurenga* around
aiming with the precision of
Afrikana *chimurenga* women of:

Haiti and Cuba
Algeria and Kenya
Mozambique and Angola
Guinea Bissau and Namibia
Zimbabwe and South Afrika.

They will explode imperialist history

incarcerating myths
They will light undying flames
                    of liberating visions
They will accurately shape
                    the A and Z
of our unfolding pilgrimage
through herstory
through living
through being.

                    Refrain

When we surmount
                    an attack
on the unfinished
                    business
of historical stock-taking
we shall begin
with dynamizing
                    freezing silences
                    now paralyzing
our womanful lives.

We shall recount
                    herstory

dramatizing it
and illustrating it
with rainbow colours.

We will pour lavish
       libation
       honouring
named
un-namable
yet to be named
Mother Afrika's matriots.

We will sing
       without counting time
We will dance
       hearts touching earth
We will feast
       on nourishing visions
nourishing visions
of womanful living
through womanful
       herstory.

We will map
       the A and the Z
of our unfolding
epic journey
       of womanful struggles
We will compose
       immortal verse
in living praise of
Mother Afrika's matriots.

Refrain

Ego Tripping *(there may be a reason why)*
Nikki Giovanni| *United States*

I was born in the congo
I walked to the fertile crescent and built
    the sphinx
I designed a pyramid so tough that a star
    that only glows every one hundred years falls
    into the center giving divine perfect light
I am bad

I sat on the throne
    drinking nectar with allah
I got hot and sent an ice age to europe
    to cool my thirst
My oldest daughter is nefertiti
    the tears from my birth pains
    created the nile
I am a beautiful woman

I gazed on the forest and burned
    out the sahara desert
    with a packet of goat's meat
    and a change of clothes
I crossed it in two hours
I am a gazelle so swift
    so swift you can't catch me

    For a birthday present when he was three
I gave my son hannibal an elephant
    He gave me rome for mother's day
My strength flows ever on

My son noah built new/ark and
I stood proudly at the helm
    as we sailed on a soft summer day

I turned myself into myself and was
    jesus
    men intone my loving name

    All praises All praises
I am the one who would save

I sowed diamonds in my back yard
My bowels deliver uranium
    the filings from my fingernails are
    semi-precious jewels
    On a trip north
I caught a cold and blew
My nose giving oil to the arab world
I am so hip even my errors are correct
I sailed west to reach east and had to round off
    the earth as I went
    The hair from my head thinned and gold was laid
    across three continents

I am so perfect so divine so ethereal so surreal
I cannot be comprehended
    except by my permission

I mean ... I ... can fly
    like a bird in the sky ...

Epilogue

Grace Nichols | *Guyana/England*

I have crossed an ocean
I have lost my tongue
from the root of the old one
a new one has sprung